EYEWITNESS COMPANIONS

Hiking

KAREN BERGER

"GIVE ME THE CLEAR BLUE SKY OVER MY HEAD, AND THE GREEN TURF BENEATH MY FEET"

William Hazlitt

LONDON, NEW YORK,
MUNICH, MELBOURNE, DELHI

Project Editor	Richard Gilbert
Art Editor	Michael Duffy
Managing Editor	Miranda Smith
Managing Art Editor	Karen Self
Art Director	Bryn Walls
Publishing Director	Corinne Roberts
DTP Designer	Karen Constanti
Production Controller	Kevin Ward
Illustrator	Julian Brown
Map Illustrators	Richard Burgess and Iorwerth Watkins
Studio Photography	Gary Ombler
Location Photography	Gerard Brown

Produced for Dorling Kindersley by
The Bridgewater Book Company Ltd

Project Editor	Emily Casey Bailey
Designer	Lisa McCormick

First published in 2005 by
Dorling Kindersley Limited
80 Strand, London WC2R ORL

A Penguin Company

2 4 6 8 10 9 7 5 3 1

A CIP catalogue record for this book is
available from the British Library

ISBN 1 4053 0252 6

Colour reproduction by GRB, Italy
Printed and bound in China by
South China Printing

See our complete catalogue at
www.dk.com

CONTENTS

HIKING HELPS YOU TO ESCAPE FROM A FAST-PACED, COMPLEX, AND OFTEN STRESSFUL WORLD. SOME HIKERS ENJOY A SLOW, RELAXED WALK, TAKING IN THE SCENERY, WHILE OTHERS LIKE TO TAKE ON NATURE AND PUSH THEMSELVES TO THE LIMIT. HOWEVER YOU CHOOSE TO HIKE, IT SHOULD BE A SAFE, ENJOYABLE, AND UNFORGETTABLE EXPERIENCE.

First and foremost, hiking is about enjoying yourself. Whether you choose to hike close to home, or travel to the other side of the world, you can find a host of trails that will lead you to areas of natural beauty. The combined pleasures of rhythmic walking, beautiful scenery, the sun on your back, and a path stretching away from you are what make hiking so popular.

EXPANSIVE VIEWS
Stunning vistas, far beyond the reach of motor transport, are on offer to the hiker.

Walking has long been considered one of the most effective forms of exercise. It is low impact, making it suitable for virtually everyone, yet if undertaken at a brisk pace it can provide good aerobic exercise, as well as toning your muscles, and improving your general physical condition. Begin with easy, level walks. To build your fitness further, go hiking in the hills, where the terrain will make you push yourself a bit harder. Once you are confident at this level, it may be time to tackle a mountain.

Travelling by car and train can take you to many wonderful places, but parking the car or getting off the train, and setting out on a footpath enables you to see many places that lie away from the beaten track. You will see the area more intimately than most visitors, and be given the chance to leave the well-travelled tourist routes and visit tiny villages, hidden beaches, and secret waterfalls.

As a hiker you will be exposed to the weather, with no car window or air-conditioning between you and nature. If it is sunny, you will probably get hot; if it is windy, you will be blown about; and if it is raining, you will get wet. But being out in the elements in this way appeals to many hikers, who relish just being outside, away from the indoor world, whatever the conditions. In addition to being closer to the elements, you will also be closer to the wildlife, enjoying the sights and sounds of birds and animals in their natural environment. Nature

ONWARDS AND UPWARDS
There is a great satisfaction to be gained from conquering a peak and scaling rough terrain – and it is also excellent all-round exercise.

reserves and trails in remote areas are especially good places to experience nature without any of the intrusions of modern-day life.

Hiking can be a very sociable activity. Whether you go for a day or a month, hiking offers an opportunity to spend uninterrupted time with friends and family, exploring new places together. If you enjoy the social side of hiking and want to meet like-minded people with whom you can swap stories and tips, choose a popular trail where hikers congregate in shelters, huts, lean-tos, or designated camping areas. You will find these on long distance trails such as the Appalachian Trail in the USA as well as throughout Europe and New Zealand. Popular Asian trekking routes are also good places to meet hikers from many countries. For hikes that are guaranteed to be sociable, join a hiking club and go on a group hike.

If you are more inclined to treat hiking as quiet, personal time, then a trip with only one or two carefully chosen companions is for you. You and your friends can choose your own route, camp and eat where and when you want, and be as spontaneous as you like. To avoid even the chance of sharing the trail with other hikers, take the opportunity to explore remote, uninhabited areas, sometimes by

following cross-country routes you design yourselves. With some prior research it is possible to go off the beaten track and walk on a very quiet trail, while staying within a reasonable distance of popular destinations.

Many hikers like to push themselves to the limit, both physically and mentally. They enjoy climbing to mountain summits – which offer challenges from steep climbs and snowy slopes to unpredictable weather – or completing a long trail, which can be arduous, and require determination and resolve. But you can find immense satisfaction in meeting these challenges, and there is the ultimate reward of knowing that you have succeeded.

To begin hiking you need to learn hiking skills in the comfort and safety of a familiar environment. If you live in a town or city, you may be surprised to find a wide choice of trails in public parks. These tend to be short, easy, and well-marked, making them perfect for beginners aiming to do two- or three-hour hikes. If you live in the country you will have an even wider network of hiking opportunities, including nature reserves and private land, which may

QUALITY TIME
Getting away from the pressures and distractions of modern life with the people who matter most to you is one of the great appeals of hiking.

have well-established hiking trails, or rights of way that connect sections of longer trails. Riverbanks, canal towpaths, and abandoned railway tracks are also suitable for hiking – especially those that have been turned into trails by local trail organizations. They are usually flat and easy to follow, making them ideal for families with children.

Think of your local paths and trails as a small-scale way to experiment with your hiking equipment in various weather conditions, before you venture further afield. Take a few local trips to test that your clothes and your gear are

Once you decide to travel away from home, your choices of environment are almost limitless

suitable. You can even cut short a hike and return home if the weather takes a sudden turn for the worse.

For a weekend trip, it is practical to choose a destination that is no more than three or four hours away from home. These one-night hikes are ideal opportunities for perfecting your tent erecting and striking skills, as well as your outdoor culinary talents. Short hikes can help you to learn the skills that you will need for a multi-day

EASY DOES IT
Hiking is not only for the super fit – there are many less rugged trails to follow that offer plenty in the way of natural interest for the beginner.

A HOME AWAY FROM HOME
Modern camping offers the hiker the benefit of many home comforts, even when staying in the most remote and beautiful areas of the world.

camping trip, without having to cope with the unexpected challenges of an unfamiliar environment.

When you are ready to travel away from home to hike for several days or more, your choices of environment and terrain are almost limitless. Rural regions, especially in mountainous areas, often have extensive trail systems, some with car parks, so that different sections can be easily accessed. There are many styles of long-distance hiking that may involve traditional camping, staying at local inns, or base camping in one place at night in order to explore different trails during the day.

Anywhere you might choose for a holiday is a potential hiking destination, and hiking is a wonderful way to explore foreign countries. Trail guides and hiking guidebooks are usually available for tourist areas. Guide services in many parts of the world will arrange longer expeditions to remote areas where you might have to travel off-trail.

With so much choice available, you can enjoy hiking in easy conditions, or if you are a more experienced hiker, in challenging environments. Wherever you hike, you will need to know what conditions to expect and what gear to take with you. Knowledge and skill can help you to be comfortable in all conditions, from reading a map in thick fog to staying warm and dry in an all-day downpour. You should also be able to cross rough terrain and set up camp quickly when caught in a sudden storm, know how to find food and water in the toughest conditions, and be prepared to deal with the variety of difficult situations you may meet on the trail.

Acquiring these skills will improve your safety and comfort when hiking. They will also help to ensure that your hiking trip is as memorable and adventurous as you would like it to be.

Karen Berger

KAREN BERGER

CHOOSING
A DESTINATION

GLOBAL HIKES

Any ten-best list is subject to personal opinion and preference, but the following hikes have been chosen for their variety, scenery, unique offerings, and popularity. There are many more routes that could be included; some of them make up the Trails directory (*see* pp.241–8).

Appalachian Trail

MAINE TO GEORGIA, USA

The so-called "grand-daddy" of long-distance trails, the Appalachian Trail (AT) runs 3,499 km (2,174 miles) along the ridgeline of the gentle mountains of eastern America. It offers both a backcountry hiking experience and a glimpse into small-town rural American life. Also noteworthy is the AT's vibrant community of long-distance hikers.

LUSH FOLIAGE
The Appalachian Trail is biologically rich – the Great Smoky Mountains National Park alone contains more species of trees than all of western Europe.

ROLLING TERRAIN
Those rolling hills are deceptive – some stretches of this hike are among the most strenuous to be found anywhere on earth. The AT's other nickname, the "long green tunnel", accurately describes the trail's long stretches of deciduous forest. But in spring, wildflowers colour the hills, in autumn the foliage is brilliantly coloured, and many parts of the trail can be hiked in the white of winter snow. Elevations range from near sea level in New York to 2,019 metres (6,625 ft) in Tennessee. The Tennessee-North Carolina border, and northern New England (New Hampshire and Maine) are the most remote and mountainous stretches.

Mount Katahdin
Green Mountain National Forest
White Mountain National Forest
Appalachian Mountains
NEW YORK
Shenandoah National Park
WASHINGTON
USA
Great Smoky Mountains National Park
Springer Mountain
ATLANTA

KM
0   1,000
0   1,000
MILES

ESSENTIAL INFORMATION

START/FINISH Mount Katahdin, Maine/Springer Mountain, Georgia

DISTANCE 3,499 km (2,174 miles)

AVERAGE TIME TO COMPLETE 5 months

ACCESSIBILITY A 3-hour drive (often less) from most east coast cities

RESOURCES Appalachian Trail Conference: www.ATConf.org

Pacific Crest Trail

CALIFORNIA TO WASHINGTON, USA

Known as "the Everest of backpacking", the Pacific Crest Trail (PCT) runs for 4,345 km (2,700 miles) through some of America's most stunning wildernesses, including Yosemite National Park, the John Muir Wilderness, and the Glacier Peak Wilderness. The PCT is less crowded, more remote, and more scenic than the Appalachian Trail.

EXTREME TERRAIN

The landscape of the PCT varies from scorching desert in southern California – you may have to carry water for 32–48 kms (20–30 miles) at a time – to alpine peaks in the High Sierra of California and northern Washington, and old-growth forests in the Pacific Northwest. Elevations range from near sea-level to 4,023 metres (13,200 ft). In the high mountains, snow can be a problem well into June and July.

ESSENTIAL INFORMATION

START/FINISH Campo, Mexico/Manning Provincial Park, Canada

DISTANCE 4,345 km (2,700 miles)

AVERAGE TIME TO COMPLETE 5 months in total (shorter options are available)

ACCESSIBILITY A 3-hour drive from most of the west coast's urban centres

RESOURCES Pacific Crest Trail Association: www.pcta.org

SUMMER WILDFLOWERS

Wildflowers carpet alpine meadows throughout the Pacific Crest Trail from after the annual springtime snowmelt until early autumn each year.

SNOWY SUMMIT

Glacier Peak in northern Washington lies at the heart of a harsh and remote landscape of snow, ice, rock, evergreen forests, and tumbling rivers.

Inca Trail

THE ANDES, PERU

The Incas built more than 23,000 km (14,290 miles) of roads in South America, 67 kms (42 miles) of which form the Inca Trail. Leading to the sacred city of the Incas in the cloud forests of Machu Picchu, the trail climbs two highland passes via a series of Inca ruins before reaching Machu Picchu through the *Inti Punku* (Gateway of the Sun).

STEEP TERRAIN

The Inca Trail crosses steep, precipitous terrain with long climbs and high passes. This is a high-altitude route: the staging town of Cusco (where guides and porters can be hired) sits at 3,400 m (11,150 ft), the highest pass tops 4,200 m (13,780 ft), and Machu Picchu lies at 2,400 m (7,840 ft). Many hikers suffer from *soroche* – the local name for altitude sickness – so spend at least one day acclimatizating in Cusco before you start.

ESSENTIAL INFORMATION

START/FINISH Piscacucho (also known as "Km82")/Machu Picchu

DISTANCE 67 km (42 miles)

AVERAGE TIME TO COMPLETE 4 to 5 days – routes of varying length are possible

ACCESSIBILITY Train or bus from Cusco

RESOURCES *Explore the Inca Trail*, Jacquetta Megarry and Roy Davies, 2002

RUINED CITY

The well-preserved ruins of Machu Picchu, the sacred capital city of the Incas, is a fascinating archaeological site that lies at the end of the trail.

Pyrenean Haute Route

ATLANTIC TO MEDITERRANEAN, FRANCE AND SPAIN

The Pyrenean Haute Route straddles the Franco-Spanish border, running from the Atlantic Ocean to the Mediterranean Sea. It is a route rather than a trail, following marked hiking trails, unmarked cross-country routes, and other footways. Lodgings can be found along most of the route, but you will need to camp in the remote central section.

MOUNTAINOUS TERRAIN

The Pyrenees mountains are tightly serrated and extremely steep, with long and sometimes treacherous climbs and descents. Cross-country navigation skills are required. Some of the route follows the GR-10, which traverses the mountain range on the French side, and the GR-11, which offers a sunnier, more remote alternative on the Spanish side.

JAGGED PEAKS
You should be prepared for ascents and descents of 1,000 m (3,200 ft) or more each day, and snowfields that last well into the summer months.

ESSENTIAL INFORMATION

START/FINISH Hendaye/Bagnul-sur-Mer

DISTANCE over 965 km (600 miles)

AVERAGE TIME TO COMPLETE 42 to 50 days

ACCESSIBILITY Start and finish can be reached by road and local rail and bus services

RESOURCES *Pyrenean Haute Route,* Ton Joosten, 2004; *Pyrenees: High Level Route,* Georges Veron, 1998

ISOLATED ROUTE
Parts of the Pyrenees mountain range, such as the Posets-Maladeta Nature Park, are among the most remote, least-populated areas in western Europe.

Swiss Haute Route

THE ALPS, FRANCE AND SWITZERLAND

This classic winter ski tour from Chamonix in France to Zermatt in Switzerland has become a popular summer hike, although there are several route variations. The 177-km (110-mile) version offers every Swiss fantasy, from tinkling cowbells and glacial tarns to 3,800-m (12,470-ft) passes and views of 10 of the 12 highest peaks in the Alps.

HIGH-ALTITUDE TERRAIN

High mountains and steep climbs are common on the Swiss Haute Route. Lodgings are available in alpine huts and village hotels, and guided treks are available. July and August are the best months to visit; in June trails may still be blocked by snow and many huts are closed.

CLAWED SUMMIT

At a height of 4,478 m (14,691 ft), the famous profile of the Matterhorn frames the eastern section of the Swiss Haute Route.

GLACIATED MOUNTAINS

At 4,810 m (15,781 ft), Mont Blanc is the highest peak in Western Europe. A side trip to the summit can be arranged with local mountain guides.

ESSENTIAL INFORMATION

START/FINISH Chamonix, France/ Zermatt, Switzerland

DISTANCE 177 km (110 miles)

AVERAGE TIME TO COMPLETE 7 to 13 days, depending on exact route

ACCESSIBILITY Start/finish can be reached by road and local rail and bus services

RESOURCES *Chamonix–Zermatt: The Walker's Haute Route*, Kev Reynolds, 2003; *Haute Route Chamonix–Zermatt: A Guide for Skiers & Mountain Walkers*, Peter Cliff, 1993

West Highland Way

SCOTTISH HIGHLANDS, UK

The oldest hiking path in Scotland runs from Milngavie near Glasgow to Fort William. It runs along the shores of the largest freshwater loch in the UK and follows old drove roads, military roads, and coach roads. Lodgings are available in villages along the route, but camping is only permitted in designated areas.

BLEAK TERRAIN

This route offers a little bit of everything: lochs, glens, farmland, and moors. It can be hiked at any time of year, although the summer months are milder. May is the most popular month, but summer can be crowded. Rain is common all-year round and midges are rife in the summer, so ensure you pack rain gear and insect repellent.

ESSENTIAL INFORMATION

START/FINISH Milngavie/Fort William

DISTANCE 152 km (95 miles)

AVERAGE TIME TO COMPLETE Roughly one week

ACCESSIBILITY Start/finish can be reached by road and local rail and bus services

RESOURCES Walk the West Highland Way: www.west-highland-way.co.uk

STILL WATERS

The route crosses the barren expanse of Rannoch Moor, a wild area of peat bogs and lochans (small lakes). Wear waterproof footwear and rain gear.

OPEN MOORLAND

After crossing Rannoch Moor, the trail passes the head of the valley of Glencoe, which is guarded by the looming pyramid of Buichaille Etive Mor (right).

Mount Kenya Circuit

KENYA, EAST AFRICA

The second-highest summit in Africa is scenically second to none. The best route is a slow circuit, largely at and above the treeline, which offers unceasing, spectacular views. Point Lenana – 4,985 m (16,300 ft) high – is the highest point on the mountain that can be climbed without mountaineering skills, and can be scaled in a weekend by a fit hiker.

DIVERSE TERRAIN

The lower slopes of Mount Kenya feature tropical rainforest and bamboo forest, while the middle slopes are moorland. Above the treeline the terrain is stark and glaciated, with fantastic canyons and spires. Altitude sickness is a common problem because the gentle lower slopes mean it is easy to ascend too quickly. Ensure you acclimatize fully.

GIANT VEGETATION

Especially noteworthy is the Afro-alpine vegetation, such as lobelias the size of bushes and groundsels as big as small cars.

KM
0 ____ 30
0 ____ 30
MILES

NARO MORU   ▲   CHOGORIA
            Mt. Kenya
                EMBU

KENYA

ESSENTIAL INFORMATION

START/FINISH Embu (summit can be reached via Naro Moru or Chogoria)

DISTANCE 48–96 km (30–60 miles)

AVERAGE TIME TO COMPLETE 4 to 5 days

ACCESSIBILITY About 200 km (125 miles) from Nairobi, where buses and shared vans are available. The trip can take several hours

RESOURCES Mountain Club of Kenya: www.mck.or.ke

LOOMING PEAKS

Mount Kenya is an extinct volcano and the summit area is a barren landscape of serrated rock, glaciers, and snowfields.

Annapurna Sanctuary

THE HIMALAYAS, NEPAL

A sacred valley ringed by enormous peaks, the Annapurna Sanctuary is a snowy hollow surrounded by towering mountain walls. The trail begins in lowland forest before climbing past rhododendron, which bloom dramatically in spring. Finally, the trek arrives in one of the world's most awesome mountain cirques (a natural ampitheatre).

HIGH-ALTITUDE TERRAIN

After starting in the humid conditions of a bamboo forest, the trek climbs, leaving behind the heat, humidity, and vegetation. The last day is spent in deep snow at about 4,877 m (16,000 ft). Porters and guides are available, and lodging is in teahouses or tents. Spring and autumn are the best seasons to visit; summer is the monsoon season and in winter snow blocks the paths.

ESSENTIAL INFORMATION

START/FINISH Phodi/Naya Pul

DISTANCE Varies according to exact route

AVERAGE TIME TO COMPLETE Approximately 11 days. Can be combined with all or part of the 3-week long Annapurna Circuit, which encircles the Annapurna Massif

ACCESSIBILITY Treks can be organised in Pokhara, which can be reached by road or plane from Kathmandu

RESOURCES *Lonely Planet Trekking in the Nepal Himalaya*, Stan Armington, 2001

SPRINGTIME BLOOM

Marigolds provide a colourful foreground to the glistening white peaks of Annapurna South (left) and Hiunchuli (right).

SNOWY SANCTUARY

High peaks ring the Sanctuary. Hikers who stay overnight at Annapurna base camp may lie awake listening to nearby avalanches.

Great Wall of China

NORTHEAST CHINA

Lying on the landscape like a giant dragon, the Great Wall of China is one of the wonders of the world. The oldest parts of the wall were built as defensive fortifications over 2,000 years ago, but much of the current wall was built during the Ming Dynasty (1368–1644). You can hike along parts of the wall as it winds through rugged, mountainous terrain.

HARSH TERRAIN

The wall climbs and descends with the landscape. Much of the walking is on hard granite and brick, so wear well-padded shoes. Some sections of the wall are in ruins, so your route may include walking on the wall itself, alongside it, or on nearby roads. Both guided and independent trekking is possible.

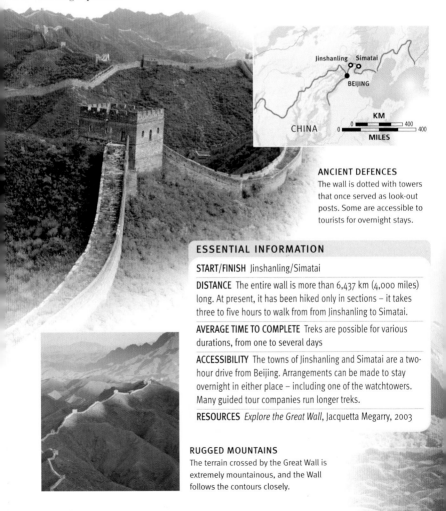

ANCIENT DEFENCES

The wall is dotted with towers that once served as look-out posts. Some are accessible to tourists for overnight stays.

ESSENTIAL INFORMATION

START/FINISH Jinshanling/Simatai

DISTANCE The entire wall is more than 6,437 km (4,000 miles) long. At present, it has been hiked only in sections – it takes three to five hours to walk from from Jinshanling to Simatai.

AVERAGE TIME TO COMPLETE Treks are possible for various durations, from one to several days

ACCESSIBILITY The towns of Jinshanling and Simatai are a two-hour drive from Beijing. Arrangements can be made to stay overnight in either place – including one of the watchtowers. Many guided tour companies run longer treks.

RESOURCES *Explore the Great Wall*, Jacquetta Megarry, 2003

RUGGED MOUNTAINS

The terrain crossed by the Great Wall is extremely mountainous, and the Wall follows the contours closely.

Milford Track

SOUTH ISLAND, NEW ZEALAND

In 1908, a British newspaper called the Milford Track "the finest walk in the world", and the accolade has stuck. Beginning at Lake Te Anau, the trail crosses Mackinnon Pass before descending into Milford Sound. The region is claimed to be the third wettest in the world, with rainfall causing dozens of waterfalls to cascade down vertical canyon walls.

DAMP TERRAIN

The trail passes through lowland temperate rainforest and climbs an exposed alpine pass, then descends to sea-level. Good raingear and insect repellent are essential. Permits are required, but both guided and independent trekking is possible. Accommodation is restricted to designated huts.

ESSENTIAL INFORMATION

START/FINISH Lake Te Anau/Milford Sound

DISTANCE 54 km (33 miles)

AVERAGE TIME TO COMPLETE 3–4 days

ACCESSIBILITY Start/finish can be reached by road, local bus services, and ferry

RESOURCES Milford Track.net: www.milfordtrack.net New Zealand Department of Conservation: www.doc.govt.nz/Explore/002~Tracks-and-Walks/ Great-Walks/Milford-Track

VERDANT MOUNTAINS

Carry good rain gear – these mountains are emerald green due to frequent rainfall, which will only add to the drama of your hike.

FLOWING WATERFALLS

During storms, the valleys roar with the sound of scores of swollen cascades tumbling from the mountain peaks.

Places to hike

Trying to determine the best place to hike is like trying to decide on the best place for any kind of holiday: once you start researching the choices, you realize that they are virtually endless. The range of opportunities for hiking is as varied as the world's terrain.

Hiking in protected areas

Parks and reserves make ideal hiking destinations and can be found all over the world, usually in highly scenic areas. Recreation is commonly one of their management priorities, which means that trails are frequently well marked and easy to find. Wildlife is often abundant, making these places ideal if you want to enjoy the variety of flora and fauna they contain.

NATIONAL PARKS

Many of the world's areas of stunning natural beauty, such as the Pyrenees mountains in France and Spain, the Annapurna Sanctuary in Nepal, Yosemite Valley in the US, and Mt. Kenya in Africa, are located in national parks. Parks may be managed very differently from one country to another. Some park authorities emphasize the protection of the natural environment, while others value traditional human uses. National parks vary widely in size, but those favoured by hikers tend to be large, with extensive trail systems. Permits and reservations may be required.

FORESTS AND RESERVES

Forests and reserves are more numerous than national parks. They are often managed both for recreation and other uses, so hikers may encounter activities such as tree-felling, arable farming, or mining. Nonetheless, these areas often have extensive networks of trails, and may offer an alternative to more heavily used national parks. For hikers seeking solitude, the forests offer vast wilderness areas with plenty of wildlife. The condition of the trails varies widely from forest to forest, which can make hiking in these areas more challenging.

NATIONAL PARK

The Grand Canyon National Park, with its deep gorge, is one of the world's premier outdoor destinations. National parks often offer well-maintained hiking trails in some of the world's most scenic locations.

WOODLAND TRAIL

Forests are often less crowded than national parks. Trails used by hikers are typically a single track that winds its way through the undergrowth.

WILDERNESS AREAS

These places offer hikers the advantages of both national parks and forests or reserves. As in national parks, extractive uses such as logging or mining are usually not permitted, and since recreation is the main activity, the trail systems are often well maintained. Wilderness areas may be less crowded than national parks, giving hikers more solitude and the opportunity to see abundant wildlife. However, travelling in true wilderness requires advanced skills because there are no roads or permanent structures in which to shelter.

NATURE AND WILDLIFE RESERVES

Although wildlife reserves are managed for the benefit of conserving wildlife, in many cases hiking is permitted and hiking trails exist. However, travelling and camping regulations vary, and in many wildlife refuges, overnight camping is not permitted.

SPECIAL AREAS

In some countries, special protected areas have been established to preserve cultural and historic sites. Some of these may be part of, or affiliated to, a national park. For example, visitors to the Lake District in England see not only the scenery of the region but also old stone walls and traditional farms, while visitors to the Annapurna region in Nepal pass through traditional villages.

TIPS FOR NEWCOMERS

FIND OUT ABOUT PERMITS

In parks and reserves, permit systems range from the non-existent to extremely strict. You may have to camp in designated areas. Some charge a fee.

BOOK IN ADVANCE

On some popular trails, reservations to hike must be booked months in advance – especially in the high season. However, last-minute arrivals can be accommodated if people with permits do not show up, so it is always worth asking.

USE THE AMENITIES

Many national parks have reception areas with outfitting shops, hotels, or camping sites with showers. Some also have on-trail huts and refuges. The provision of such amenities allows you to hike with a lighter pack.

KNOW THE RULES

Rules, procedures, and terrain vary among parks, even those in the same country. Rules may cover issues such as whether or not you may build a fire, hike with a dog, camp close to a water source, or put up a tent in the daytime. Check locally.

DO YOUR HOMEWORK

Many national parks have one or two well-known trails that are crowded during the tourist season. Look through guidebooks or ask rangers about other less well-known but equally beautiful trails.

Hiking in the mountains

There is no type of terrain that excites a hiker's imagination as much as an Alpine peak piercing the sky. Pictures of snow-capped summits, flower-filled meadows, and deep blue tarns fill the pages of hiking magazines to inspire readers. So if outstanding scenery, a physical challenge, or a sense of rejuvenation are what you seek, be prepared to climb.

THE MOUNTAIN ENVIRONMENT

Mountains have their own climatic zones and can present enormous challenges to the hiker. As altitude increases, the temperature falls, and precipitation becomes more likely. But different mountain ranges have their own character: some are predictably sunny in certain months of the year; others are predictably rainy at other times of the year. In some mountain ranges, thunderstorms roll in every afternoon during the summer, yet in others, storms are completely unpredictable. Above the treeline, winds can be fierce, the sun strong, and shelter non-existent – you will need to wear sunscreen. As the elevation increases it is important to be aware of the decreasing temperature, and acclimatize your body to changes slowly. Weather patterns are usually well documented, so research your destination thoroughly before you set off. Good guidebooks contain this information.

MOUNTAINS AND SNOW COVER

In most parts of the world, high mountains are suitable for hiking only in the summer. However, in hot and tropical climates, mountains may offer cool respites at any time of year, and may even be snow-covered throughout

CHALLENGING MOUNTAINS

Mountain environments are challenging and require skill, but the well-prepared hiker is rewarded with plenty of opportunities to stop and enjoy the view.

WINTER HIKING
It is advisable to take a winter hike in the middle of the season when the weather has stabilized, and snow and ice on the ground have become compacted to provide a safer footing.

the summer. In most areas, snow begins to melt in late spring or early summer (depending on variable factors such as winter snowfall and early summer heat), and begins to accumulate again in early autumn. The further north or south from the equator and the higher the mountain range, the shorter the hiking season – in many ranges, some snow lingers year-round, and the occasional summer blizzard may occur.

SEASONAL HAZARDS
In late spring and early summer, you may have to cross large fields of ice and snow (*see* pp.167–169). Finding a safe route requires special skills and equipment, such as an ice axe. Another annual hazard in high mountains is the seasonal thaw. Melting snow from glaciers and snowfields fills rivers and streams, making them difficult – and sometimes dangerous – to cross with any degree of safety (*see* pp.164–166).

CHALLENGE AND ACHIEVEMENT
Mountains can offer strenuous physical challenges to hikers of all ages and abilities, and an incomparable sense of achievement when reaching a summit. It is possible to hike to mountain summits, including some of the highest peaks on each continent, without special equipment. The summits of Mt. Whitney in California, US, at 4,418 m (14,495 ft), Kilimanjaro in Tanzania at 5,895 m (19,340 ft), and even Aconcagua in Argentina at 6,960 m (22,835 ft), can all be reached if you are in good physical shape. However, hiking uphill is enormously challenging. The world's tallest high-rise buildings are about 366 m (1,200 ft) tall – ascending a mountain may mean you have to climb three times higher than that in a single day.

Hiking in hot zones

Hot deserts include some very striking landscapes. They have a harsh and arid beauty that is both subtle and dramatic, and an almost complete absence of rain for most of the year.

By contrast, jungles and rainforests offer lush vegetation, a humid climate, and a fascinating array of wildlife. Both require special gear, and tolerance for uncomfortable weather conditions.

THE DESERT ENVIRONMENT

Deserts are defined as areas that receive less than 23 cm (9 in) of annual rainfall, where evaporation of the limited water it receives exceeds the amount lost by precipitation. This means that deserts are places where water is scarce and must often be carried. Arid and semi-arid climates are areas that receive more rainfall than true deserts, or may be arid for only part of the year. For hikers, their characteristcs and challenges are similar to those of true deserts.

DESERT HIKING

Walking through deserts requires appropriate gear to protect the skin from the relentless sun. A wide-brimmed hat protects the face and neck.

HIKING IN THE DESERT

At first glance, walking for long distances in a barren, desolate, hot, and waterless landscape is not an inviting prospect. Yet a desert offers its own special beauty, such as cacti flowering after a desert storm, wild flowers blooming in the spring, and animal life in abundance. If a feeling of almost limitless wilderness and the expansive beauty of an endless sky appeal to you, then a desert hike could be a good choice.

SEASONAL INFORMATION

In many deserts, there is a brief rainy or monsoon season, in which sudden storms produce much of the annual rainfall. Hiking after the wet season gives you the best chance of finding water in ephemeral streams and springs. There is a danger of flash floods, particularly in canyons and steep-sided dry river beds.

SPECIAL GEAR

In addition to high factor sunscreen, you will need full-body sun protection. You must also carry water containers and a good filter, because desert water is often polluted. In the dry season you may not need a tent. A rain jacket is needed only to shield you from strong desert winds, and a tarpaulin just to provide shade. You will also need warm clothes for night-time, as the temperature drops dramatically when the sun goes down.

TROPICAL RAINFORESTS AND JUNGLES

Jungles and rainforests are unique and diminishing environments. Both are found in the tropics and subtropics near the equator, in Latin America, Africa, and Southeast Asia. Technically, a rainforest and a jungle are different – the tropical rainforest is generally shielded by a canopy, which prevents dense undergrowth, whereas a jungle

HIKING IN TEMPERATE RAINFOREST
Walking in the dappled light of these ancient forests can be a magical experience, but come prepared for both wet and dry conditions. Even in the short dry seasons, the climate is cool and the air moist.

usually has a tangle of dense vegetation. Jungles and rainforests are both wet and humid, although jungles do have a dry season. If you are interested in wildlife and ecology, you will be amply rewarded. Enormous flowers and trees, delicate orchids, and dramatic insect and bird life are found in abundance in these regions.

TEMPERATE RAINFORESTS

Temperate rainforests contain some of the largest trees in the world and are found in places such as New Zealand, Tasmania, Chile, Norway, and the Pacific coast of North America, where annual rainfall is high and evaporation is low. However, like jungles and rainforests, these ecosytems are threatened by human activities, such as logging. Travelling off-trail through these forests is impossible, since the forest floor is a carpet of soft, decomposing stumps and new vegetation growth from fallen trees. On some trails wooden boardwalks shield fragile plants from walkers' boots in wet weather, and also protect hikers from mud.

SPECIAL GEAR

You will need good raingear and a tent with full flysheet coverage. To protect against insects take mosquito netting, insect-proof head nets, and insect repellent. Warm clothing is essential, and rubber jungle boots can help you wade through deep jungle mud. Other useful items are walking sticks, waterproof zip-lock bags for cameras, maps, and guidebooks.

TIPS FOR NEWCOMERS: DESERTS

RESPECT THE SUN
Wear a hat, and protective clothing. Put on sunscreen and take a break at midday.

CARRY ENOUGH WATER
Carry 1 litre (1¾ pt) of water per person for every hour of hiking.

SNACK REGULARLY
Take easily digestible snacks, such as a trail mix of nuts and dried fruits.

KEEP WARM AT NIGHT
Ensure your sleeping bag is warm enough to stop you becoming chilled at night.

CHOOSE COOLER WEATHER
Visit in a cooler season, if there is one, for more comfortable conditions.

TIPS FOR NEWCOMERS: JUNGLES/RAINFORESTS

HIRE A GUIDE
Pick a guide who can plan a route to include the flora and fauna of the region.

USE A DETAILED MAP
Take a good map with you to help you pinpoint your exact position.

CARRY A GPS RECEIVER
Navigating through the dense vegetation of a forest is easier with a GPS receiver, used alongside your map. Keep it in a waterproof case.

CHOOSE DRIER WEATHER
Visit jungles during the dry season when trails are least muddy. Check the conditions locally.

Hiking off the beaten track

Different types of landscape can provide magnificent scenic views for hikers. Rugged coastline, moorland, uninhabited bush or outback, or arctic and sub-arctic environments are just a few of the great variety of places that can be hiked, depending on your interests and goals. Each terrain has its own character and may require special skills or equipment.

COASTAL PATHS

Some coastal paths simply follow along a stretch of coastline, while others may be slightly inland and elevated from the high-tide mark, which means they remain passable during times of high water. Plan your route carefully in consultation with tide tables in order to gauge the time you arrive at tidal flats, otherwise you risk a long wait until low tide. Remember that walking on soft sand is tiring and requires endurance. Camping may be on a soft beach – although on some seashore trails, you may choose to stay at an inn or hostel in a nearby town. Take boots, hat, sunscreen, water, and insect repellent.

HIKING ALONG THE COAST
While not as common as mountain trails, coastal paths can be every bit as dramatic and challenging for the hiker.

MOORLAND

This landscape is open, rolling, heath-covered upland. In good weather, moorland is beautiful, wild, and desolate, but prone to sudden thick fog. In foggy conditions there will be little or no visibility, so navigation skills are essential. Knowing how to use a GPS receiver will help you to find your way in fog.

Sudden downpours of rain are fairly common on moorland. Muddy bogs can slow travel at any time of year, and can also form dangerous areas where the saturated earth cannot hold the weight of a human. For these reasons, hiking on moors is always best undertaken with at least one other hiking partner, who can assist you if you get into difficulties.

HIKING ON MOORS

You need to pack good raingear, including pack-covers and waterproof cases for maps and cameras. Your tent should have full rainfly coverage.

OUTBACK AND BUSH

Some parts of the globe have enormous expanses of open, sparsely inhabited land. Hiking across areas of wild and rugged country can be an exhilarating experience. The first skill you need is an ability to plan a cross-country route and follow it using a map, compass, and GPS receiver. There are usually no hiking trails, and you will need to estimate how far you can walk and what provisions you will need daily, including your water supply. You will be able to buy food in remote bush towns but choice will be limited. Use a local guide to help with route selection and advice on avoiding wild animals, especially in Africa.

HIKING IN THE OUTBACK
Sunscreen and clothing that offers sun protection during the day are vital. It can be very cold at night, so you will need a thickly filled sleeping bag.

ARCTIC AND SUB-ARCTIC AREAS

These challenging environments range from vast frozen plains to major mountain ranges, and from narrow fjords to wide glacial valleys. Advanced navigation skills are essential, since there are few marked hiking trails (and those that exist are usually under snow). You will need a sleeping bag suitable for low temperatures (at least a three- or four-season bag), warm layers, bear-proof canisters, and a map, compass, and GPS receiver. Insect protection, such as a mosquito head net, is essential. Plan your trip to the Arctic to coincide with animal migrations of reindeer and caribous, but be aware of dangerous animals, such as brown and polar bears, which pose a danger to hikers. The Arctic's ecosystem is fragile, so you should follow a "no-trace" policy – everything you take in must be brought out.

CAMPING IN THE ARCTIC
You will need advanced camping skills, such as how to build snow shelters, stay warm, and prepare hot meals.

Styles of hiking trip

Your choice of trail is almost limitless. You can set off with a pack full of gear and fend for yourself, trekking for days or even weeks. Or you may choose to visit a developing country and hire porters to carry your gear. Accommodation varies greatly according to where you go.

Hiking on multi-day trails

Multi-day trails may be up to several thousand kilometres in length and offer benefits to hikers, irrespective of their level of experience or how long they plan to hike. They tend to be well-marked and well-maintained, with car parks provided along the way so that different sections can be accessed. Long trails are ideal places to stretch your hiking legs, even if only for a day.

TYPES OF LONG TRAIL
Long trails are found worldwide, and vary from a network of traditional footpaths in developing nations to trails built specifically for recreation in the US. In European mountains, long trails often follow old trade routes and shepherd paths. Trail clubs build and maintain these mountain trails, choosing the most scenic routes available. These clubs often fight to protect the trails and their environment from development. Because these trails are mostly used for recreation, and other uses are limited, they are generally well maintained and in excellent condition for hiking.

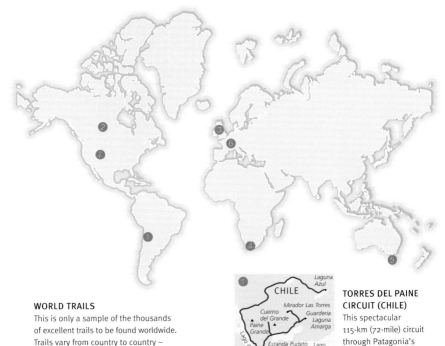

WORLD TRAILS
This is only a sample of the thousands of excellent trails to be found worldwide. Trails vary from country to country – some run along footpaths, others use roads. Accommodation ranges from huts or shelters to camping in the wild.

TORRES DEL PAINE CIRCUIT (CHILE)
This spectacular 115-km (72-mile) circuit through Patagonia's remote national park traverses glaciers, forests, and lakes.

TRANS-CANADA TRAIL (CANADA)

This route, which is still under construction, will be the longest trail in the world – a network totalling more than 18,000 km (11,200 miles) when it is completed.

COAST-TO-COAST TRAIL (UK)

This 304-km (190-mile) scenic walk crosses famous landscapes such as the Pennines, the Yorkshire Dales, and the Lake District. It has long upland stretches.

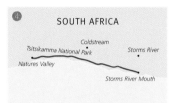

OTTER TRAIL (SOUTH AFRICA)

Although only 42 km (26 miles) long, this trail connects with the Dolphin Trail and the Tsitsikamma Trail, giving the option to explore inland mountain areas.

SOUTH COAST TRACK (AUSTRALIA)

Tasmania's stunning 83-km (52-mile) coastal trek passes through some of the world's last remaining temperate rainforest and crosses two mountain ranges.

GR5 (EUROPE)

This trail runs from the North Sea to the Mediterranean, passing through Holland, Belgium, Luxembourg, Switzerland, and France. Highlights include Alpine peaks, the dykes of Holland, and the vineyards of Alsace.

CONTINENTAL DIVIDE TRAIL (US)

Following the American watershed boundary between east and west, this is the most difficult and remote trail in the US. Much of the trail is in place; when complete it will run for 5,000 km (3,100 miles).

TIPS FOR NEWCOMERS

USE THE TRAIL CLUBS

Long trails frequently have trail clubs that co-ordinate maintenance, arrange group hikes, and provide information about everything from parking areas to trail conditions.

CHOOSE THE BEST PARTS

Scenic sections of long trails are sometimes connected via a less scenic path. There is no reason to hike along an uninteresting connecting trail unless you intend to hike the entire distance. Contact trail clubs for recommendations on the most scenic sections of each trail.

CHECK TRAIL CONDITION

Long trails pass through land managed by a variety of agencies, such as national parks, nature reserves, private land, farmland, and national forests. As such, parts may not be well-maintained. The trail club is the best source of information.

CREATE A LOOP

In many larger areas such as national parks, long trails are only one of the options available. You may be able to create a loop using a section of the long trail as your route away from your vehicle, and another, interconnecting part of the trail as your way back, with perhaps a connecting trail to join the two. This adds variety and avoids the difficult transport logistics of one-way hikes.

Deciding on accommodation

There are many types of hiking accommodation to choose between – from tents to huts, bed and breakfasts, hostels, and trail shelters. Once you are aware of all the options, you should be able to choose the type that suits you best, depending on the amount of comfort you want and what is available. Many hikers plan a long trip to include a variety of lodgings.

CAMPING IN THE WILDERNESS

Many hikers on multi-day trips carry lightweight tents. In North America, tents are usually pitched in the wilderness – preferably out of the sight of other campers and hikers. If you are hiking in any of the North American wilderness areas, you will have to use your tent for shelter because there are no permanent structures, lean-tos, hostels, refuges, bed and breakfasts, or inns to stay in. The lack of accommodation is generally not a hardship because most wilderness hikers prefer to camp in solitude. You will be expected to clean up your site when you go, leaving no trace of your stay.

DESIGNATED CAMPSITES

Some hikers prefer to camp close to other people. In Europe, campsite areas are often situated next to refuges or other amenities where hikers can buy meals or prepare their own. In some US parks, hikers are required to pitch their tents in designated group sites.

HUT-TO-HUT HIKING

Huts and refuges are popular in Europe (especially in the Alps) and in New Zealand, but, with few exceptions, are rare in North America. Huts are found on trails away from populated areas and roads, and are usually only accessible on foot. They typically offer dormitory-style accommodation, and cooking facilities, or alternatively, hearty meals for a reasonable price. You may need to make reservations in high season on popular trails – always check in advance.

HUT ACCOMMODATION
Offering simple, comfortable accommodation, staying in huts means you do not have to carry a tent or, usually, cooking gear.

EMERGENCY SHELTER
Situated above the treeline in New Zealand, this modern shelter is for emergency use in storms.

BASIC TRAIL SHELTER
Shelters are run on a first-come, first-served basis. This shelter lies next to a mountain trail in Peru.

PERMANENT HUT
One of North America's rare mountain huts offers food and lodging to hikers arriving on foot.

BED & BREAKFASTS AND HIKER HOSTELS

Along popular hiking routes, inns have sprung up to accommodate hikers, and can be less basic than huts. They include family homes, B&Bs, and hostels that cater to hikers at low cost, offering generous portions of food, and laundry facilities. Most trail guides make note of such hiker-friendly lodgings. If you stay in such accommodation, you do not need to carry sleeping or cooking gear, and can take side trips to local cultural attractions. Accommodation varies in quality and cleanliness – from spotless B&Bs to insect-infested shacks.

TRAIL SHELTERS

These differ from huts, B&Bs, and hiker hostels in that there are no services (such as meals, laundry, or cooking facilities). Shelters are fairly basic and range from disused cabins and huts to structures purpose built for hikers. Scotland, for example, has a long tradition of trail shelters, while in the Alps, hikers often use old shepherds' huts.

TENT ACCOMMODATION

Hikers must carry supplies and a tent when hiking in the wilderness, but gain the opportunity to camp in peace and solitude, away from other hikers.

Trekking in developing countries

A popular way to explore developing nations is by travelling on foot. It helps you to avoid the sometimes inefficient and overburdened local transport systems, while allowing you to interact directly with local people, and to visit interesting cultural and religious sites. Taking porters or pack animals with you makes this quite a different experience from a domestic hike.

ORGANIZED TREKS

An organized trek can range from a simple trip to a huge expedition. A guide leads the group while porters show the way, haul gear and equipment, cook food, and set up camp. The number of porters employed depends on the size of the group. Such organized trips can be booked from your home country or arranged when you arrive. Using porters and guides supports the economy and encourages local people to preserve the surrounding area, because it generates income from tourists (*see* pp.126–9).

PACK ANIMALS

Animals such as llamas, donkeys, mules, horses, and even goats can be used to carry supplies. In a similar style to a trip with porters and guides, a trip with pack animals requires more planning and scheduling than a normal group hiking trip, but it does allow you to carry more equipment and food. If you intend to use pack animals to carry equipment, hire a guide and animal handlers.

INDEPENDENT TREKS

You can also trek independently in developing countries, and many experienced hikers prefer an unguided trek to an organized one. There are many guidebooks available for the independent traveller that describe routes, hostels, restaurants, and food restocking opportunities for trekking in popular destinations. You can also trek independently with a local guide, many of whom will enhance the trek with cultural insights and local knowledge (*see* pp.118–25).

MEETING THE LOCAL PEOPLE
Because many trekking routes pass through towns and villages, hikers often have an opportunity to interact with the people that live in those places.

BUDDHIST PRAYER STONES IN NEPAL
Use a guidebook to advise you of customs relating to visiting religious shrines, such as acceptable dress, photography, or rituals of behaviour.

SECURITY AND PERSONAL SAFETY

The cost of your plane ticket might well be equal to the cost of a local person's house, while the money you paid for your hiking gear could feed a local family for a year. With such disparity in wealth, visitors are sometimes targets for thieves. It is sensible to consider the wide range of security products available to help guard your belongings. These include cable-reinforced money-belts, small padlocks, steel nets to encase your backpack, and secret zipped compartments. But none of these is as effective as common sense – do not display expensive electronic equipment or large amounts of cash, and keep an eye on your belongings at all times. Take care when travelling in politically unstable areas. Remember that there is safety in numbers, and local guides can help you avoid known trouble spots.

LOCAL CUSTOMS AND ETIQUETTE

Many cultures have what may seem a bewildering array of cultural and religious taboos, and an uninformed visitor may frequently, if inadvertently, give offence. In Nepal, for example, even walking on the incorrect or correct side of a prayer wall can offend or endear you to your hosts. Many countries have similar customs that may be hard to understand. For this reason, you should buy a good guidebook that explains the local customs, and make sure that you are aware of them before you arrive.

LOCAL FOOD

Hiking can be an opportunity to try authentic local food – which can be much better than restaurant meals made for tourists. However, hikers with food allergies, restricted diets, or aversions to spices may find that their selections are limited in remote locations. You need to carry some packaged food just in case.

HYGIENE AND SANITATION

Despite usually having poorer standards of sanitation, many hikers prefer to stay in lodgings found along trekking routes in remote rural areas rather than big hotels. There are many destinations where the water supply is not clean nor the street food safe to eat. If you have no previous experience of travelling independently in developing countries, find out which destinations to avoid when planning your trip. If comfort and sanitation are a priority for you, travelling with a tour company will help you to find the best available local amenities.

RURAL TOILET
Sanitary facilities in remote rural parts of many developing nations are frequently quite basic, and in some cases may be less than hygienic.

Deciding when to go

Some people first choose a destination, then consider which time of year is the best for hiking in that location. Those with more restricted holiday options may choose their dates first. In either case, time of year can make a huge difference to the quality of your experience.

Assessing the weather

Weather – heat, cold, dryness, precipitation, and wind – can be a major factor in the enjoyment of any hiking trip. The well-equipped and experienced hiker often learns to cope with and acclimatize to challenging weather conditions, but it still makes sense to choose your destination with a view to avoiding predictable or seasonal climatic problems.

RAIN AND DRIZZLE

In many regions, certain times of the year have much more rain than others. Local rainy seasons may feature all-day drizzles or more dramatic afternoon thunderstorms. In summer, walking through an afternoon shower can be refreshing, but in spring or autumn, an all-day drizzle can be debilitating. If your destination has seasons that are typically rainy, take adequate raingear or avoid visiting at that time.

REGULAR DOWNPOURS
Clouds regularly gather over mountaintops. Be prepared for localized downpours, but avoid times of year when rain is predictably constant or heavy.

HEAT AND SUN

Most hikers find that walking strenuously in temperatures much higher than 24–27°C (75–80°F) soon becomes uncomfortable. This is a problem in hot deserts, and also in mountainous regions above the treeline where the air is thin and the sun reflects off the snow. In some parts of the world, such as New Zealand, ozone-depletion makes sunburn a serious problem. Humidity is also a factor that increases discomfort – summer hiking in both tropical rainforests and temperate deciduous forests can be a distinctly sweaty experience that you may wish to avoid.

EXTREME HEAT
The summer sun may be overpowering in hot, arid regions. Hiking in the cooler winter or early spring may be more comfortable.

MONSOONS

Many tropical and subtropical regions (as well as some temperate rainforests and some desert regions) have dry- and wet-season cycles. In a desert region, the local "monsoon" season may simply bring afternoon thunderstorms, but in the tropics, it can mean day after day of drenching, unceasing rain, that leaves you little chance to dry your clothes. Such conditions make hiking unpleasant, so do your best to avoid them.

HURRICANES AND TYPHOONS

Many tropical destinations have seasons when small, violent tropical storms are likely to occur. Such storms are known as typhoons in the China seas and western Pacific, and hurricanes in the rest of the world. They can cause extensive damage over a wide area, so avoid travelling to affected areas at these times of year.

SMOG AND DUST

Air can be polluted by industry or by dry- and wet-season cycles in some regions, which affect breathing and visibility. In many cases, seasonal cycles are predictable because they follow weather patterns. When planning a hike, choose times when the air is clearest.

INSECTS

In cold regions, the insect season reaches its peak during the first two weeks after snow has melted, in spring and early summer, although in hot, humid regions insects can be a problem all year round.

FREEZING NIGHTS
Temperatures can drop below freezing during the night at high elevations, even in spring. Some trails will be closed during the winter months.

In drier climates, there is very little humidity to hold the day's heat once the sun goes down, so nights can be bitterly cold – even though daytime temperatures are uncomfortably hot.

SNOW AND ICE

Mountainsides can be covered by snow and ice clinging on to the slopes well into the summer months. This increases the chance of avalanches, which pose a threat to hikers. If you decide to hike in Alpine areas in early summer, always check with local trail clubs or land managers to find out the condition of the snow and ice.

AVOIDING AREAS AFFECTED BY SEASONAL CONDITIONS

Unless you are a very experienced hiker looking for a challenge, it is worth choosing your visiting dates carefully to avoid the worst of the weather in the most extreme climates of the world such as deserts, mountains, or arctic conditions.

SEASON	RECOMMENDED DESTINATIONS	PLACES TO AVOID
Winter	Deserts, destinations in the opposite hemisphere, the tropics and sub-tropics	High mountains
Spring	Deserts, hill country and low mountains, forests	High mountains, cold climate
Summer	High mountains, cold-climate forests, arctic and sub-arctic regions	Deserts, tropics, sub-tropics, hot lowlands
Autumn	Temperate deciduous forests	High mountains

Choosing when to visit

In addition to weather conditions and patterns, other local factors may affect the planning of your trip. You may wish to avoid the height of the tourist season. Knowing when plants and flowers are at their best, when a special holiday or festival is taking place, or when animal migrations occur can help you plan a trip that meets your expectations.

HIGH TOURIST SEASON

The tourist season varies from country to country, but high season usually coincides with school holidays. In midwinter, many tourists choose to go to warm destinations and ski areas, while in summer, outdoor-oriented holidaymakers may prefer high mountains. In high season, tourist services and facilities such as mountain huts, B&Bs, and information offices are open. The disadvantages, of course, are that prices are much higher and there are more hikers on the trail. You may have to limit your flexibility by making reservations to secure a place in hiker hostels and inns.

CAPTURING THE HERD

If your destination is known for wild animals, be sure to choose a season when the animals are in residence, or migrating through the area.

FLOWER AND FOLIAGE DISPLAYS

The timing of natural spectacles, such as wildflower blooms or colourful autumn leaves, may vary from year to year because of variances in weather, or because of the elevation. It is always best to check locally for up-to-date information on the best time to visit.

ANIMAL MIGRATIONS

You may plan your visit to coincide with animal migrations – the sight of a sky full of hundreds of birds of prey riding the thermals, the sound of a herd of elk bugling, or the hooves of tens of thousands of African wildebeest thundering across the vast Serengeti National Park. Some of these displays are world renowned, so require planning and early reservations.

LOCAL FESTIVALS AND HOLIDAYS

If you plan to stay in a town during a local event – whether it is a celebration of a delicacy such as a local wine, a fête honouring a patron saint, or a music festival – it is best to make hotel reservations in advance. Regular

LOCAL FESTIVAL
This Buddhist festival in a small village in Myanmar gives visitors the opportunity to hear traditional music and sample local delicacies.

campsites also become full, although temporary sites are set up to cater for the large influx of visitors at major sporting or cultural events. Consider how national holidays may affect local facilities. In France, for example, August is regarded as the month in which local people go on holiday, so it is common to find shops in certain parts of the country shut for the whole month.

ELECTIONS AND POLITICAL UNREST
Political unrest is a global concern. Some countries may be less safe or comfortable to travel in due to cultural or political conflicts. In others, special events such as elections may carry with them the potential for unrest. A rosy picture is often portrayed in guidebooks, so check with your country's foreign office or state department for an update on the current political climate.

SEASONAL SAFETY
Brightly coloured clothing visible from far away is advisable for hikers during the hunting season. Safety vests can also be worn over your clothing.

HUNTING SEASON
This season is best avoided. During the hunting season, you may have to share the countryside with hunters looking for game, including deer, wild boar, bears, grouse, and partridge. In addition, there may be different seasons for hunting with particular kinds of weapon. The best source of information is a local land management agency. If you do decide to hike during the hunting season, be aware of any activity going on around you, and wear bright orange clothing, which can be seen from far away.

CLOTHING AND EQUIPMENT

Choosing gear

With thousands of items to choose from, your first visit to an outdoor retailer's shop may be confusing. Choosing gear is not about buying the latest, trendiest, or even the most expensive equipment, it is all about buying affordable equipment that matches your needs.

Narrowing the choices

Start by evaluating the weather and terrain you will encounter on your hike, then consider what is – and is not – essential. A tight budget may restrict your choices, but you will still find many functional and practical choices in all price ranges. Do not be seduced by things that you may never use – focus instead on solid gear that meets the needs you have identified.

EVALUATING CONDITIONS
Gear made for climbing Mount Everest may be indestructible, but it is not what you need on a hike through the English Lake District or the American Southwest. In fact, the strongest equipment may be heavy and lack the features you need. Read guidebooks and contact the local tourist office to find out about the weather conditions and terrain you will encounter, then choose the clothing and equipment that suits your hike.

CHANGING CONDITIONS
The weather and terrain at the top of a climb are often quite different from those encountered at the outset. It may not be cold, though, and since the exertion will warm your body, you do not want to become overheated. Ensure your backpack is large enough to carry strong, heavy equipment and any extra clothing.

UNSETTLED WEATHER
In changeable climates you need head-to-toe raingear for safety and comfort in case of a sudden downpour. Pack your gear in a waterproof backpack to ensure it remains dry.

MAKING A CHECKLIST OF ESSENTIAL ITEMS

To make sure you do not carry too much, keep a checklist of the gear that you take. After each hike, make a note of what you did and did not use, then alter your gear list accordingly. (You should always carry emergency equipment such as raingear and a first-aid kit.) Your checklist may change from hike to hike, as you encounter different conditions or as you gain experience. It will become a gear log, in which you make notes about the conditions and how well your gear worked. For example, if you slept comfortably on a sub-freezing night in a particular sleeping bag while wearing certain items of clothing, the next time you go out in similar conditions, you will know exactly what to bring. Likewise, you might make a note of items you wished you had – for example, a thicker sleeping mat, a rain hat, or gloves. Also note how much you used of items such as sunscreen, stove fuel, and insect repellent – next time, you might be able to manage with less.

MILD WEATHER
If you are camping in warm weather you will need a well-ventilated tent that allows air to circulate.

SETTING GOALS

Understanding your hiking goals will make it easier to choose the right gear for your trip.

ARE YOU HIKING SOLO OR AS PART OF A GROUP?

Solo hiking can be as lightweight and spontaneous as you like, but group hikes mean larger tents, more cooking equipment, and careful planning.

HOW MUCH DISTANCE DO YOU PLAN TO COVER?

For long-distance hikes, keep your pack weight low and only carry what is truly necessary.

WHAT WILL WEATHER CONDITIONS BE LIKE?

Weather reports will determine whether you need light or heavy clothing and gear.

DO YOU HAVE ANY SPECIALIST INTERESTS?

If you are a keen bird-watcher or photographer, you will need to consider the extra weight of binoculars or a camera.

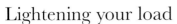

Lightening your load

Hiking "light" is the biggest backpacking trend in recent years. New materials and designs have made it possible to cut the weight of loads, making hiking much more enjoyable.

When choosing gear, always check to see if there are lighter alternatives that will perform the same function. Also, choose gear that serves multiple purposes, so that you carry less weight.

INCREASING COMFORT AND FITNESS

Lightweight hiking is simply a case of choosing lighter and often smaller versions of equipment. It does not mean sacrificing essentials in order to save weight. A lighter pack is easier and more comfortable to carry, especially on long, uphill hikes. It also puts less stress on knees, neck, shoulders, and back muscles. In an emergency, a lighter backpack will help you to walk more quickly to safety.

Your own personal fitness and weight are also part of the equation – just as a light, streamlined backpack makes hiking easier, being fit means that your body works more efficiently because there is no extra body weight to carry.

REDUCING PACK WEIGHT IN STAGES

Gradually reduce your backpack weight over a number of hikes, rather than cutting down to the bare minimum in one go. Try leaving behind your non-essentials on a hike in sunny weather. What can you comfortably live without? When hiking in bad weather, notice how much of your gear you are using. Gear that remains unused during a cold, wet weekend can probably be left at home in the future.

WEIGHT GUIDELINES

Hiking gear comes in a wide range of weights. In average hiking conditions in a temperate climate, keep within the guidelines below for a comfortable trip.

ITEM	MAX. WEIGHT
Backpack	2 kg (4½ lb)
Two-person tent	2.5 kg (5½ lb)
Sleeping bag	1 kg (2¼ lb)
Hiking boots	1 kg (2¼ lb)
Solo tent	1.3 kg (3 lb)
Sleeping mat	650 g (1½ lb)
Raingear (jacket and trousers)	550 g (1¼ lb)
Food (per day, per person)	900 g (2 lb)

HIKING LIGHT
You can travel more quickly and cover greater distances with a lightweight backpack.

IMPROVIZED SHELTER
A tarpaulin can be strung on a rope tied between two trees to make an impromptu shelter that is much lighter than a tent. If there are no trees, use trekking poles as supports instead.

STREAMLINING YOUR GEAR

The following five strategies will help you to keep down the weight and size of your gear. Follow them sensibly and your pack weight will drop without compromising safety.

■ You can easily get rid of excess and cut several kilos from your load by closely examining the contents of your pack. Do not bring extra changes of clothing – instead, rinse clothes in a stream. Also, trim your cooking kit to bare essentials – a single cooking pot will often do.

■ When hiking with a partner, assess what gear you can conveniently share. You can save several kilos by sharing a tent, stove, cooking kit, first-aid kit, penknife, and even personal items such as a toilet trowel, sunscreen, and insect repellent.

■ Consider weight when replacing old equipment. Look for newer lightweight components such as siliconized nylon and titanium, and for simple designs that maximize function while minimizing weight.

■ Some equipment can do several jobs, which makes it weight-efficient. For example, a trekking pole helps you to walk during the day and can be used as a tarpaulin support at night. Similarly, a foam mat can be folded to make a backpack frame during the day and then used as a mattress at night.

■ Measure out portions of all consumables. Buy insect repellent in small plastic bottles, or use insect repellent that has built in sunscreen. Travel- or sample-sized soap, toothpaste, and first-aid ointments are lighter than standard sizes. Pack spices in miniature zip-locking bags (available at many food stores) and minimize all packaging (such as cardboard food boxes).

LIGHTWEIGHT GEAR

Lightweight equipment lightens your load without having to leave behind essentials and emergency items.

TORCH

Slimline, lightweight torches are useful on a hike and at a campsite, but always remember to take spare batteries.

BACKPACK

The lack of a rigid metal frame makes this backpack a lighter and more flexible way of carrying gear if the load is not too heavy.

SLEEPING BAG

Lightweight sleeping bags come with both down and synthetic fillings, but down bags compress more easily and pack down smaller.

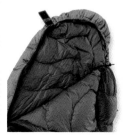

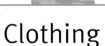

Clothing

Today's outdoor clothing is technologically advanced and highly sophisticated – new materials and designs are extremely lightweight, durable, and versatile. To make the most of your gear, choose the fabrics and combinations of clothes appropriate to the conditions.

Layering clothes

The rule of layering is simple – it is better to choose several light layers than one heavy layer. Wearing multiple layers gives you the flexibility to fine-tune exactly how warm you are by taking off and putting on layers as you work harder, as you rest, or as the temperature changes. Choose fabrics such as wool, microfleece, fleece, or down, which are good insulators.

HOW LAYERING WORKS

Layering is effective because it traps air between the clothing layers, which means that you stay warm. If you wear the correct layers in the correct order, your clothing will move sweat away from your body, keep moisture out, and insulate you. Wear wicking fabrics in both hot and cold weather.

The base layer provides warmth and wicks moisture away from your skin

The mid-layer provides warmth. Use insulating fabrics in cold weather, or when resting in camp

Lightweight fitted gloves worn under bulkier fleece gloves protect fingers from the wet and cold

The outer layer of waterproof, breathable fabric keeps rain out and allows water vapour from sweat to escape

Raindrops are repelled

Perspiration is drawn away from the skin

Gore-tex® outer layer

Fleece mid-layer

Synthetic mesh or lightweight layer

Polypropylene base layer

Skin

Heat

Wicking long underwear worn under a protective outer layer gives legs extra warmth

Two pairs of socks can be worn under boots. A lightweight inner sock draws moisture away from feet and lessens friction

LAYERING SYSTEM
The top (outer) layer repels rain water, while dampness is wicked away. The lower layers retain body warmth.

FABRIC	PROPERTIES	USES
COTTON Comfortable for temperate climates, cotton absorbs water and dries slowly, so is less suitable for cool or wet climates.	Absorbs water Provides ventilation	■ Shorts ■ Trousers ■ T-shirts ■ Bandanas ■ Sun-protection hats
WOOL A good insulator, wool next to the skin can be itchy. Merino and cashmere are lightweight, warm for their weight, and do not itch.	High water repellency Warm when wet	■ Socks ■ Sweaters ■ Hats ■ Gloves ■ Long underwear
SILK Though comfortable and lightweight, silk retains moisture. Because of this, it has lost ground to newer, faster-drying synthetics.	Comfortable against skin Lightweight	■ Long underwear ■ Sleeping bag liners
POLYPROPYLENE Both inexpensive and warm, polypropylene wicks moisture away from the skin, keeping you warm, dry and comfortable.	Wicks moisture away Dries quickly	■ Long underwear ■ Raingear ■ Balaclavas ■ Gloves ■ Hats ■ Insulating shirts
FLEECE A bulky, lightweight fabric, fleece keeps you warm. Microfleece is a tighter weave, and weighs less, but is not quite as warm.	Retains warmth when wet Warm for weight	■ Vests ■ Hats ■ Gloves ■ Trousers ■ Jackets ■ Balaclavas
MICROFIBRE A stretchy, tightly woven fibre that allows clothing to fit tightly to the body, microfibre repels wind and some moisture.	Tightly woven Repels moisture	■ Vests ■ Wind jackets ■ Shorts ■ Raingear ■ Towels
GORE-TEX® A water-repellent coating and microscopic holes in Gore-tex® fabrics prevent moisture from entering while allowing sweat to escape.	Coating repels water Breathable	■ Rain jackets ■ Rain trousers ■ Gloves ■ Hats ■ Gaiters ■ Boot linings
SOFT-SHELL Similar to an insulating fleece, soft-shell offers excellent breathability, but is inadequate protection in a heavy storm.	Some water repellency Good breathability	■ Jackets ■ Water resistant leggings

Clothes for hot weather

Hiking can be hard exercise that raises your body temperature and can make you uncomfortable. In very warm weather, it is vital to stay as cool as possible to avoid heat exhaustion and possibly heatstroke – and to enjoy yourself. Your choice of clothing can help. Choose breathable fabrics, which will keep you cool while protecting your skin from the heat of the sun.

COPING WITH THE HEAT

Too much exposure to direct sunlight can cause sunburn and dehydration. If you are hiking in very warm weather, pay special attention to your body temperature and make sure you stay hydrated. Heat rashes can also be exacerbated if sweat is not able to evaporate properly.

HOT WEATHER CLOTHING

Protect your skin by covering as much of your body as you can with a thin layer of clothing. Remember to wear a hat as well.

SUN PROTECTION

Clothing should be loose and light coloured to protect your skin from sun and insects.

Synthetic materials wick away moisture and dry more quickly than cotton

Sleeves should be loose so they can be rolled up and secured by a button

A shirt with ventilation flaps allows air to circulate, helping sweat to escape

Check zips have a fabric flap inside so they do not chafe your skin

Waterproof boot linings are not necessary in warm weather, particularly in dry climates

KEEPING COOL

Your choice of clothing should help you to keep cool when hiking in the heat and humidity.

A loose fitting t-shirt made from moisture-wicking fabric is good for air flow and comfort

A wide brim shades the face and neck. Light colours reflect the sun's rays

Convertible trousers
Lightweight, full-length trousers shade the skin from blazing sun. Convertible trousers have legs that can be unzipped for those who prefer hiking in shorts

HOT, RAINY WEATHER
You might not need full raingear on a summer hike, so take a water-resistant wind shirt or lightweight rain jacket to protect you from a shower.

WIND SHIRT
This type of shirt is not waterproof but it is water-resistant, which may be sufficient in light summer rain and for the cool nights that usually follow hot days in the desert.

WIND PROTECTION
A wind shirt is useful in warm deserts where strong, dry seasonal winds are common.

A high collar protects the neck

Tightly woven wind shirt fabrics keep out wind and some water

LIGHTWEIGHT RAIN JACKET
In hot, rainy conditions an inexpensive rain jacket made of polypropylene is an excellent choice, as it is breathable as well as waterproof. An ultralight jacket will fold away to a tiny pack size.

RAIN PROTECTION
Look for loose-fitting, well-ventilated, lightweight jackets. A breathable fabric allows sweat to escape.

All rain jackets should have a hood. Some have a peak in the front, which helps keep water off the face

Underarm zips, which are an advanced feature, and a loose fit ensure good ventilation

Lightweight fabrics can tear easily, so take care when rock scrambling or hiking through vegetation

HATS FOR THE HEAT
Hats protect your head and neck from both the sun's rays and insects. They also absorb sweat.

BASEBALL CAP
The wide brim of a baseball cap shelters the eyes from the sun.

BANDANA
A bandana can be rinsed in cool water and worn on top of the head, or worn under a baseball cap to shade the neck.

DESERT HAT
A desert hat combines the sheltering brim of a baseball cap with the neck protection of a bandana.

LIGHTWEIGHT RAIN HAT
A lightweight rain hat gives protection from both sun and rain, so is a good choice for tropical regions.

Clothes for wet weather

Sudden downpours can occur just about anywhere and most hikers have been accidentally caught out in rainstorms or monsoons. Many regions that offer attractive hiking may experience periods of unsettled weather. If you carry the gear necessary to stay warm and dry, and make sure you keep it dry and accessible, you will be prepared for any wet conditions.

FABRICS THAT KEEP OUT MOISTURE

Garments that are breathable and waterproof keep out moisture while allowing sweat to escape. Gore-tex® is the best known of such laminates and used in many outdoor products. Polypropylene is also used to make inexpensive raingear that is both waterproof and breathable.

DRESSING FOR WET WEATHER

Choose raingear that fits loosely enough to allow free movement and to accommodate insulating layers if necessary.

A breathable, waterproof jacket allows sweat to escape while keeping rain out

Hood keeps the rain off and your neck warm

Rain leggings are essential in cold weather

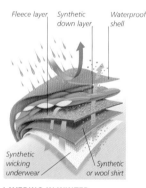

Fleece layer   Synthetic down layer   Waterproof shell

Synthetic wicking underwear   Synthetic or wool shirt

LAYERING IN WINTER

Wearing layers of clothes in cold and wet winter weather will help to keep you both warm and dry.

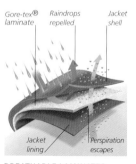

Gore-tex® laminate   Raindrops repelled   Jacket shell

Jacket lining   Perspiration escapes

BREATHABLE LAMINATES

The tiny holes in Gore-tex® laminate allow droplets of perspiration to escape, while keeping raindrops out.

LIGHT PONCHO

Ponchos, usually made from inexpensive coated nylon, are useful in warm weather because they provide plenty of ventilation. The back of a poncho can be draped over a backpack or daypack as a rain cover.

A hood retains heat around the head and neck

Drawstring fastening keeps the rain out

PONCHO

Choose the lightest poncho available. Very thin ponchos may not last for more than a season, but are worth buying because they are lightweight and inexpensive. They allow free movement and can accommodate extra layers underneath if needed.

Waterproof case
A waterproof map case is essential for navigating in rain.

RAIN HAT

The hat shown has a wide brim, which will prevent water dripping on to the face and down the back of the neck.

A chin strap will keep a rain hat from blowing off in a strong wind

KEEPING COOL AND DRY

In warm weather, a rain hat will keep your head dry, allow the neck to be ventilated, and also offer protection from the sun.

KEEPING RAINGEAR ACCESSIBLE

Always pack your raingear where you can retrieve it quickly if there is a sudden downpour. Keeping it in a side pocket or front compartment avoids having to open the main pack, which avoids letting in rain.

Multiple compartments allow you to organize your raingear

DAYPACK CHOICE

This should be big enough to hold lunch, emergency gear, essentials, and an extra layer of clothing.

Contents kept inside a drawstring pouch are easily accessible when the weather turns bad

CHOOSING GEAR FOR DIFFERENT CONDITIONS

For warm weather, good conditions, or light showers:

- Lightweight rain jacket or poncho
- Wind shirt
- Loose fitting t-shirt
- Rain/sun hat
- Water-resistant footwear

For cold weather, difficult conditions, or downpours:

- Insulating layers
- Waterproof jacket with hood
- Waterproof leggings
- Gaiters
- Boots
- Rain hat

Clothes for cold weather

Hiking in cold weather can be both exhilarating and enjoyable. There are fewer insects than in hot weather and you are not subject to the debilitating exhaustion resulting from steep climbs in high temperatures. Usually, fewer people are out walking, so you can appreciate the solitude. But to enjoy yourself, you need to wear clothes that suit the conditions.

SNOWY WEATHER

You need to pay careful attention to clothing layers. Use a lightweight base layer to wick away moisture from your skin, several layers of warm insulating clothing, and an outer shell that is waterproof and windproof for weather protection. Be sure to brush away snow so that it does not creep inside your clothing, where it will melt. Walk at a slow, steady pace that you can maintain – this will avoid the need to stop and get cold.

A waterproof, insulated jacket with watertight zip forms part of the outer layer

HIKING IN SNOW

When active in cold conditions, wear a waterproof outer layer to keep warm and dry.

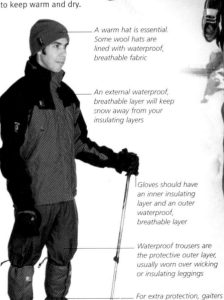

A warm hat is essential. Some wool hats are lined with waterproof, breathable fabric

An external waterproof, breathable layer will keep snow away from your insulating layers

Gloves should have an inner insulating layer and an outer waterproof, breathable layer

Waterproof trousers are the protective outer layer, usually worn over wicking or insulating leggings

For extra protection, gaiters cover your boots and keep snow away from your feet

Heavy leather boots will keep your feet warm and dry

Waterproof, lightweight trousers will keep your legs dry in deep snow

PLANNING AHEAD

Put on the clothing you plan to wear, go outdoors and stand still. If you are slightly chilled, you are dressed appropriately for walking. If you are comfortable, or too hot, remove some clothes.

COOL AND COLD DRY WEATHER

Be sure to wear a wicking base layer to keep moisture away from your skin. When the weather is dry but blustery, use a windproof outer layer (either a wind shirt or a windproof microfibre) to help stay warm. Keep a hat and gloves handy in case the temperature drops further. The secret to staying comfortable is to constantly adjust your layers as your body temperature changes. When you are going uphill and working hard, remove layers to avoid sweating. When you are walking easily downhill, add a layer to stay warm.

A hat helps you regulate your body temperature

Wicking base layers come in several different weights; colder temperatures require heavier weights

A windproof outer layer will help you to stay warm, especially in exposed surroundings

DRESSING FOR THE COLD
Use multiple layers so you can quickly adapt to changing temperatures.

COOL AND COLD RAINY WEATHER

Wear a wicking base layer next to the skin, and an outer layer consisting of a waterproof, breathable jacket and trousers. In very exposed conditions where you encounter cold, wind-driven rain, you may need to add another insulating layer to keep your body warm. Most hikers chill quickly in cold weather when they are not walking, so the fewer breaks you take, the better. Try to set a moderate pace that you can keep up all day, even going uphill.

A hood can be worn over a hat for extra protection, if necessary

Draw cords prevent warm air escaping from the vulnerable neck area

A rain jacket needs to cover the hips and fit over insulating layers

DRESSING FOR THE COLD AND WET
Do not over-dress – sweat can soak you as much as rain.

STAYING COMFORTABLE IN COOL AND COLD WEATHER

Your clothing can help to keep you comfortable while you are hiking in cold conditions.
■ **Pick a pace that is comfortable,** even going uphill. If you move too fast you may work up a sweat, which can condense when you stop to take a break, leaving you damp.
■ **Have easily accessible quick snacks** that you can eat while walking. These will enable you to keep up a steady pace.
■ **Once you have picked your pace,** adjust your clothing so that you are comfortable.

This may involve putting on or taking off layers, or using clothing features such as venting pockets and zips to adjust your temperature and ventilation.
■ **Remember that adding or removing** a hat and gloves is the quickest and most effective way to adjust your body's core temperature.
■ **If it is raining, use a waterproof hat** with a brim to keep water away from your face (and glasses, if you wear them) and to stop it going down your neck.

Clothes for camping

At the end of a rigorous day of hiking, you will probably be tired and hungry. You may also be cold. In the cooler evening hours, you can chill quickly because your clothes have become damp with sweat or rain. Being warm and dry in camp is a matter of safety, comfort, and enjoyment, so having dry clothes available at all times is very important. Also, hiking is hard on outdoor clothing – it will perform better and last longer if well cared for.

CHANGING OUT OF DAY CLOTHES
As soon as you get to camp, change into warm, dry clothes as the clothing you wore in the day is probably damp and dirty. Changing avoids catching a chill and the possibility of hypothermia. Use a wicking layer of polypropylene long underwear and, if needed, a fleece jacket and a hat. If you expect to be camping in temperatures below freezing, a down jacket is ideal for evening warmth. Spread your day clothes out to air, so that they are dry for the next day.

CLOTHES FOR SLEEPING
To stay warm in a sleeping bag, you need to wear layers. Ideally, you should wear a layer of clean polypropylene long underwear. This not only protects your sleeping bag against dirt (to increase the bag's longevity) but also keeps you more comfortable and warm. In low temperatures, add a hat and gloves, do up all the zips and collars on your sleeping bag, or add another layer of clothing. If you have only two sets of clothes, wear your camp clothes at night.

UNEXPECTED COLD NIGHTS
Occasionally, a surprise cold front will reduce night-time temperatures to well below expectations. You can add several layers of clothing – including raingear, if it is dry. Raingear will hold some of your body heat close to your skin while you are sleeping.

WASHING CLOTHES
When you set up camp, rinse out your hiking clothes, if time allows. Synthetics dry quickly in sunshine, but cotton and wool take many hours.

DRYING CLOTHES

To shorten drying time, wring clothes several times and hang them on a clothesline. When your clothes are dry, a clothesline can be used to hang food safely away from animals. It can also be used for emergencies, or to lash items to your pack.

CARING FOR CLOTHES IN CAMP

When you have finished hiking for the day, rinse out your hiking clothes if you have time – many synthetic fabrics dry very quickly, especially on a sunny afternoon. When washing clothes, never use soap directly in a water source and dispose of it carefully into the ground. If you do not have a container big enough to wash clothes in, settle for a quick rinse, then hang to dry from a length of clothesline tied between two trees. If you do not have time to clean or rinse your clothes, give them a good airing – hang them from a line, a tree branch, or lay them out on a rock.

CARING FOR CLOTHES AT HOME

Regard the care you take of clothing as an investment. Treat expensive fabrics properly with recommended cleaning products, to ensure their long life.

■ **Read fabric labels carefully** for care instructions. Outdoor fabrics must be washed at specific temperatures with mild soap (not detergents) and most should not be dry cleaned. Polypropylene and many wool products must be washed in cold water, never hot water.

■ **Dry clothes according** to manufacturers' directions. Most fleece clothing can be dried in a machine, as can many Gore-tex® garments. Polypropylene can never be dried in a clothes drier, and neither should most wool garments.

■ **The durable water-repellent coating** of Gore-tex® and other waterproof, breathable fabrics can wear off. If your jacket appears to be absorbing water, the problem is most likely to be this. Ironing it may help. Also, compounds that rejuvenate the water repellency coating are available from companies such as Nikwax®. These wash-in solutions restore the ability of the fabric to repel water. You will see the difference as water on a restored jacket will "bead" and run off. Check that the treatment does not contain a waterproofing agent that might reduce the garment's breathability.

■ **Use specialist cleaning products** to restore clothing made of fleece, soft-shell fabric, or down. Nikwax® produces a complete line of cleaners that prolong the longevity of your gear.

■ **Always clean and thoroughly dry** outdoor clothing before storing it for any length of time. Gear should be stored in a dry, well-ventilated area, where mould will not grow.

Footwear

Choosing suitable footwear involves matching your needs to one of the many different styles available. Hiking footwear ranges from lightweight trekking sandals to fully fledged mountaineering boots. However, by far the most important factor is a correct fit.

Understanding footwear

Choosing the right boot may be the most important decision you make when selecting gear. An ill-fitting boot can cause nothing but misery, and more hikes are ruined by blisters and foot pain than by anything else. Evaluate the conditions in which you plan to hike, and also consider your own history of footwear use, footwear problems, and fit difficulties.

THE ANATOMY OF A BOOT

Understanding the ways in which the different types of boots are constructed, and the importance – and relevance – of all the different features, means that you can choose the boots that will most suit the conditions in which you plan to hike.

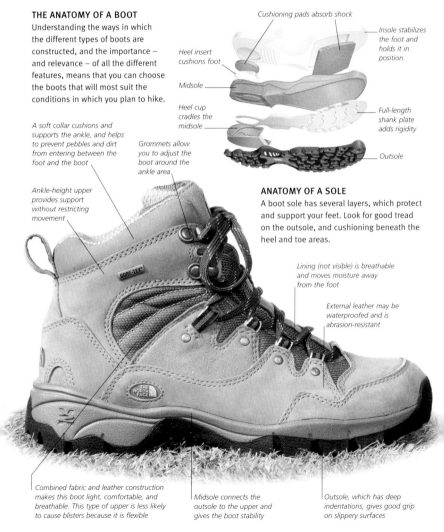

Cushioning pads absorb shock

Insole stabilizes the foot and holds it in position

Heel insert cushions foot

Midsole

Heel cup cradles the midsole

Full-length shank plate adds rigidity

Outsole

A soft collar cushions and supports the ankle, and helps to prevent pebbles and dirt from entering between the foot and the boot

Grommets allow you to adjust the boot around the ankle area

Ankle-height upper provides support without restricting movement

ANATOMY OF A SOLE

A boot sole has several layers, which protect and support your feet. Look for good tread on the outsole, and cushioning beneath the heel and toe areas.

Lining (not visible) is breathable and moves moisture away from the foot

External leather may be waterproofed and is abrasion-resistant

Combined fabric and leather construction makes this boot light, comfortable, and breathable. This type of upper is less likely to cause blisters because it is flexible

Midsole connects the outsole to the upper and gives the boot stability

Outsole, which has deep indentations, gives good grip on slippery surfaces

Choosing socks

Socks are an important part of your footwear system. Their function is to wick sweat away from your feet, and to provide cushioning. They also provide warmth and can be used to fine-tune the fit of a boot. Try wearing a thicker sock with a slightly large boot, a thinner sock with a slightly tight boot, or two pairs of socks if there is room.

WICKING SOCKS

A lightweight inner sock made from a wicking fabric draws moisture away from your feet, helping to prevent blisters. Lightweight wool and polypropylene socks also do not cause friction, so are less likely to rub.

INNER SOCKS

Socks made from wool and polypropylene are smooth against the skin, and are more comfortable to wear if you have blisters.

SUMMER SOCKS

Summer-weight socks can be made of wool or a wool-nylon blend. Wool is a good choice even in hot weather, because it draws moisture away from the foot and provides cushioning. Socks that contain nylon will last longer.

LIGHT SOCKS

These socks are thick under the sole and heel, but are lighter and thinner around the ankle and over the top of the foot.

THREE-SEASON SOCKS

These are also called trekking socks, and are thicker than summer-weight socks. Thicker socks are used by many hikers in the summer because their added cushioning is highly effective in preventing blisters.

TREKKING SOCKS

These long-lasting socks are a good choice for long-distance hikers.

WINTER SOCKS

Winter-weight socks are thicker than three-season socks. Like other wool socks, they should be worn with a lightweight wicking inner sock. Be sure your boots are big enough to accommodate them. Socks that are too thick for the boot can constrict circulation.

WINTER-WEIGHT SOCKS

These socks are only needed in temperatures well below freezing.

ADDING COMFORT

To ensure long-term comfort, you can adjust your footwear by adding insoles, heel pads, or sock liners.

■ Insoles are shaped liners that slide into your boot or shoe. They improve fit, and so reduce chafing and help prevent blisters.

■ Custom-fitted insoles for your boots may be recommended by a chiropodist. If you have recurring foot pain, consult a specialist and take your boots to the appointment.

■ Soft, heel-shaped pads made of rubber, foam, or gel can help to alleviate heel pain while walking.

■ Thin sock liners fit between your inner sock and outer sock to hold in the heat in very cold weather.

Types of boot

There are two factors that determine the type of boot you select. The first concerns your personal requirements. These include the shape of your feet and how much support they need.

You also need to consider how far you are travelling and the terrain. Keep the weight of your boots as light as possible because unnecessary weight on your feet can be extremely tiring.

LIGHT TRAINER BOOT

Fabric and leather hybrids are popular on trails worldwide because they combine the support and traction of a boot with the weight and flexibility of a trainer. Many have waterproof, breathable linings. These boots tend to cause fewer blisters because of their flexible construction.

Flexible fabric uppers allow the boot to breathe

FABRIC AND LEATHER HYBRID

Hybrids are a good choice for day and overnight hikers on moderate terrain because of their comfort and light weight.

MIDDLEWEIGHT BOOT

A good compromise between the new trainer boots and the traditional heavier, higher-cut leather boots, middleweight boots are cut lower on the ankle, are made of lighter-weight materials, and are more flexible than traditional leather.

The boot is cut low on the ankle, so it is more flexible

LIGHT LEATHER BOOT

Nubuck leather boots provide more support and water repellency than a hybrid, and are a reasonable weight for hiking.

TRADITIONAL HEAVY LEATHER BOOT

Heavier boots have fallen out of favour with the arrival of new, lighter types. However, they are frequently preferred by hikers who carry heavy loads on rough terrain.

A high cut gives good ankle support

HEAVY LEATHER BOOT

Three-season full-grain leather boots are heavier, but provide excellent support and good protection in snow.

SNOWSHOEING BOOT

Traditional snowshoeing boots are lined with thick felt. Most modern boots have an insulated foot bed, to reduce heatloss through the sole of the boot. The waterproof leather upper and rubber outsole keep feet warm and dry.

Flexible uppers are comfortable, but do not give enough support for long hikes

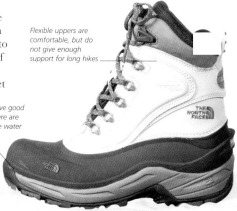

Rubber soles have good traction and there are no seams where water can seep in

SNOWSHOEING BOOT
Snowshoeing boots usually have an inner insulating boot made of felt or a synthetic material such as Thinsulate®.

CLIMBING AND HIKING HYBRID

Modern climbing boots have a more flexible construction than traditional boots. They are designed to be worn with crampons and to keep feet warm in very cold temperatures, but they can also be worn without crampons for hiking on approach trails.

Crampons can be worn to give extra grip when walking on snow and ice

CLIMBING BOOT
The weight and stiffness of climbing boots make them inappropriate choices for very long-distance treks.

JUNGLE-TREKKING BOOT

These are high boots made with rubber soles, leather toes, and heels, with canvas and nylon uppers. They should fit sufficiently snugly that the suction of thick mud cannot pull them off your feet. Jungle boots can cause the feet to sweat and swell, so make sure they are not too tight, and wear moisture-wicking socks. In hot weather, carry alternative footwear such as light trainers or trekking sandals for camp and for use on easier terrain.

High uppers keep mud off your trousers

Leather provides waterproofing

JUNGLE-TREKKING BOOT
Jungle boots are waterproof, fit high on the lower leg, and are tight-fitting.

Fitting boots

The most important aspect of choosing the correct footwear is fit. However, a boot that feels fine in the shop may cause blisters later. A skilled salesperson can help you to find the right boot, but knowledge of the fitting process can help. Above all, do not rush – you will pay for your haste on the trail.

FINDING THE PERFECT FIT

Shop for boots in the afternoon, when your feet are naturally slightly swollen from walking. Wear the socks you plan to wear while trekking and if you use therapeutic insoles or orthotics, bring them too. Be sure to have your feet measured while you sit and stand. Alert the salesperson to any problems or fit issues, such as a common blister point.

The boot should fit snugly. When you push your foot all the way forward, you should be able to fit one finger between the back of your foot and the boot. Check that the forefoot is wide enough for your toes to move.

Stand on a slope (most shops can provide this) to check that your toes do not bang against the front of the boot when you are facing downhill. When facing uphill, push your heel up as far as it will go. It should not come up more than about 1 cm ($\frac{1}{2}$ in).

Try on several pairs of boots for comparison. Wear the boots in the shop for a while to feel for any trouble spots, such as rubbing, squeezing, or tingling.

At home, wear the boots indoors for a few days to continue to check the fit. Most retailers will allow you to return boots if you have not worn them outside. When you are completely happy with your boots, start breaking them in, on short walks at first, then on longer ones.

ADJUSTING FIT

Sometimes you can adjust the fit of old boots. If they are too big, add an insole or wear thicker socks. Moleskin can be used to pad parts of the foot where the boot is loose and rubbing. If boots are too tight, try wearing a lighter pair of socks. Some boots can be stretched by a cobbler, or you can rub a coin on the inside of the boot to push out and stretch uncomfortable areas.

CURING PRONATION AND SUPPINATION

Pronation and suppination are common problems. In pronation, the ankle bends inwards as you walk. In suppination, which is less common, the ankle bends outwards.

This can lead to ongoing foot pain. Use special insoles to keep the foot firmly in place inside the boot. These insoles also help to hold the foot in a straighter position.

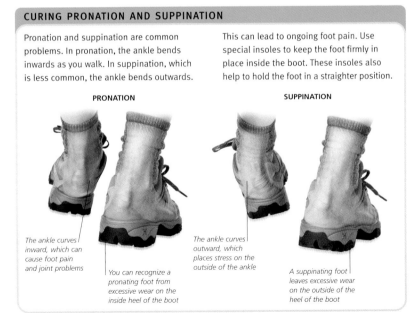

PRONATION

SUPPINATION

The ankle curves inward, which can cause foot pain and joint problems

You can recognize a pronating foot from excessive wear on the inside heel of the boot

The ankle curves outward, which places stress on the outside of the ankle

A suppinating foot leaves excessive wear on the outside of the heel of the boot

Caring for boots

Boots take every step of a hike with you, and can come into contact with mud, water, snow, ice, rocks, and dirt. Leather is durable and water repellent, but without care it will weaken, shrink, and dry out, leading to cracks in the surface. With proper care, however, a pair of boots can last for years.

MAINTAINING WATER REPELLENCY

Many fabric and leather hybrids need no preparation and can simply be worn straight out of the box, but leather boots need treating with a waterproofing solution. A few manufacturers recommend, or even provide, specific waterproofing products – follow their directions or you may void your boot guarantee. With many manufacturers, you may safely use one of the variety of waterproofing and leather conditioning products that are commercially available. Be sure the product is formulated for the type of leather in your boot.

Reapplication will be necessary to maintain waterproofing and suppleness, especially after heavy wear. Rub in the waterproofing treatment thoroughly and allow the boots to dry before using them again.

CLEANING LEATHER BOOTS

Regular cleaning prevents particles of dirt from working their way into the leather. Whenever possible, brush, wipe, or rinse away mud and dirt with water. To remove stubborn grime, you may need to use a boot-cleaning solution.

CLEANING BOOT LININGS

Wipe the inner lining of your boots clean after each hike to remove dirt and salt from perspiration, which breaks down the lining. Sprinkle bicarbonate of soda inside boots to help control odours.

DRYING BOOTS

Never dry boots near a direct heat source such as a radiator, fire, or an oven. Fast drying will permanently damage the leather as well as the adhesives that hold the sole in place. Remove the laces and insoles, and stuff the boots with newspaper. Allow them to dry slowly at normal room temperature.

MENDING A DELAMINATED SOLE

Delamination occurs when the sole of the boot starts to peel away from the boot upper, usually near the toe. Repairing delaminated soles requires a strong glue.

1 Clean the area thoroughly with alcohol, as glue will not be effective if dirt is present. When the area to be repaired is dry, apply a generous amount of glue.

2 Leave the glue for a few minutes to become tacky, then fix the sole back in place by pressing it against the boot.

3 Hold the repair in place with duct tape and allow the glue to dry for at least 24 hours before wearing.

Footwear for day hikes

Not everyone needs hiking boots – day hikers may find that cross-trainers are more comfortable and less expensive. Trekking shoes, sandals, or other lighter alternatives are often sufficient for overnight hikes, and many hikers now favour these alternatives to the heavy, traditional boot. On longer treks, lightweight footwear will support you best if you carry less pack weight.

CROSS-TRAINER

It is perfectly feasible to go hiking without wearing boots. On many kinds of terrain, such as well-maintained footpaths, cross-trainers are adequate. However, they lack the traction and ankle support of trekking shoes or hiking boots, and so are not a good choice on muddy or uneven routes.

Cross-trainers should be roomy enough for hiking socks

A MULTI-PURPOSE SHOE

Cross-trainers usually have less cushioning and support in the forefoot than trekking shoes.

TREKKING SHOE

This type of shoe is lightweight, durable, and usually made of breathable material. Trekking shoes are often less expensive than hiking boots, and provide good traction and lateral support on a variety of terrain. They are often adequate for day hikers or overnight hikers with light backpacks.

SUPPORTIVE YET LIGHTWEIGHT

A cross between light trainer boots and trail-running shoes, trekking shoes offer more support than cross-trainers.

A stiff footbed and sole help prevent the foot from twisting

TRAIL-RUNNING SHOE

Many boot manufacturers now offer a line of trail-running shoes designed with trail conditions in mind. The rubber outsole gives good traction and cushioning to the base of the shoe, while a two-tier lace system keeps the shoe firmly in place.

A LIGHTER OPTION

Although lightweight and flexible, trail-running shoes lack the necessary support for all-day hiking with a fully-loaded backpack.

A cushioned heel adds to comfort

Rubber, abrasion-resistant outsole gives good traction and durability

DECIDING BETWEEN SHOES AND BOOTS

Wear shoes if the following applies:
- You are prone to blisters
- You will be hiking on easy terrain or well-maintained footpaths
- You will be carrying only a daypack

Wear boots if the following applies:
- Your ankles are prone to twisting
- You will be hiking on rocky or muddy terrain, or you will be hiking cross-country
- You will be carrying a heavy backpack

TREKKING SANDALS

The traditional amphibious sandal worn by kayakers has recently been adapted for hiking on warm days. Some models have toe bumpers to protect toes from rocks and roots, a strapping system that holds the foot in place even on uneven terrain, and arch supports, which help to hold the sandal in position.

TRAIL SANDAL

Sandals that are designed for use when hiking have rugged soles to grip the trail surface and a strong construction.

A strapping system holds the foot in place

An adjustable fastener ensures a snug fit

Solidly constructed sole, but no protection for toes

LIGHTWEIGHT SANDAL

A pair of lightweight sandals is a good choice as back-up footwear, or for day hiking on well-groomed trails.

Some models have back fastenings, making the sandal easy to slip on

Ridged sole helps to prevent the foot from slipping in the sandal

The sole is lighter, but also thinner and less rugged than the trail model

THE NORTH FACE

CAMPSITE WEAR

Some hikers additionally carry very light footwear for use when camping in mild weather. Inexpensive flip-flops and lightweight sandals are good choices that can also be used on the beach or in water.

Slip-on style is convenient for use at camp

An open heel makes flip-flops unsuitable for trail hiking

FLIP-FLOPS

With no support or cushioning, these lightweight slip-on shoes should not be worn on the trail.

Backpacks

Whether on a day hike or a week-long trek, you will be probably be wearing a backpack, so choosing the right one for your equipment and your body is important. The backpack is one of your most essential items of hiking gear, and it needs to fit comfortably.

Choosing a backpack

Backpacks are essentially fabric sacks attached to a frame. The sack holds the equipment while the frame distributes the weight. An internal frame is lightweight and comfortable.

Traditional external frame backpacks are used by hikers who carry heavy loads. Modular backpacks give you the flexibility of a large backpack, a holdall, and a daypack.

INTERNAL FRAME BACKPACK

This type of pack has its origins in the mountaineering world, where an external frame would be a dangerous liability because it could catch on rock or ice. Most of your gear rides securely inside an internal frame backpack, although some expedition packs have external ice axe loops, crampon guards, ski pockets, and lashing points for carrying extra gear.

BACKPACK CAPACITY

In Europe, pack capacity is measured in litres. Your backpack size depends on how many days of hiking you plan to do, the climate, how much gear you plan to take, and your body size. A large pack capacity is usually between 75 and 95 litres.

FROM MOUNTAINEERING TO THE TRAIL

Internal frames have become increasingly popular in recent years and are now more widely available than external frame packs.

Top lid compartment, ideal for raingear

Compression strap to reduce bulk

Additional compartment makes items accessible

Fully adjustable harness for support

Padded shoulder strap for comfort

Lashing points for extra gear

Straps for lashing extra items

Fully adjustable hip belt

EXTERNAL FRAME BACKPACK

These backpacks are the classic hiking carry-alls. Essentially, they consist of a rigid frame, usually made of aluminium, that rides on your back. Suspended from the frame is a sack, normally divided into several compartments. Additional gear can be strapped on the frame, usually above and below the main compartment.

CLASSIC BACKPACK

A light external frame allows you to carry heavy loads.

Additional compartment makes items accessible

Frame is strong and lightweight

Hour-glass shape of frame allows weight to sit high on the back

Uppermost compartment is ideal for raingear

Side pockets for daily necessities

Sleeping bag compartment for easy access to contents

Hip belt attached to lower frame of backpack

BACKPACK FEATURES

Consider these factors before choosing between an internal or external frame.

INTERNAL FRAME

- Carries load weight low and closer to the back
- Ideal for rough terrain because close fit reduces bouncing and helps to maintain balance
- Preferred by women because the low centre of gravity makes the weight more comfortable

EXTERNAL FRAME

- Carries weight high up
- Good for ventilation as frame holds pack away from the back
- Often less expensive than comparable internal frame packs
- More compartments for organizing gear

MODULAR BACKPACKS

Modular packs represent a new innovation in backpack design. These packs can be expanded depending on your trip. Take off the daypack if you do not need it, so that you have a smaller, lighter pack on a summer hike. Re-attach it for a longer trip.

Main pack is big enough for weekend jaunts

Zip off daypack can be used separately

MAIN PACK AND DAYPACK

FLEXIBLE PACK

This backpack can be used as a traditional backack, holdall, or daypack.

Zipped to the main pack, the daypack adds extra space

Zipped compartment gives easy access to contents

Shoulder straps and hip straps operate like those of a traditional backpack

Shoulder straps and waist band are tucked in and secured

EXPANDED MODULAR BACKPACK

Pack can be carried by a handle on its side

HOLDALL

Fitting and packing your backpack

How comfortable a backpack is depends on how well it fits, how well it is packed, and how much it weighs. Packs come in different sizes, with components such as hip belts, harnesses, and frames, so be sure to allow time for fitting when buying. Aim for a pack that rides comfortably on your back without chafing, hurting your shoulders, or pulling on your neck.

MEASURING PACK SIZE

Backpack sizing is based on torso length, which runs from the bony protrusion at the base of your neck to the small of the back. Each manufacturer has its own sizing scale, with some offering different sizes of shoulder harnesses and hip belts.

FITTING YOUR PACK

Fitting should be done with a lightly loaded pack. Shops often have pillows and sacks on hand for this purpose.

Loosen all the straps, fit the pack onto your shoulders, then tighten the lower shoulder straps and the hip belt until they feel snug. You can alter the load lifter straps (behind your shoulders) to transfer weight from the shoulders to the hips and vice versa. Some packs have load stabilizer straps, which pull the backpack more tightly on the hips. Women in particular find this a useful adjustment to make for comfort because of their lower centre of gravity.

SIZING UP YOUR BACKPACK

For an accurate fit, your back should first be measured. Select a pack based on your torso length and try it on.

Measure from the prominent vertebrae at the base of the neck

Measure to the point in the small of the back level with the top of the hip bones

ADJUSTING THE FIT

Be sure that all parts of the pack fit comfortably with straps adjusted to allow for any changes in your weight or bulky clothing.

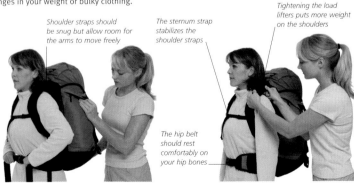

Shoulder straps should be snug but allow room for the arms to move freely

The sternum strap stabilizes the shoulder straps

Tightening the load lifters puts more weight on the shoulders

The hip belt should rest comfortably on your hip bones

PACKING YOUR BACKPACK

Keep your gear organized in waterproof stuff sacks to protect it from rain and keep it clean. Your daily essentials should be readily available, and the bulk of your heavy items should be as close to your back as possible in order to avoid the backpack pulling away from your shoulders. Lighter items should be towards the bottom of the pack.

ORGANIZING A BACKPACK

This is one of several ways to organize a backpack; every hiker takes slightly different gear and must fit it into a slightly different size and shape of pack.

Use a ditty (cloth) bag to hold personal essentials such as a roll of toilet paper

Store daily essentials such as lip balm, snacks, sunglasses, a compass, a pocket knife, maps and guidebooks, insect repellent, and sunscreen in an outer pocket

Carry your water bottle where it is upright and accessible

Keep your sleeping bag in a waterproof stuff sack

Use the bottom compartment of your pack for your sleeping mat and sleeping bag

Put your tent in a waterproof stuff sack and strap it to the outside of your pack

Pack raingear and a waterproof sack containing extra layers, gloves, and a hat at the top of your pack where they are accessible

Put your first-aid kit where the contents are secure, and yet accessible

Place bags containing stove, eating utensils, and cook set near to the back, as they are heavy

Store food bags close to the back because they are likely to be heavy

Keep your clothing in a waterproof stuff sack to ensure it stays dry

Secure your fuel bottle outside the pack in an upright position to minimize the risk of leakage

Tent poles are durable so can be strapped on to the bottom of your pack

CARRYING SPARE PARTS

Packs are usually well made, but even the best construction cannot protect against a hiker who steps on a belt buckle or drops them down a rocky slope. A few simple items allow you to make necessary repairs:

■ Heavy-duty carpet needle and thread strong enough that you cannot break it with your hands
■ Extra belt buckle
■ Extra shoulder strap buckles
■ Clevis pins (for external-frame packs)
■ Pliers (for manipulating broken parts of external-frame packs)

WET WEATHER

Store items in protective bags in case of wet weather. Use the pouches of your pack to carry items you will need on a rainy day.

■ A top compartment is handy for items such as raingear, pack cover, and lunch.
■ A small pouch worn on your hip belt can be used to stow guidebook pages, a pocket knife, your compass, and insect repellent.
■ Be sure to protect electronic equipment in zip-locking bags or waterproof pouches.
■ A bin liner is useful for waterproofing your sleeping bag or reinforcing your clothing bag stuff sacks.

Backpacks for short trips

You do not always need a huge pack. Smaller backpacks are easier to carry and lighter when hiking. Bags that can be used both as traditional holdalls and as internal frame backpacks are more convenient for travellers with varied itineraries. Daypacks and lightweight backpacks with lashing-points for attaching gear can be useful for overnight hikes with small loads.

CONVERTIBLE TRAVEL PACK

A versatile travel pack has long been a favourite with backpackers who move from hostel to hostel. They can be carried as a backpack, but can also be converted into a holdall, which can be a useful alternative in towns.

AS A HOLDALL

Using a convertible travel pack makes sense if you will be travelling on planes or buses, when exposed pack straps can be damaged in transit.

For rigidity, a backpack is supported by an internal frame

Thin hip belt is best suited to short hikes with light loads

With straps tucked in, the holdall can be carried like a suitcase

Shoulder straps and waist belt are safely stowed away under fabric flaps

AS A BACKPACK

If the convertible pack is to be used primarily for hiking, choose one with comfort features, such as a padded hip belt and a supporting internal frame for rigidity.

DAYPACK

Carrying a full-size backpack on a day hike is a waste of effort – the pack would be only half full and the extra weight of the bag would be an unnecessary burden. Instead, choose a daypack. Ensure it can carry a full day's supplies for hiking in challenging terrain with unsettled weather. A small daypack need not have a hip belt; but those meant for heavier loads should have one.

Elastic cord strapping can be used to attach items to the outside of the pack

Second zipped compartment helps you keep gear organized

HOW LARGE?

Daypacks range in capacity from 20 to 45 litres. Choose a pack that is big enough to hold extra clothes, raingear, food, and emergency supplies.

Side pouch can be used to carry a water bottle

DAYPACK ON BACK

CONVERTIBLE COMPARTMENTS

Some backpacks have a top compartment, or lid, that can be removed from the main pack, strapped around your waist, and worn as a cross between a daypack and a belt bag. These are especially useful if you are base-camping and want to do a short day hike, or walk with only minimal supplies.

LID WORN AS BELT BAG

THREE PACKS IN ONE

You have the choice of using the backpack and compartment together, the backpack alone, or the belt bag alone.

BACKPACK AND LID

LIGHTWEIGHT BACKPACK

A lightweight backpack does not have a rigid frame, so it is easy to travel with it packed inside a suitcase. These backpacks are used by hikers with light loads, and are convenient if you are travelling by train or car, but want the option of taking a hiking trip as well.

The top compartment folds over the pack and is secured with compression straps

A frameless pack is light and flexible, but heavy loads may be uncomfortable

Belts on lightweight packs are less padded than belts on standard packs

PACKS FOR LIGHT LOADS

Lightweight backpacks are well-suited to weekend use but not recommended for extended trips

BELT BAG

When day-hiking in warm weather with minimal equipment, a belt bag is ideal.

THE LIGHTWEIGHT CHOICE

A belt bag is big enough for snacks and personal items, but not to carry extra clothes such as raingear.

BELT BAG ON WAIST

STUFF SACK

A stuff sack is useful for short, impromptu side-trips from a base camp. The straps used on some compression sacks can also be used to carry the sack over the shoulder knapsack-style.

Drawstrings are pulled to close the top of the bag

TWO USES FOR ONE SACK

Compression sacks, commonly used to carry sleeping bags, also double as light daypacks.

Pull up on the straps to compress the bag

Tents

Choosing your wilderness home is a matter of matching your needs to the many types of tent on the market. Look for the lightest tent available that meets your requirements. A two-person tent for temperate weather should weigh less than 2.5 kg (5^1/$_2$ lb).

Tent construction

Three-season tents are designed for use in a variety of climates and have construction features found on most types of tent. The inner layer is made of lightweight material, which offers both insect protection and ventilation.

The flysheet and floor are made of waterproof fabric, which should extend about 10 cm (4 in) above the ground. Most tents use two or three poles, depending on whether they are built for low weight or stability.

THREE-SEASON TENT INNER
Typical of most tent designs, the three-season tent demonstrates how lightweight materials and innovative design features combine to give a secure, portable shelter.

Pole separates inner tent and flysheet, allowing air to circulate

Inner-tent material is uncoated to aid ventilation and disperse condensation

Swift clip
Securely attaches inner tent to poles quickly and easily

Panels of material allow tent to take an irregular shape

Seams are double-stitched to withstand tension

Pole sleeve
Guides pole around inner tent to distribute strain on sleeve evenly

Flysheet attachment
Colour coded to allow each pole to be matched quickly to the right grommet

THREE-SEASON TENT WITH FLYSHEET

The flysheet extends in front of the tent to form a vestibule for gear storage, and provides good protection from the rain. When closed, an extended flysheet may result in poor ventilation.

Guy rope anchors tent securely against high winds

Outer door can be rolled horizontally and fixed to flysheet

Flysheet extends to the ground

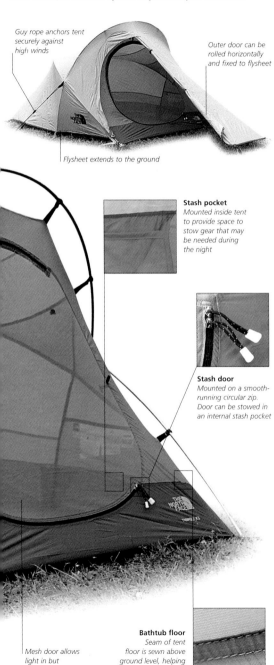

Stash pocket
Mounted inside tent to provide space to stow gear that may be needed during the night

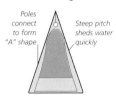

Stash door
Mounted on a smooth-running circular zip. Door can be stowed in an internal stash pocket

Bathtub floor
Seam of tent floor is sewn above ground level, helping to prevent leakage during storms

Mesh door allows light in but prevents insects from entering

TENT FRAME DESIGN

Most tents use one of three basic frame designs. Innovative tent designs often incorporate elements from one or more of these basic shapes.

A-FRAME

The oldest design is the A-frame. Easy to pitch in poor weather, it does not suffer from condensation and is reasonably priced compared to tents using other frame designs.

Poles connect to form "A" shape

Steep pitch sheds water quickly

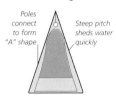

TUNNEL

The tunnel frame uses curved poles to achieve a greater internal volume than the A-frame, and tends to be less heavy.

Curved poles provide headroom

Only two poles means less weight

DOME

The dome frame also uses curved poles, but achieves greater rigidity by single or multiple crossings of the poles.

Rounded shape sheds snow

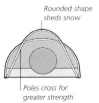

Poles cross for greater strength

Choosing a tent

The secret to choosing the right tent is to have a clear idea of the terrain and weather you expect to be camping in. Tents are categorized according to the conditions they can be used in –

a summer tent will be adequate for warm-weather trips, a three-season tent for both warm and cold conditions, and a winter tent for camping in severe weather.

SUMMER TENT

Sacrificing complete weather protection for views and ventilation, summer tents weigh less than three-season or winter tents. The inner tent is usually made of insect-proof netting, while the flysheet gives adequate coverage for warm-weather squalls, but may not withstand a mountain storm. Summer tents are best used in temperate climates below the treeline, since they are less stable in fierce storms than three-season and winter tents. Pitch them near sheltering trees or windbreaks.

LIGHTWEIGHT SUMMER TENT

Weight is saved by using two poles in a crossed pattern, and lightweight mesh in place of heavier material.

Flysheet does not reach the ground, giving good air circulation

Mesh fabric allows air to circulate

Buckle

SUMMER TENT WITH FLYSHEET

THREE-SEASON TENT

The most versatile and popular tents available are three-season tents. They are suitable for use in a wide range of climates and terrain, including light snowfall and high mountains. Most versions have vestibule areas for gear storage, two or more poles for stability, and good flysheet coverage. Three-season tents can be either freestanding or secured with stakes; the latter are less convenient to pitch – especially when camping on rocky ground – but are lighter in weight.

VERSATILE THREE-SEASON TENT

A balance is achieved between weight and durability by the use of mesh wherever possible, and an innovative, lightweight pole design.

Flysheet extends all the way to the ground for good weather protection

Low rear of tent provides stability when it is pitched against the wind

THREE-SEASON TENT WITH FLYSHEET

WINTER TENT

In winter, heavy snowfall and high winds mean that safety as well as comfort are the primary factors in tent selection. For hiking in severe winter conditions, look for a tent that offers extra-strong poles, storm windows, and ample pockets for gear storage. The dome shape sheds snow well, and withstands high winds and heavy snow accumulation. But beware – these extra features can push the weight of a tent to more than 4.5 kg (10 lb). Choose the lightest tent with the features you need.

ROBUST WINTER TENT

Strength is more important than low weight, so three aluminium poles are used, and durable ripstop nylon replaces lightweight mesh.

Front vestibule provides space for gear storage

Doorway allows hikers to cook in the vestibule without leaving their sleeping bags

WINTER TENT WITH FLYSHEET

QUESTIONS TO ASK BEFORE YOU BUY

Before you decide what type of tent to look for, ask yourself the following questions:
- In what terrain and weather conditions will the tent be used?
- Is comfort or low weight more important?

- How many people will it need to sleep?
- How much storage space will you require?
- Who will carry it? (If hiking with a partner, you can share the load of your tent, but if you plan to hike solo weight must be kept down.)

Pole crossing

Dome shape offers good head room

Doors on either side allow easy entry and exit when sharing a tent

Colour-coded attachment point

SUMMER TENT WITHOUT FLYSHEET

Poles cross at a single point for light weight and stability.

Buckle is a lightweight method of attaching the flysheet to the inner tent.

Colour-coded attachment point and poles allow easy tent erection.

Hook

Cam-lock clip

Mesh fabric

Pockets mounted inside the tent provide space to stow gear

Floor extends to give water protection

THREE-SEASON TENT WITHOUT FLYSHEET

Cam-lock clip attaches the inner tent to the poles for added security in poor weather.

Hook attaches the inner tent to the poles for quick erection in poor weather.

Mesh fabric and sealed-seam zip combine ventilation and waterproofing.

Ventilation zip

Three criss-crossed poles provide excellent stability in strong winds and heavy snow

Condensation sponge

Fully enclosed pole sleeve provides extra stability in poor weather

Zip tag

WINTER TENT WITHOUT FLYSHEET

Ventilation zip increases air circulation and dries wet gear in poor weather.

Condensation sponge absorbs moisture and stops the flysheet from touching the inner under snowfall.

Zip tag allows the tent door to be easily opened and shut when wearing thick winter gloves.

Tents for special conditions

Sometimes, a standard two-person tent is not necessary. It may be too large for your backpack, or too heavy for one person to carry. If you are anticipating good weather, or if you are expecting to sleep primarily in refuges, shelters, or hiker hostels, carry a smaller or a lighter tent, or other kind of shelter. It can be used for occasional or emergency use only.

SHELTER

This kiva shelter is a versatile tent. It can be traditionally rigged by using the adjustable pole or can be suspended from a branch. The tent has no floor so the ground can be dug out to provide standing and sleeping space for three or four people.

A single tent pole supports the structure

Upper zipped vent sits above opening to tent

Tent is supported in a pyramid shape

LIGHTWEIGHT SHELTER
The shelter is lightweight and suitable for most conditions. Flaps can be pegged down or buried.

The ground can be dug out for standing or sleeping

Ground level snow flaps can be folded under, or pegged out

BIVVY BAG

A bivvy bag is even smaller than a one-person tent. Bivvy bags usually consist of a single layer of waterproof, breathable fabric in the shape of a loose sleeping bag. While light to carry, they have little headroom and are prone to condensation.

One or more small tent poles can usually be inserted to hold the fabric up and away from your face

Limited height means you are restricted to a prone position

Ensure the bag is long enough for your height

SMALL SHELTER
A bivvy bag is most useful in a cool, dry climate, such as in high mountains.

At least two stakes are needed in the front

A vestibule provides storage space for gear

ONE-PERSON TENT

A solo tent is heavier than a tarpaulin, but provides greater protection in extremely wet weather. Like bivvy bags, they can be prone to condensation, and some of them have very limited headroom, making it difficult to eat when inside.

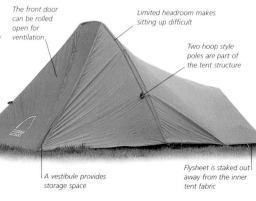

The front door can be rolled open for ventilation

Limited headroom makes sitting up difficult

Two hoop style poles are part of the tent structure

SOLO TENT
With more breathability than a bivvy bag, this is a good tent for wet, humid climates.

A vestibule provides storage space

Flysheet is staked out away from the inner tent fabric

Caring for your tent

To ensure that your tent will continue to keep you warm and dry in cold, wet weather, you must take care of it. Care includes preparing it, treating it gently during use, and cleaning and storing it properly after your hike. The useful life of a tent can be prolonged by using waterproofing treatments, and a groundsheet can help to protect it from damage.

PREPARING A TENT

Many modern tents are factory seam-sealed, which means a piece of tape is placed over the seams to prevent droplets of moisture entering through the stitching. However, your tent may need additional sealing because most manufacturers seal only the major seams, leaving the minor ones unprotected.

Sealant glue is available to purchase that can be pressed into the needle holes. A tube may come with your tent.

USING A GROUNDSHEET

A groundsheet is a piece of lightweight waterproof fabric placed under a tent to protect the fragile fabric from being damaged. It also helps to keep out any water that may pool under the tent.

PROTECTING AGAINST SUN AND FIRE

Tent fabric is lightweight, which makes it fragile. Over time, the fabric will degrade with exposure to direct sunlight. To prolong its life, try not to leave your tent pitched during the day. If you intend to pitch it in one place for several days, choose a well-shaded area. Also, be attentive to sparks from fires, which can damage the tent fabric.

CLEANING A TENT

Rinse your tent with water when you get home. If possible, do this in the evening to reduce exposure to direct sunlight. Pitch it, hose it, and let it stand until it dries. Never dry-clean a tent or put it in a washing machine or a tumble drier.

RESTORING WATER REPELLENCY

After many uses, some tents may lose their water repellency. This can be restored with commercially available waterproofing treatment and is usually applied to the uncoated side of the fabric.

STORING A TENT

Correct storage can prolong the life of your tent for many years. Ensure the tent is completely dry before putting it into a stuff sack. Alternatively, store it loose in a cool dry place.

SEAM SEALING

Work in a well-ventilated area. Pitch the tent so that the seams are taut, on a protected soft surface such as grass or a groundsheet. Do not pitch the tent on concrete or cement because, when you turn it upside down to seal the bottom, you could damage the fabric.

1 Keeping the seam taut, carefully brush the sealant on to all untaped seams, one by one.

2 Spread the sealant liberally and evenly on to the fabric so that it fills the holes in the stitching.

3 Wipe away excess and allow to dry, then apply a second coat. Do not store until it is completely dry.

Sleeping gear

After a hard day hiking, a good night's sleep is both appreciated and necessary. Choosing the right sleeping bag can help you to sleep comfortably – it should be warm enough for cold nights, yet not so warm that you are uncomfortably hot in milder conditions.

Sleeping bag features

A sleeping bag traps the air heated by your body and surrounds you with a protective shell of warm air. Fine filaments of down or synthetic fibres in the sleeping bag trap pockets of air, providing insulation. Thickly filled bags are the warmest, but quality and weight also need to be considered.

CHOOSING A SLEEPING BAG
When selecting a sleeping bag, you need to take into account its shape, insulating material, loft, construction methods, and individual features.

Cord lock
A locking mechanism secures the hood closed in cold weather, and can be loosened in mild weather

To retain body heat, a hood is essential for sleeping in colder weather. It should be roomy enough for you to turn your head

The sleeping bag should close securely around your shoulders, preventing warm air from escaping

Baffles are channels sewn into the bag to prevent the down from collecting in one area

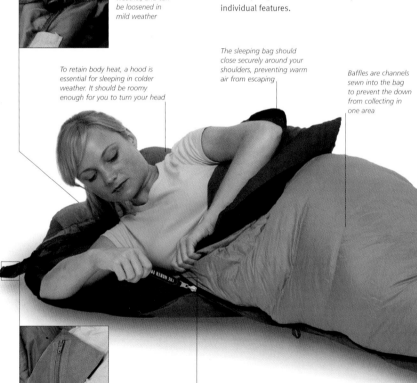

Pocket
Some sleeping bags come equipped with accessory pockets, which can be used to store small items such as a key or wallet

Zip
Ideally, a zip should be snag resistant and have a draught tube – a thin strip of down that fits over the zip on the inside of the bag, preventing heat from escaping and cold air from seeping in

SLEEPING BAG FILLINGS

Sleeping bags are made with either a down filling or a synthetic filling. Down sleeping bags are often used on high mountain expeditions because, for its weight, down is warmer than synthetic alternatives. It is also easier to compress, which is important when you have a lot of gear to fit into a small amount of space.

Goose down is better quality than duck down because it has more loft, which means that a goose down bag is warmer than a duck down bag of equivalent weight. Synthetic bags are preferable in damp climates because, unlike down, they retain some of their insulating value if they accidentally get wet. They also dry more quickly than down bags.

TEMPERATURE RATINGS

The warmth of a sleeping bag is identified by its temperature rating. In theory, a 0°C (32°F) bag should keep you warm in the stated temperature. If you are buying a three-season bag, look for the 0°C (32°F) rating. However, be aware that manufacturers differ in their standards, and hikers differ in their metabolisms, making temperature ratings an inexact science. Some manufacturers give a comfort rating and a survival rating, but these, too, are inexact.

In general, on a good quality bag, the fluffier the bag, the warmer it will be. In addition, the temperature rating can be affected by a number of design features, such as draught tubes on zips and the shape of the hood. Where the top of the sleeping bag wraps around your shoulders is another important area – a snug fit here will stop warm air from seeping out.

DOWN FILLING

Down filling consists of very small, light, down feathers. The quality of down is measured according to fill and loft:
■ Fill is another name for the down. It is rated according to its loft number (the volume). Known as the fill power rating, the loft is measured according to how much volume (in cubic inches) an ounce of fill takes up. Each manufacturer of down bags attaches a fill power rating to its insulation.
■ The higher the loft number the more efficient the insulation, so less filling is needed to fill a sleeping bag. This also means that the bag is lighter and more compact.

BAFFLES

Baffles are a feature of bag design that ensure an even spread of down.

SEWN-THROUGH

In this inexpensive construction, warm air may escape through uninsulated stitching.

BOXWALL

Mesh partitions at quilt lines prevent cold spots. It is costly, but very warm.

Try out a bag for fit before you buy. If it is too snug, you will feel constricted and your body will compress the filling, making it less effective

Extra baffles are often added to the foot section to help eliminate cold spots. The foot box should be big enough to allow for natural foot positions

Sleeping mats and accessories

In addition to a sleeping bag rated for the appropriate temperature, you will need a foam or air sleeping mat to ensure a comfortable and dry night's rest. Specialized gear, such as a mosquito net, a hammock, a space blanket, or an inflatable pillow may be needed in some environments.

SLEEPING MATS

An air or foam mat will not only help you to sleep more comfortably on hard or uneven ground, but will also provide insulation, preventing body heat from being lost through contact with the ground. The thicker the mat, the warmer it will be. Mats also act as a barrier between you and any moisture that may have seeped inside your tent.

AIR MATS

Available in different thicknesses, with some also containing a layer of foam, air mats provide superior comfort and thermal insulation. However, they are heavier and more expensive than foam mats. Self-inflating versions and blow-up versions are available, although most self-inflating mattresses do need topping up. Full-length mattresses are necessary in winter. In summer, a shorter length may suffice.

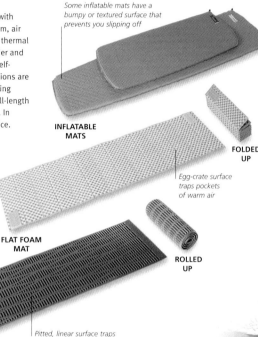

Some inflatable mats have a bumpy or textured surface that prevents you slipping off

INFLATABLE MATS

FOLDED UP

Egg-crate surface traps pockets of warm air

FOAM MATS

The lightest and simplest type, foam mats simply roll up and may be strapped under a backpack. They are most comfortable when used on soft ground, such as sand or pine needles. Foam mats can also be used underneath an air mat for extra ground insulation in winter.

FLAT FOAM MAT

ROLLED UP

Pitted, linear surface traps pockets of warm air

RIDGED FOAM MAT

PILLOW

An inflatable pillow is certainly not a necessity, but will add to your comfort. Alternatively, use a stuff sack filled with spare clothing or a rolled-up fleece top.

SLEEPING EASY

An inflatable pillow is an optional item – choose the lightest one available.

Rubberized cotton exterior can be wiped clean

Inflate according to comfort

SPACE BLANKET

A space blanket is made from lightweight heat-reflecting metallic material. It weighs only a few grammes, folds away easily, and gives emergency protection from poor weather.

QUICK WARM-UP

For maximum effect, wrap yourself up with the reflective side next to your body.

Aluminium coating reflects heat back to body

MOSQUITO NET

If you are sleeping under the stars, a mosquito net, which can be hung tarpaulin-like from a rope suspended between two trees, protects against insects.

Some are treated with insecticides

BUG PROTECTION

For comfort, mosquito nets provide protection from biting insects and allow air flow.

HAMMOCK

Carrying a hammock means that you can camp even if the ground is muddy, rocky, or inclined. With a hammock, anywhere with trees can be a campsite – a lightweight tarpaulin can be hung above you and staked to the ground in case of rain. Modern hammocks are designed to enable users to sleep in an almost flat position. If a hammock sags, lying diagonally flattens the hammock, giving more support to the spine.

HANGING A HAMMOCK

Situate your hammock safely – somewhere with no dead tree branches above. Make sure the tree or upright is strong enough and that ropes are tied securely and will not slip.

Use an air mat for insulation and warmth, or a heat-reflecting pad. These can be ordered from some suppliers, or homemade by taping reflective metal foil to a foam mat

Secure the hammock tightly to the trees. The wide webbing on this hammock reduces damage to the bark

Caring for sleeping bags and air mats

Sleeping bags are subject to daily wear and tear and can become grubby after a few hikes. But cleaning them can be a delicate operation, and repeated washing will reduce their insulating properties. Both sleeping bags and air mats may need repairing in the field, so always carry some repair tape and a repair kit with you. Careful handling prolongs the life of sleeping gear.

USING YOUR SLEEPING BAG

When setting up camp for the night, lay your sleeping bag out to give it time to loft fully before you go to bed. Place your bag on a sleeping mat for added comfort and insulation from the ground when you lie down. Wear thermal underwear that is reserved for sleeping in, or use a cotton or silk sleeping bag liner. This reduces the amount of skin oils and other dirt that get on to your sleeping bag, which will eventually contaminate the down and affect its loft and insulation. In hot weather, sleep in lightweight trousers and a long-sleeved shirt (which will also protect you from mosquitos or other insects in the evening hours). Sleeping bag zips frequently malfunction, but crimping them with pliers usually fixes the problem.

TIME FOR A SHAKEDOWN

Give your sleeping bag a daily shake. This will help to keep it fresh and ensure that the filling remains evenly distributed.

SLEEPING BAG CARE IN THE FIELD

When airing a sleeping bag, do not put it on bare ground, which may be dirty or damp. Find a dry, clean area such as a large rock. Keep your sleeping bag away from wet and dirty clothes. On a damp night, store wet raingear away from where you are sleeping, and ensure that your sleeping bag is not touching any moist surfaces.

SLEEPING BAG REPAIR

Always try to repair any tears to your sleeping bag shell or lining immediately.

■ Use Gaffa tape or duct tape for temporary repairs. Cut the tape in a circle rather than a square, so the edges do not snag the fabric.

■ More permanent repairs can be made with nylon repair tape or patches. Most outdoor retailers sell patch kits.

■ There are a number of companies that will repair your sleeping bag professionally. They can, for example, repair tears and separating seams, replace zips, and put new drawstrings into hoods.

MAINTAINING YOUR SLEEPING BAG AT HOME

WASHING AND DRYING YOUR SLEEPING BAG

■ Wash sleeping bags frequently to keep them clean, but not more than necessary. The soap strips the oils away from the down, and they are essential for the down's loft and therefore its warmth retention. Fill in synthetic bags also starts to break down with excessive washing.

■ Use a mild soap and follow the manufacturer's directions. Sleeping bags can be hand-washed, or washed in the gentle cycle of a washing machine. If too bulky for your machine, wash your sleeping bag in a large machine in a launderette. Never dry-clean a sleeping bag.

■ In a tumble dryer, use the delicate or lowest setting. To prevent the down clumping, put a tennis ball into the machine for a few minutes during the drying cycle – the action of the ball will help to dissipate the clumps.

■ Handle wet sleeping bags extremely gently. They can be air-dried, but not on a clothesline. You need a surface that can support the weight of the bag so that its delicate baffles do not tear. The simplest way is to drape the open bag across a rotary dryer so that it is well supported. Or, lie it on a sports net (such as a badminton net) that has been laid parallel to and off the ground.

STORING YOUR SLEEPING BAG

■ In between hiking trips it is best to store your sleeping bag in a large cotton storage sack. The bag should sit loosely in the sack. Do not store a sleeping bag in the stuff sack for long periods because compressing it in its stuff sack will reduce its loft.

■ Do not store the sleeping bag in a plastic sack because it can trap moisture and encourage mould, mildew, and bacteria to grow. Make sure the bag is completely dry (*see above*) before it is stored – even for a short period of time.

CARING FOR YOUR AIR MAT AT HOME

Air mats are low maintenance and taking care of yours will give it a longer life. Take your air mat out of its stuff sack and remove any stains with a soft cloth and warm, soapy water. Air-dry the mat and then store it, flat if possible, in a cool, dry place. Always store your air mat with the valve open and keep it dry to prevent mildew forming.

REPAIRING AIR MATS

Although comfortable and warm, air mats are vulnerable to being pierced or snagged by large brambles, burrs, rocks, or flying embers. Even the tiniest of holes allows all the air to escape. Most air mats come with a repair kit that includes patches and specially formulated glue. If you cannot find the leak by sight and sound, fill the mat with air and place it in a tub of water. Check for bubbles to locate the damaged area.

1 Locate the spot and mark it with a pen or crayon. If the hole is not visible, immerse the mat in water.

2 Let the air mat dry if wet, then undo the valve. Rub the glue into and around the hole.

3 Place a piece of repair tape over the hole. Stand a pot of hot water on top to help it cure.

Cooking equipment

If hikers have anything in common, it is the appreciation of a good meal. Portable stoves and carefully chosen utensils make the cooking process quick and easy. Consider the complexity of the meals you want to cook, and the weight and bulk you are willing to carry.

Stoves

A portable stove allows you to cook anywhere you like without having to make a fire. Cooking over a stove is easier and safer than cooking over a fire, and is more environmentally friendly. Fires can cause unsightly scars on the landscape, especially in fragile environments such as arid regions and tundra. Your choice of stove may depend on what fuel is available.

ESTIMATING FUEL USE

Each type of stove requires a different amount of fuel, and each hiker has different cooking needs, so gauging fuel use is a matter of trial and error. Most stove manufacturers suggest how much fuel to take. Keep a record of what you cooked and how long your fuel lasted, to gauge your fuel consumption. A 325 ml (11 fl oz) bottle of fuel or a 190 g (6.7 oz) cylinder is usually more than adequate for a weekend hike. Make sure fuel bottles are free from leaks, as they will spoil food and damage other equipment.

FUEL AVAILABILITY

If hiking abroad, check with a local hiking organization or guidebook to find out which fuel is available locally. Fuel types most widely available may be paraffin, dry-cleaning fluid (which works in white gas stoves), and gas in cylinders.

HOW A LIQUID FUEL STOVE WORKS

Once primed – or pre-heated – a typical liquid fuel stove vaporizes fuel, mixes it with oxygen, and then burns it.

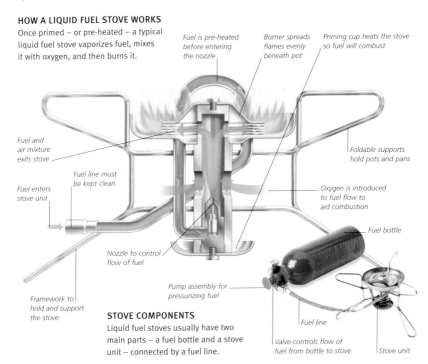

Fuel is pre-heated before entering the nozzle

Burner spreads flames evenly beneath pot

Priming cup heats the stove so fuel will combust

Fuel and air mixture exits stove

Foldable supports hold pots and pans

Fuel line must be kept clean

Fuel enters stove unit

Oxygen is introduced to fuel flow to aid combustion

Fuel bottle

Nozzle to control flow of fuel

Framework to hold and support the stove

Pump assembly for pressurizing fuel

STOVE COMPONENTS

Liquid fuel stoves usually have two main parts – a fuel bottle and a stove unit – connected by a fuel line.

Fuel line

Valve controls flow of fuel from bottle to stove

Stove unit

LIQUID FUEL STOVE

Most types of liquid fuel stove function on white gas, and may also be able to use unleaded petrol, white spirits, and even dry cleaning fluid.

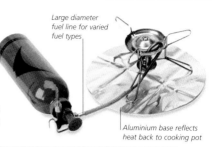

Large diameter fuel line for varied fuel types

Aluminium base reflects heat back to cooking pot

RELIABLE STOVE

Popular with mountaineering expeditions because of reliable performance, liquid fuel stoves perform well even in extreme cold and high altitudes.

CYLINDER STOVE

Easy to operate and lightweight, cylinder stoves use a blend of pressurized butane and propane. As the burners are small, these stoves are only suitable for use with small pots and pans.

Valve opens to allow gas to flow to burner

Stove snaps or twists onto cylinder

Use only small pots on small pot supports – oversize pots may topple over

SIMPLE STOVE

Although great when hiking in recreation-intensive areas where fuel is widely available, cylinder stoves do not perform well in very cold temperatures.

COMBINATION STOVE

While all combination stoves can use a variety of fuel types, such as white gas and unleaded petrol, some models also take standard gas cylinders. Although heavy, these stoves are highly adaptable.

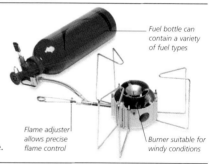

Fuel bottle can contain a variety of fuel types

Flame adjuster allows precise flame control

Burner suitable for windy conditions

VERSATILE STOVE

For journeys when your fuel sources are uncertain, and if travelling to several different regions where fuel availability varies, choose a combination stove.

ALCOHOL STOVE

These are extremely lightweight and run on methylated spirits, which is sold in lightweight plastic bottles and is widely available in ironmongers and DIY shops.

Heat output is low so use a lid to conserve heat

Burner unit includes a simmering ring to regulate heat

LIGHTWEIGHT STOVE

If your meals require simple cooking, and if you are more concerned with saving weight than convenience, alcohol stoves are useful. Heat output is low, so boiling times are long.

QUESTIONS TO ASK BEFORE YOU BUY

Before you decide what type of stove to buy ask yourself the following questions:
- Are you looking for a lightweight stove?
- Will you be cooking simple meals that require only a low heat output?

- Are you hiking abroad and relying on the availability of local fuel?
- Will your stove perform well if you are hiking in cold conditions or at high altitudes?
- What size pots and pans will you be using?

Utensils and accessories

Successful cooking on the trail is a case of planning ahead, choosing your equipment, and being prepared to minimize. You can make a delicious meal with one small pot and a few simple ingredients – or you can pack a spice cabinet and a bevy of home-hydrated food for a gourmet feast.

ESSENTIAL COOKING ITEMS

Cooking gear should be lightweight. You will find multipurpose knives, cutlery, dishes, food carriers, pots and pans sets, mugs, cups, and cleaning supplies at your local retailers. However, you should be able to use some of the supplies you have at home, if they are not too heavy.

MULTIPURPOSE KNIFE

In addition to a blade, a multipurpose knife should have a screwdriver, scissors, awl, can opener, wire cutters, and corkscrew. Its uses range from peeling carrots to whittling sticks. Look out for a miniature, lightweight model.

The corkscrew is an optional feature

A can opener is a useful feature for hikers

CUTLERY

A spoon usually suffices for most camping meals, although a combined spoon and fork is available, which does two jobs for the price and weight of one piece of cutlery. Choose cutlery that is heatproof, lightweight, and robust.

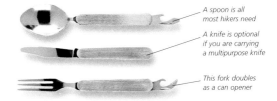

A spoon is all most hikers need

A knife is optional if you are carrying a multipurpose knife

This fork doubles as a can opener

DISHES

A plastic bowl meets almost all outdoor eating needs. Choose one that fits inside your cooking pot to save space. If hiking with a partner, choose nesting bowls (one bowl fits inside the other) to save even more space.

FOOD CARRIERS

The best way to carry food is in a nylon stuff sack. Count out precise portions of the major ingredients for each meal, discard removable packaging, and pack the food into plastic zip-lock bags. Staples such as dried milk, sugar, and spices can also be stored in these bags, although small quantities of spices can be kept in miniature plastic containers.

A waterproof sack is a good choice. Hang it from a tree to keep your food safe from animals

Buy small containers for storing spices, but do not carry too many as they add weight and take up space

QUESTIONS TO ASK BEFORE YOU BUY

Before you choose your equipment, ask yourself the following questions:
- How much storage space do you have?
- What kind of meals will you be cooking and what do you need to prepare them?

- How many people will you be cooking for?
- Is there anything on your list that you can do without – for example, a frying pan?
- Can you share any of the equipment with hiking partners to avoid doubling up?

POTS AND PANS SETS

A billy-can set of pots that stack inside each other is a popular choice, but there is a danger of taking more pots than you actually need. Assess your cooking requirements, and if possible, take just one pot. Always take the lid – it saves fuel and cuts down on the cooking time. Aluminium pans are a good choice because they heat quickly – but they can burn food if not attended. Titanium pots are expensive, but are extremely durable and light.

Clip is designed to be used with a pot-grabber, which hooks on to the clip and becomes a handle

Rounded edges encourage even heat distribution up the sides

Tight-fitting lid makes cooking quicker and more economical

Lids with flat tops can also double up as plates or shallow bowls

A pot-grabber can be attached to the pan, making it safer to pick up when hot

A large pot is a good choice if you will be cooking for more than one person

MUGS AND CUPS

Insulated mugs keep soups and drinks hot in cold weather. Nesting cups made of Lexan® are tough and heatproof, yet light and easy to pack. Avoid using enamel or metal mugs, which are often the cause of burned lips.

Lid to keep in warmth

Insulation keeps drinks and soups hot

Lightweight plastic is inexpensive and does not break

CLEANING SUPPLIES

A scouring-pad will keep your pot and eating utensils clean. A synthetic pad will last longer than a sponge and does not retain odours. Use a few drops of multi-use liquid soap (carried in a small plastic bottle) for washing up.

Metal scouring-pad for pots used on a fire

Synthetic pads for dishes and pots used on a stove

Essential equipment

A clean supply of water is essential on a hike, and carrying enough fresh water or being able to purify supplies is a requirement. A first-aid kit is also invaluable, while a torch, a watch, a wash kit, a map case, and an air mat repair kit are all worth finding space for.

Water carriers

Carrying water for a short day hike is usually no problem – you need only a lightweight water bottle with a tight lid. Most packs have external pockets to slot a bottle into, or attach it to your pack or belt with a loop-top lid. To stay hydrated on the move, a sport bottle top makes drinking easier, or choose a hydration system. For camp, a water carrier bag can be packed.

WATER BOTTLES
For a longer hike choose a durable bottle. Nalgene™ polycarbonate bottles can withstand freezing cold or boiling hot liquids. Aluminium bottles are lightweight and virtually unbreakable.

MAKING A PRACTICAL CHOICE
A bottle with a wide mouth means you can more easily scoop water from a shallow source. A narrow-necked bottle is easier to drink from.

WATER CARRIER BAG
Large bags are convenient for long waterless stretches and for carrying water from a water source to a campsite. Small bags are useful as they can be balanced in different parts of your pack.

CARRYING WATER
These water carrying bags weigh very little when empty, but can carry up to several litres of water. Each litre of water weighs 1 kg (1 lb per pint).

Bag folds neatly away when not carrying water

Opening for filling combined with tap for easy pouring

HYDRATION SYSTEMS
Consisting of a lightweight plastic bladder and drinking tube, these are built into a pack. Alternatively, they can be bought separately and put inside your daypack or waist pack. The drinking tube allows you to take a drink of water effortlessly while on the move, making it easier to stay hydrated.

HYDRATION PACK
An integrated water carrier is built into the pack. Water is sipped through a tube that passes over the shoulder.

Drink tube with bite-valve

Durable plastic bladder carries 1.8 litres (70 fl oz) water

HYDRATION BAG

Equipment for treating water

If you have to find drinking water in the wild, it is always best to treat it. Micro-organisms that can cause intestinal problems may be present, caused by contamination by wildlife, farm animals, pollutants, or other hikers. Spring water taken directly from the source in high mountain wildernesses may be uncontaminated, but to be safe, treat all drinking water.

SAUCEPAN
The most basic way to kill parasites is to bring water to a rolling boil for at least a minute – the only gear required is a pan and a stove. This works well when purifying cooking water and water for hot drinks, but it is not practical for refilling water bottles during a hike.

CHEMICAL PURIFIER TABLETS
Iodine tablets will enable you to clean water in a container such as your water bottle, without the need for any extra equipment. Simply add the tablets to your water, then leave for up to 20 minutes (*see* p.189). Additional tablets are available to counteract the distinctive taste of iodine. Alternatively, keep some lemon peel in your water bottle.

FILTER
To strain out most parasites and micro-organisms you can use a ceramic or charcoal based filter. It will not, however, remove viruses (which are common in less-developed countries).

COMBINED FILTER AND PURIFIER
These units contain an iodine element, which kills viruses, as well as a filtering system, which strains out parasites and micro-organisms. Some units are modified water bottles – water passes through a filtering and purifying system before emerging clean from the spout.

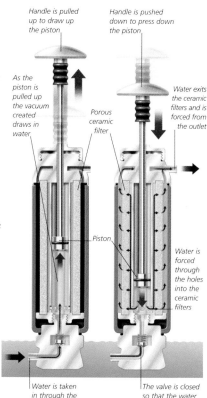

Handle is pulled up to draw up the piston

Handle is pushed down to press down the piston

As the piston is pulled up the vacuum created draws in water

Porous ceramic filter

Water exits the ceramic filters and is forced from the outlet

Piston

Water is forced through the holes into the ceramic filters

Water is taken in through the open valve

The valve is closed so that the water cannot escape

THE WATER FILTER
Water is drawn in when the handle pulls the piston upwards. When the piston is pushed downwards the water is forced through the ceramic filter.

CARING FOR YOUR FILTER

■ Filters clog when contaminants build up in the filter. If using one with a replaceable cartridge, always carry a spare. Cartridges can sometimes be cleaned in the field.
■ Follow the manufacturer's directions for cleaning whenever your filter becomes sluggish or difficult to operate.

■ Some filters can be scrubbed clean with a brush. Others can be back-washed, by which contaminants are removed by running clean water and bleach back through the filter element, which is then rinsed thoroughly.
■ To prolong a filter's working life, use a pre-filter to strain out the largest contaminants.

First-aid kit

Like a spare tyre, a first-aid kit is something you hope you will never have to use. Both items share another quality – they need to be checked regularly. Adhesives can deteriorate in humid conditions, so replace items such as plasters every few trips. Also, check use-by dates on medication.

KIT CONTENTS

Commercially available first-aid kits are useful, but the contents need to be tailored for a wilderness setting and the length of your hike. You may need to add more pain killers, and some items that are not commonly included, such as itch relief for insect bites. Specially designed kits for hikers are available at outdoor retailers.

Scissors, which may be on a multipurpose knife, are essential for cutting tape and trimming nails

Micropore or zinc oxide tape is useful for holding dressings in place

Sterile wound dressings are used to cover bleeding wounds

Adhesive strips are perfect for covering small cuts, and are also useful for holding bandages in place

LIFESYSTEMS™

Crêpe bandage is used to support muscle or joint injuries, secure dressings, or to apply pressure to control bleeding

Conforming gauze bandages stretch, so are ideal for joint support where some mobility is still required

Antiseptic cleaning swabs (not visible) are essential for cleaning wounds – and your hands

A disposable syringe can be used to irrigate a wound

Pain killers, such as paracetamol, should be saved for emergencies

FIRST-AID KIT
Pack a small torch in your first-aid kit to ensure you can find what you need in the dark.

Hypodermic needles are especially useful when travelling in developing countries – if you need an injection, a clean needle protects against infections

---

CARRYING ADDITIONAL MEDICAL SUPPLIES

Remember to take any personal medications, including any that you use only infrequently but might need while on your hike. Take copies of doctor's prescriptions that you may need to replenish during your trip. You should also take:

■ Malaria tablets if you are travelling in a region of the world where it is prevalent.

■ Plastic face shield or pocket mask to protect you and a casualty from infections when giving rescue breaths.
■ Survival bag to provide immediate warmth in almost any emergency.
■ Treatment for rashes and insect bites including sprays, antihistamine pills, and anti-inflammatory ointments to stop itching.

Useful extras

The items required for a trip will usually differ from person to person. Over time, develop a list of items you generally find useful (and jettison items that you find you never need). Your list will also change depending on the climate, the terrain, the length of trip, and the likelihood of finding supplies en route.

ITEMS TO CONSIDER

Good personal hygiene can help prevent minor cuts becoming infected, so you may want to take biodegradable soap in a container. Multi-purpose items are particularly useful – a watch can double up as an alarm clock or a barometer. Zip-lock bags are ideal for protecting items from damp, dust, and insects, and for organizing items in your pack.

WASH KIT

Personal requirements will vary, but a basic kit could contain a small travel comb, a razor, a small tube of toothpaste, and a travel toothbrush. You may also need a small amount of biodegradable soap measured into a plastic container.

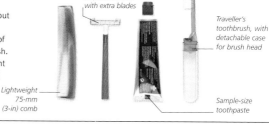

Disposable razor with extra blades

Traveller's toothbrush, with detachable case for brush head

Lightweight 75-mm (3-in) comb

Sample-size toothpaste

WATCH

Choose a watch with an alarm. Some watches also have features such as a compass, barometer, and altimeter, which can help you monitor your progress and location.

Water-resistant case with a large-digit, back-lit display

AIR MAT REPAIR KIT

If you have an air mat, a repair kit is essential in case of punctures. It can also be used to patch other items, such as raingear, tents, and sleeping bags.

Air mat repair kit includes patches and glue

ZIP-LOCK BAGS

You can protect everything from clothing to matches, and food to electronic equipment, with a zip-lock bag. The zip seals tightly while allowing the contents to stay flat. The fastenings are not very robust, so take spare bags.

WATERPROOF MAP CASE

A see-through waterproof map case enables you to navigate even in bad weather without worrying about ruining your maps.

A rolldown Velcro® closure keeps out the water

Clear plastic case means your map stays visible

Toggle allows you to adjust length of neck cord

Specialist equipment

Extreme weather and challenging conditions require extra equipment.
Make sure you are prepared, especially for the cold, and know how
to use the equipment. Items such as trekking poles, a GPS, and a
camera can make the whole experience more enjoyable.

Cold-weather equipment

Being comfortable in the cold is
largely a matter of having the right
equipment and knowing how to use
it to keep yourself warm and dry.

Wear layers for maximum warmth.
If carrying an ice axe or poles, make
sure you can move your arms freely
when wearing your pack.

WHAT TO TAKE

Cover your head, neck, hands, and feet
with light, insulating layers to protect
your extremities from the cold. Gaiters
should be made of a waterproof,
breathable material or your feet will be
too hot. Crampons and traction devices
help to prevent falls on snow and ice.

GAITERS

Designed to keep out moisture, snow, and debris,
these are fabric boot coverings. Winter gaiters
extend to just under the knee, and are made of
waterproof, breathable material. A back zip makes
them easy to get on and off. Some feature a velcro
front panel that can be adjusted to tighten the gaiter.

*Adjustable drawcord
prevents snow and
dirt entering the gaiter*

*Abrasion-resistant
fabric minimizes
scuffing and tears
from crampons*

*Strap goes under the boot
to hold the gaiter in place*

INSULATING SOCKS

Pile or fleece socks can be worn inside your
sleeping bag at night. They will keep your feet warm,
and also ensure that any dirt and moisture that
might be on your feet stays away from the inside of
your sleeping bag. Dry your feet before you put on
your bedsocks, and do not wear them for hiking.

*Microfleece socks are
lightweight and warm*

INSTEP CRAMPONS

Modified crampons help you to keep your footing
on slippery slopes at only a fraction of the weight
of fully fledged climber's crampons.
Instep crampons fit just under the
instep of the boot.

*Straps around
the boot hold the
crampon in place*

*Instep crampons usually have four
points, which dig into the ice*

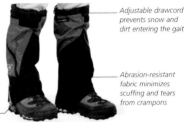

TRACTION DEVICES

Consisting of small metal grips coiled around a
rubber-blend web that stretches over the sole of
your boot, traction devices act like studded snow
tyres. They are designed for moderately
icy trails, not dangerous mountain
slopes, so do not use them in
place of crampons.

*Removable strap
fits over the top
of your boot for
greater stability*

*A rubber strap
goes under the boot*

*Studs grip
the snow*

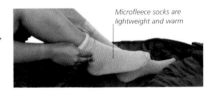

BALACLAVA

A balaclava covers the head, neck, and part of the face. It can be worn alone, with a hat, or under the hood of a jacket for extra warmth. Balaclavas are also useful on cold nights, because they will not fall off when you roll around in bed. They are made of polypropylene, fleece, microfleece, and other wicking, insulating synthetics. Weights vary – except in extreme conditions, the lightest weights are adequate for most hikers.

A wicking, insulating material is ideal

The fabric around the neck can be pulled up to cover the chin

NECKWEAR

Ordinary scarves tend to catch on backpack frames and other equipment, so tube scarves are sewn in a circle so that they hug your neck snugly without becoming tangled. The neck tube can also be pulled up over the back of the head to cover the ears, or pulled up over the chin to act as a face mask. Microfleece versions are comfortable, warm, and easy to pack. Some neckwarmers feature a front zip, which you can open to allow in air if too warm.

A neck tube can be worn alone or with a hat

SUNGLASSES

It is essential to wear sunglasses in snow, especially when hiking above the treeline. Use glacier glasses, which filter out UV light and have side panels that prevent the strong sunlight and harmful rays from coming in at the sides. In very windy weather, snowgoggles offer better protection as they cover more of the face. Sunglasses should fit securely. If they mist over due to condensation, pull them away from your face briefly to clear.

Lenses must filter out UV rays

Snug, flexible frames will keep glasses in place during movement

GLOVES

A layering system is useful for your hands as well as your body. An insulating layer of fleece or polypropylene gloves or mittens provides warmth, while outer mittens made of a waterproof, breathable fabric keep out moisture. Thin liner gloves allow you to do delicate tasks such as operating a stove or putting tent poles together. They can also be worn as an extra layer for warmth.

Thin liner gloves can be worn next to the skin as a third layer

Insulating gloves provide warmth

Waterproof, breathable outer mittens keep out snow and rain

ICE AXE

Because you can use it to cut steps in the icy surface as you go, an ice axe is necessary when crossing steep slopes. You can also use it to perform an ice-axe arrest if you start to slip. You may need an ice axe in summer if you are hiking at high elevations in snow-covered terrain. If you expect to need an ice axe, it is best to learn how to use it at a class before you set off.

The curved pick set with teeth can be used as a brake

Sharp spike used to plunge the axe into snow for stability, balance, and safety

Trekking poles and hiking sticks

Poles and sticks can help to prevent the aches and pains that affect many hikers, especially any who are older or overweight, or who have injury-prone knees. While walking, poles reduce the pressure on the back, legs, and especially the knees, by transferring weight onto the arms. A single pole can be used, but for the optimum level of support, many hikers prefer two.

TYPES OF POLES AND STICKS

Some hikers use ski poles, but traditional wooden sticks are favoured by others. Features to look for are graphite tips for better traction, spring-loaded shock absorbers to take pressure off the knees and absorb the shock of a steep step or hop downhill, and ergonomically angled cork hand grips. These will absorb sweat so the hands do not develop blisters.

USING A PAIR OF POLES

Hikers who rely on trekking poles to take pressure off their knees often prefer to use two poles. Two poles mean you are balancing your weight between four limbs. This is not always convenient if you have items to carry. Hikers who use poles primarily for balance may prefer to use just one pole.

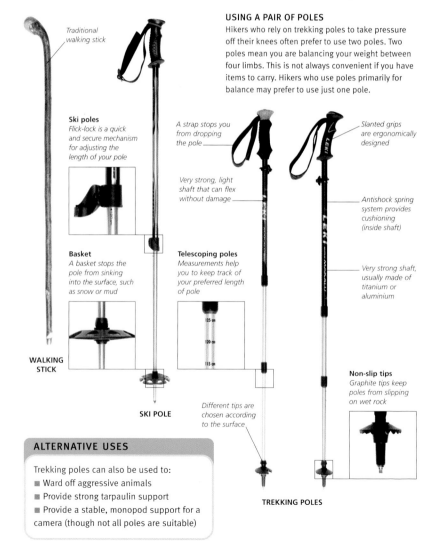

Traditional walking stick

Ski poles
Flick-lock is a quick and secure mechanism for adjusting the length of your pole

Basket
A basket stops the pole from sinking into the surface, such as snow or mud

WALKING STICK

A strap stops you from dropping the pole

Very strong, light shaft that can flex without damage

Telescoping poles
Measurements help you to keep track of your preferred length of pole

SKI POLE

Different tips are chosen according to the surface

Slanted grips are ergonomically designed

Antishock spring system provides cushioning (inside shaft)

Very strong shaft, usually made of titanium or aluminium

Non-slip tips
Graphite tips keep poles from slipping on wet rock

TREKKING POLES

ALTERNATIVE USES

Trekking poles can also be used to:
- Ward off aggressive animals
- Provide strong tarpaulin support
- Provide a stable, monopod support for a camera (though not all poles are suitable)

Animal-proof equipment

Sometimes wild animals become so used to humans that they begin to visit campsites, often with the intention of begging or stealing food. This is a problem not only for you but also for the animals, who can grow dependent on an unnatural diet. When hiking in popular recreational areas, always take the necessary equipment to guard your food from animals.

TAKING PRECAUTIONS AT CAMP

The usual method of keeping food away from animals is to hang it in a tree (*see* p.219). However, in certain regions, bears and other animals have become skilled at finding food in trees, which necessitates using alternative strategies, such as bear-proof canisters, bear-proof stuff sacks, and hanging food from poles with ropes.

BEAR-PROOF CONTAINERS

Bear-proof canisters are hard plastic carriers for food. In some parks they can be rented, and typically hold about five days' worth of food. Bear-proof stuff sacks made of the same fabric used in bullet-proof vests are also effective. For attaching food to ropes on poles, a karabiner (metal clip used in mountaineering) is useful.

KEEPING FOOD AWAY FROM ANIMALS

Choose a tree that is well away from your sleeping area and a branch that is strong enough to hold your stores. Suspend the food at least 3.5 m (12 ft) above the ground and well away from the trunk.

RODENT-PROOFING

Bears are not the only animals that steal your food. Mice and rats are often found in popular campsites, hiking shelters, and huts. A contraption that keeps rodents from your stores can be easily made on site. You will need a penknife, a tin can, 90 cm (3 ft) of cord or rope, and a small stick.

Nail / Tin can
Cord / Stick
Knot / Canvas bag

1 Use the penknife to puncture a hole in the base of an empty food can.
2 Hold the can upside down and thread a short piece of cord through the hole. Tie a knot in the rope underneath the can to hold it in place, leaving about a 30 cm (1 ft) length of rope under the knot.
3 Tie the upper part of the rope to the nail. Tie a stick to the bottom of the rope in a perpendicular position.
4 Hang your food from the stick. The mice cannot get past the can to the food.

Tools and gadgets

You do not need to load up your pack with every gadget and electronic tool that has been invented for outdoor enthusiasts. But many of these items have functions that are useful in extreme weather or difficult terrain. Make sure the ones you choose are good quality and will not let you down.

ALTIMETER

When navigating in mountainous terrain it is useful to have an altimeter. By using changes in atmospheric pressure, it measures your elevation above sea level.

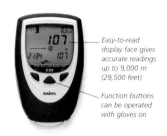

Easy-to-read display face gives accurate readings up to 9,000 m (29,500 feet)

Function buttons can be operated with gloves on

LOCATING YOUR POSITION

If properly adjusted to the correct elevation at your starting-point, you can use an altimeter, together with a map, to determine your location.

PEDOMETER

It is always interesting to record how far you have walked, and a pedometer provides this information. Knowing this distance can also help you navigate.

Digital display shows the distance and number of steps

Set your weight and stride length to begin

INDICATING DISTANCE

Most pedometers count your footsteps, then calculate distance. To be accurate, you must first measure the length of your stride.

MOBILE PHONE

When hiking solo, especially in remote areas, a mobile phone is useful in case you need to call for help. However, there may be no signal, and nowhere to recharge the battery, so it is no substitute for good judgement; or an excuse to take risks.

Most mobile phones double up as clocks

A sturdily constructed phone is more hardwearing on the trail

KEEPING IN TOUCH

Be discreet when using your mobile phone in popular wilderness areas – other hikers may not want to hear your conversations.

BINOCULARS

Although most often used for spotting wildlife and birds, or to take a closer look at features or landmarks in the distance, binoculars are also a useful navigation aid when looking for the path, or searching for a viable cross-country route.

Look for solid construction of the focus adjustment

Larger lenses gather more light to give a clear and detailed view

GETTING A GOOD VIEW

From ornithology to astronomy, a rugged but lightweight pair of binoculars will enhance your enjoyment of the natural world.

GPS

The Global Positioning System (GPS) uses multiple signals from satellites to determine your position on earth. GPS is extremely accurate – you can fix your position to within 3 m (10 ft).

Systems designed for backpackers sometimes include footpath data. You can input your own information to help you find a path or a route, or to recall a route later. GPSs can also calculate approximate travel time.

MILITARY MUSCLE

Originally developed for military use, the cost of commercial GPS systems has fallen to make them more affordable.

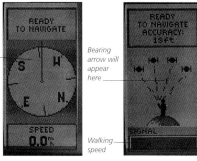

Graphic shows use of satellites to plot position

Bearing arrow will appear here

Walking speed

NAVIGATION SCREEN

COMPASS SCREEN

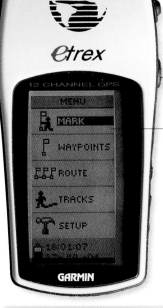

Operation buttons on side of unit

Menu screen allows the user to scroll through the unit's features

Compass arrow shows north

Animated figure 'walks' with you

ALL MAPPED OUT

Simple GPS systems are used as a navigational aid in conjunction with a map (see p.157).

MAP SCREEN

BEFORE YOU BUY

Before you decide what type of GPS to look for, consider the following questions:
■ Do you want a simple model, to be used with a traditional map, or one with map storage and download facilities?
■ Do you want to know your altitude as well as your position? If so, choose a model with an on-board barometric altimeter.
■ Is the size and weight a concern? Simpler units are often smaller and lighter.
■ Do you require other features, such as night sky information, waterproof casing, a calendar, or enhanced battery life?

Photography

Taking photographs is an excellent way to record the places you have visited on hiking trips. But if you want to bring home high-quality pictures, you face special challenges. First, weight limitations restrict the amount of equipment you can carry. And second, the rigours of being outdoors in all weather can be harmful to delicate photographic equipment and film.

DIGITAL CAMERA

A digital camera is an excellent choice because it allows you to take several shots, review them, and choose the one you like best – something that is important when shooting action pictures or wildlife, where you cannot control the photographic subject. Some digital cameras are small enough to fit in the palm of your hand (a bonus for weight-conscious hikers), but they must be carefully protected against rain and dirt. On a long trip, unless you have a laptop with you on to which you can upload images from the camera, you will need to carry additional memory cards.

FILM-FREE
The popularity of digital cameras has grown along with their picture quality and affordability.

Function dial
Manual selection of functions including automatic setting

Viewfinder
The image can be framed through the viewfinder and on a small LCD screen

Flash
Autoflash function can be turned on and off manually

AF/self-timer lamp
Helps camera to focus automatically, and to take time-delayed shots

Lens
Automatic zoom lens with 3x optical zoom on standard model

POINT-AND-SHOOT CAMERA

Point-and-shoot cameras are available in both digital and standard film formats. Some companies make point-and-shoot weatherproof models that are just as lightweight as standard versions, but can be used in wet weather and even be immersed in water up to a depth of 3 m (10 ft) or more. They allow you to take shots in challenging conditions.

MAKE IT SNAPPY
Compact, lightweight, and easy to use, a point-and-shoot camera has much to commend it to the hiker. These cameras run on batteries, so pack extras.

Shutter
Squeeze gently to take the shot

Lens
Automatic zoom lens with 3x optical zoom

Flash
Automatic function for shots taken in poor light

Viewfinder
The image is seen through a separate viewfinder lens

SINGLE LENS REFLEX CAMERA

A traditional single lens reflex (SLR) camera uses 35-mm film and has interchangeable lenses. These cameras, which can produce excellent results, are best for serious photographers, but may be too complex and heavy for the needs of most hikers.

Shutter
This must be squeezed gently, particularly on a slow aperture setting

Shutter dial
Adjusts the length of the exposure

Flash mount
Flash unit fixes here

Viewfinder
On an SLR camera you look at the subject through the lens via mirrors

Lens
The size of the aperture and the focus of the lens are adjusted here

SLR LENSES

Interchangeable lenses make SLRs the most flexible of all cameras. Fixed lenses come in different magnifications, wide-angle lenses increase the angle of view, and telephoto zoom lenses are excellent for both distant or close-up shots. Coloured filters can be added for effect.

FILM AND LENSES FOR AN SLR

FILM

■ Choose film for the light conditions you expect to encounter. Most outdoor photographers shoot ASA 60–100 in bright sun. In shadier areas, ASA 200 may give you more flexibility.
■ In warm climates, store film right in the centre of your pack, perhaps insulated in a bag full of clothing. In sub-freezing weather, handle film slowly and gently, because it can crack and tear.
■ Film can pass safely through airport X-ray machines if it is lower than ASA 800 and if you do not go through many checkpoints. Alternatively, you can ask to have your film hand-inspected. To avoid X-ray machines you can have your film developed or you can send it home via the post.

LENSES

■ Limit yourself to two or three lenses if possible, or it will significantly increase pack weight.
■ Choose suitable lenses for the type of pictures you wish to take – portraits, panoramic scenery, wildlife, or indoors with subdued lighting work well with different types of lenses.
■ Using a zoom lens allows you to magnify the subject, offering great flexibility for hikers at a reasonable weight. Telephoto lenses are heavy and often require the use of a tripod.
■ A lens hood is a parasol for your lens – it shades the lens from too much sunlight.

PERSONAL ITEMS

Ensure that you take some or all of the following personal items:

- [ ] Personal wash kit (toothbrush and paste, biodegradable soap, razor, comb, towel, women's sanitary supplies, partial roll of toilet paper, toilet trowel)
- [ ] Personal medications
- [ ] Insect repellent
- [ ] Lip balm
- [ ] Camera and film
- [ ] Spare batteries
- [ ] Journal, pen, notebook
- [ ] Sewing/repair kit
- [ ] Money
- [ ] Rope for bear bagging (optional)
- [ ] Cord for drying clothes (optional)

CLOTHING AND EQUIPMENT FOR THE TRAIL

Wear or use the following items while you are hiking:

- [ ] Shorts or trousers
- [ ] Shirt
- [ ] Sock liners
- [ ] Socks
- [ ] Hiking boots or shoes
- [ ] Hat
- [ ] Watch
- [ ] Trekking poles
- [ ] Backpack
- [ ] Compass
- [ ] GPS
- [ ] Map and/or guidebook
- [ ] Extra items of clothing (underwear, trousers, shirt, insulating layers). Include one more layer of insulation than you think you will need, an extra pair of socks, and sock liners

EQUIPMENT FOR COOKING AND EATING

You will need some of the following items if you plan to cook a meal or prepare a hot drink:

- [ ] Stove and stove accessories (pump, windscreen, heat exchange, matches)
- [ ] Fuel bottle or canister
- [ ] Pot, lid, and pot grabber
- [ ] Plastic bowl for eating
- [ ] Pot scrubber
- [ ] Utensil(s)
- [ ] Cup or mug
- [ ] Spatula or cooking spoon (optional)

EQUIPMENT FOR SLEEPING

Take the following items if you are planning to make an overnight hike:

- [ ] Tent (ensure you include poles, stakes, cord, flysheet, and tent body)
- [ ] Groundsheet
- [ ] Sleeping bag
- [ ] Sleeping mat
- [ ] Sleeping clothes; extra layers in cold weather (long-john top and bottoms)
- [ ] Inflatable pillow (optional)

RAINGEAR

Pack the following items close to the top of your bag, to allow you to put them on quickly if the weather worsens.

- [ ] Pack cover
- [ ] Raingear (jacket or poncho, trousers, gloves)
- [ ] Rain hat (optional)

TEN ESSENTIALS

The concept of ten essentials evolved from the pursuit of mountaineering, where climbers often face unexpected and challenging conditions.

- [ ] Utility knife
- [ ] Water bottle
- [ ] Water filter
- [ ] Torch
- [ ] Extra food (energy bars and a handful of nuts and dried fruit, in case of emergency or delay)
- [ ] Extra clothing (including raingear)
- [ ] Matches and firestarter
- [ ] Sunscreen and sunglasses
- [ ] Signalling device
- [ ] First-aid kit

LAST-MINUTE CHECKLIST

Keep a checklist of things to do before you leave home. Your own list may include such chores as turning down your thermostat or giving a key to a neighbour.

- [ ] Take any food you stored in your refrigerator
- [ ] Fill water bottles
- [ ] Find a safe place in your pack for your keys
- [ ] Check for an updated weather forecast
- [ ] Check trail conditions with the local land management organization or park office
- [ ] Ensure you have the appropriate papers such as permits and parking stickers
- [ ] Make two copies of your itinerary. Leave one in your car, and one with a friend
- [ ] Instruct a friend what to do and who to call if you do not return as scheduled

ORGANIZING
A HIKE

Planning a local hike

Local day or overnight hikes offer a wonderful opportunity to test your hiking legs, become familiar with your gear, and learn new skills. Hiking close to home reduces travel time, allows you to experiment in a familiar environment, and re-schedule easily if the weather turns bad.

Planning ahead

Before you set off from the start of the trail you will need information about what lies ahead. But what you need to know depends on your hike. For example, a short there-and-back hike on a well-marked trail on fairly even terrain requires minimal planning and just a day pack, whereas a long all-day loop hike in rugged wilderness needs greater planning and more gear.

FINDING TRAIL INFORMATION

On a short hike, a trail guide may be all that you need for a safe and enjoyable walk. For a longer hike, however, you will need information on trail conditions, terrain, elevation gain and loss, hazards, obstacles, and water availability. In both cases, you will need a current weather report. Such information can be obtained from a variety of sources.

Local hiking clubs often publish trail guides and local maps, or maintain websites containing information about trail conditions. Club members can offer you advice on the conditions and about equipment needs, and will sometimes organize group outings on nearby trails. Often, such hikes will be graded for difficulty, so you can choose one that matches your ambition and ability. Some outdoor clubs, especially in Europe, maintain shelters known as refuges out in the wild. You may find that they offer discounts on their use to members of fellow organizations.

Outdoor leisure shops sell local maps and guidebooks, as well as equipment suitable for local conditions. Salespeople at these shops are often enthusiastic hikers themselves, and can provide advice about their favourite local trails. Many outdoor leisure shops offer free classes or seminars, where participants can learn relevant skills. Equipment retailers may also have bulletin boards where hiking clubs post notices of their activities.

Local land management organizations often publish or sell trail guides, and wardens can provide up-to-date information about trails. For local day-hiking opportunities, contact your town's leisure department regarding suitable parks and reserves in your area.

ASSESSING TRAIL CONDITIONS

One of the advantages of hiking close to home is that you are usually aware of major events that could impact on a trail, such as local flooding, ice storms, or forest fires. Trails can also be closed for reasons that have nothing to do with hiking conditions – for example, in 2001 and 2002 many of the UK's walking trails through farmland were closed to prevent the spread of animal diseases.

It is also important to pay attention to seasonal issues. Heavier than usual rainfall can cause rivers and streams to run high and fast, making them dangerous to cross. A drought may cause usually reliable streams to run dry. A long cold winter with heavy snowfall may result in trails that are blocked by ice and snow late into spring.

Be aware that, even in a relatively small local area, trail conditions may vary considerably due to elevation, or depending on whether the trail is on the windward or the leeward side of a mountain range. However, if conditions make hiking on one trail ill-advised, do not give up – there are bound to be other trails from which you can choose.

DIFFICULT TRAIL
Steep, cross-country travel can increase your travel time by as much as 100 per cent. When planning a hike, be sure to find out about the terrain.

CROSSING A RIVER
When following a trail that involves fording a river, bear in mind that after heavy rain or a snow melt you may need to follow an alternative route.

FOLLOWING AN EASY TRAIL
On an easy trail you can make fast progress. Also, not having to worry about obstacles gives you more opportunity to enjoy the scenery.

CLEARING TRAILS

Many trails are created and maintained by volunteers who are members of hiking clubs. By participating in voluntary trail-clearing outings, you will have the chance to meet more experienced hikers and learn about other trails in the area. Volunteers help to clear overgrown vegetation, install water drainage systems, build rock stairs, and pick up litter.

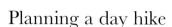

Planning a day hike

A day hike can be anything you want it to be, from a gentle foray near your home to a challenging hike further afield. It also provides a chance to prepare yourself for a longer hike – you can try out new gear, increase your level of fitness, and discover how far you can walk comfortably in a day.

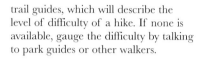

DECIDING WHERE TO GO

Plan your hike around an interesting destination such as a waterfall, a lake to swim in, or a summit. You can also hike in an area of interesting or varied landscape, such as a canyon or gorge. If you are in unfamiliar terrain, it is important to understand how to read the landscape on a map before setting out. What can start as a gentle stroll in the hills can become quite strenuous, and may even involve a perilous rock climb further along the route.

Look in outdoor leisure shops for local guidebooks, or ask the staff for their recommendations. Many large parks have extensive trail systems and publish their own maps and trail guides, which will describe the level of difficulty of a hike. If none is available, gauge the difficulty by talking to park guides or other walkers.

PLANNING SPEED AND DISTANCE

When calculating how long a hike will take, it is important to know how much ground you can cover comfortably in an hour, and for how many hours you can walk. Many people overestimate their fitness and assume that they can walk at a reasonable pace for six or seven hours. In fact, unless you are used to walking all day, your pace is likely to slow considerably towards the end of the hike.

Try several short local hikes (*see* p.12) – perhaps with a local walking group to allow you to learn from other hikers – before embarking on a full-day hike. If you are hiking in a group, it is important that you base your pace on the ability of the slowest member.

Once you are sure of your average walking pace, use the table below as a guide to judge how far, and at what speed, you can walk in a day.

GAUGING SPEED AND DISTANCE

INTENSITY OF HIKE	AVERAGE SPEED	RECOMMENDED LENGTH OF DAY HIKE
Leisurely	3 km/h (2 mph)	4.5–8 km (3–5 miles)
Moderate	4 km/h (2½ mph)	6.5–9.5 km (4–6 miles)
Strenuous	5 km/h (3 mph)	9.5 km and over (6 miles and over)

Add 30 minutes for every 300 m (1,000 ft) of elevation gain. Also allow about 10 minutes' rest time per hour of hiking.

POINT OF INTEREST

An interesting feature, such as a waterfall, makes an ideal halfway point to your hike. Ensure you are wearing adequate footwear for the conditions.

CHOOSING A ROUTE

There are several types of route from which to choose. A loop hike is a circular walk in which you return to the start without retracing your steps. Sometimes you can make a loop by stringing together segments of several different trails. If you cannot find a loop hike, you might take a there-and-back hike by walking to an interesting destination, then retracing your steps. Alternatively, if you have hiking partners and two cars, you can shuttle cars to each end of the trail, then take a one-way hike from one end to the other, to avoid incurring any transport problems.

ASSESSING THE AREA

Most areas offer several types of hike, such as the one-way and loop hikes shown below. Check your map for key features such as tricky terrain, water sources, and parking facilities.

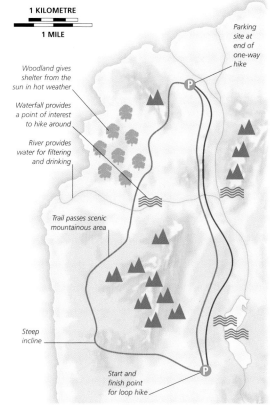

1 KILOMETRE

1 MILE

Woodland gives shelter from the sun in hot weather

Waterfall provides a point of interest to hike around

River provides water for filtering and drinking

Trail passes scenic mountainous area

Steep incline

Parking site at end of one-way hike

Start and finish point for loop hike

KEY

——— One-way hike

——— Loop hike

P Car park

Wooded area

Rocky terrain

Water feature

HIKING ESSENTIALS

PERMITS AND REGULATIONS

In most countries, permits are required only for overnight hikes, but in some places they may be needed for day hikes. Sometimes trails are closed for seasonal reasons or due to local problems. In many US national forests, you must buy a pass to park your car. Check with the land management agency for current information.

MAPS AND INFORMATION

Maps or trail guides are generally available at local outdoor shops, or from the organization that manages the trail. Never be tempted to hike without a detailed map or guidebook of some sort. If new to an area, it is easy to become disoriented, or even lost, if you fail to notice a critical turning off point. In high mountains, this is especially important, as fog and rain can obscure the view and quickly change the look of the landscape.

SAFETY

Although a day hike may be short, safety is still an important consideration:
■ Plan your hike in advance. Assess the terrain where you will be hiking.
■ Wear suitable clothing and sturdy footwear. Carry extra clothing to protect you against cold and rain.
■ Tell others where you are hiking and when you expect to return.
■ Take a mobile phone in case of emergencies.
■ Hike with a friend in remote and rough territory.

Choosing gear for a day hike

If your day hike is going to be on even terrain and in fair weather, then a good pair of boots, some comfortable clothes, and a day pack containing water and food may be all that you need. For anything more advanced, choose from the items described here according to your needs.

CLOTHING AND EQUIPMENT

Short hikes close to home give you a chance to try out clothing, footwear, and equipment. Unless you live in extreme terrain such as mountains, day hikes require only simple, functional gear that fits comfortably, moves with your body, and lies flat to avoid chafing. Inner clothing should wick sweat and moisture away from your skin; outerwear should protect you from wind and rain.

DAY HIKE BASICS

When choosing your clothes and equipment, consider the weather, sun exposure, trail conditions, insects, and the length of your hike.

A lightweight rain jacket is an essential item in mountainous areas, where weather can change quickly

Choose a daypack that is big enough to carry extra clothing, essential personal gear, and food and water

Use telescopic trekking poles if hiking on steep, rocky terrain

Water bottle
Make sure the seal is tight and store the bottle upright in your belt bag or daypack

On easy terrain, trekking shoes offer enough support and good traction

Trousers protect you against cold, sunburn, insects, and stinging plants

FABRIC ALTERNATIVES

Traditionalists wear cotton T-shirts and shorts, but synthetic T-shirts and shorts made of the newest high-tech fabrics help to regulate sweat and temperature much more efficiently than cotton. Microfleece is very lightweight, and retains warmth even when wet. Wool or wool blend socks, combined with sock liners made of a fabric such as polypropylene, add cushioning and wick the sweat away from your feet.

A synthetic T-shirt will help regulate temperature better than a cotton shirt

FEWER CLOTHES

In hot conditions, shorts and a T-shirt give more freedom of movement and are more comfortable.

Carrying a belt bag can be cooler than carrying a daypack in hot weather

The lower section of convertible trousers can be unzipped and removed to make shorts

HIKING BOOTS

A good choice for rocky terrain or deep mud, hiking boots are also essential for hikers with weak ankles.

A hat is the most effective way to regulate your body temperature

A zippered front opening enables you to adjust your temperature easily in changeable weather

Gloves are recommended when hiking above the treeline, or in cooler climates

EXTRA CLOTHES

A hat, gloves, and a microfleece sweater are recommended for hiking in unsettled climates where the temperature can change quickly.

HIKING ESSENTIALS

CLOTHING AND EQUIPMENT

Match your clothes to the weather and choose polyester or synthetic fabrics (which wick sweat away). What you carry should also be governed by the conditions and the terrain. Follow this basic checklist:

- Daypack or belt bag
- Water and food for snacks and lunch
- Rain jacket or poncho
- Trekking poles
- Map and/or guidebook
- Compass
- First-aid kit
- Extra clothes
- "Ten Essentials" if hiking above the treeline or in remote areas (*see* p.105)

Making an overnight hike

For your first overnight hike, choose a nearby destination when the weather forecast is good. By sticking to easy terrain in gentle countryside, you will have the chance to pace yourself and learn the basic techniques of camping and cooking without having to cope with unfamiliar conditions.

CHOOSING A TRAIL

A hiking guidebook to your region will probably have dozens of suggestions for trails. Look for well-marked, easy trails with established campsites and adequate sources of water. When you have narrowed your selection down to a few trails, ask members of a local hiking club, a salesperson at an outdoor leisure shop, or the organization that manages the land for their recommendations.

PLANNING FOR COMFORT AND SAFETY

Perhaps the most common mistake made by newcomers to overnight hiking is planning too ambitiously. Walking along a trail is very different from walking in a town. The constantly shifting pressure of uneven ground affects muscles very differently from the pressure of pavements, where each step is the same. Also, the added weight of a backpack increases the effort needed to take each step. Hence, new hikers are often surprised by sore muscles and blisters. For these reasons it is better to plan a short hike than to attempt a long and difficult trail on your first time out.

Safety issues should be a factor in your planning. Avoid camping above the treeline, especially in passes or on ridges, where you might be exposed to storms. If there are river fords, be sure to check on water levels before your hike. In spring, many hiking trails may retain snow or ice, or may be muddy or boggy. In arid areas, find out whether seasonal water sources are likely to be running or dry. The more information you collect about conditions beforehand, the more enjoyable your hike is likely to be.

SETTING UP CAMP

Plan to arrive at your camping destination well before nightfall, so that you have time to put up your tent and prepare your meal in daylight.

Allow sufficient time to prepare sleeping arrangements before nightfall

In order to put up your tent quickly and easily, practise erecting it before your first hike

HIKING WITH OTHERS

An overnight hike is a wonderful way to share uninterrupted time with family and friends. Another person's perspective and judgement also adds an element of safety to a hike. Several people can share the weight of gear such as tents and cooking equipment.

MAPPING A ROUTE

This circular hiking route has varied scenery and terrain, and a refuge point. It covers a total distance of about 20 km (12 miles), divided between two days.

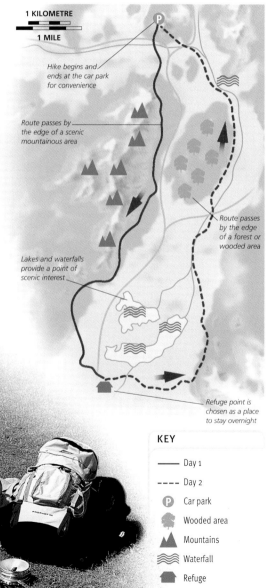

Hike begins and ends at the car park for convenience

Route passes by the edge of a scenic mountainous area

Lakes and waterfalls provide a point of scenic interest

Route passes by the edge of a forest or wooded area

Refuge point is chosen as a place to stay overnight

KEY

—— Day 1

---- Day 2

P   Car park

🌳   Wooded area

▲▲   Mountains

〰   Waterfall

⬠   Refuge

HIKING ESSENTIALS

PLANNING YOUR ROUTE

A detailed itinerary is not usually required for a simple overnight hike, although if permits are required, you may need to commit to a campsite in advance. Generally, you should decide how much distance you want to cover: 10–13 km (6–8 miles) a day is generally far enough for beginners; fit hikers can easily double that. Check the guidebook to be sure there are campsites or refuges at the distances you want to cover. Also check for water sources and whether there are any long climbs that will slow you down.

ESTIMATING DISTANCE

If you are planning an easy, conservative distance, you should have no problem making it to your campsite before dark. But if you have only half a day to hike, or are planning to cover a long distance, make sure you have enough time. Always take account of the weight of your pack, any climbs, difficult terrain, and the fitness of your companions when estimating your distance. Also factor in time for resting, eating, and stretching (see pp.142–5).

PERMITS AND REGULATIONS

Many parks, forests, and reserves regulate camping. In some regions, permits are required, reservations may be recommended, or you may have to use designated campsites each time you set up camp.

Choosing gear for an overnight hike

Overnight, you need the same basic clothing as for a day hike, but you should also allow for changes in the weather, and for night temperatures.

With modern lightweight equipment, it is possible to keep the weight of your shelter, sleeping bag, stove, utensils, and backpack to less than 5 kg (10 lb).

ASSESSING YOUR NEEDS

You will need a fairly large backpack to accommodate all your gear, but try to avoid carrying a pack that is bigger than you need. Choose a tent that provides the appropriate level of shelter for the terrain and weather you expect, and make sure you take a groundsheet to protect your fragile tent fabric from punctures. Include an air mat for a comfortable night, and a sleeping bag appropriate to the temperature. Unless you are going to cook over a fire, you will need a stove and a cooking pot, plus whatever food you plan to eat at your campsite. If trekking in a moderate climate, convertible trousers can be suitable for both daytime (as shorts) and night-time (as trousers) use. You may also need extra layers for night-time warmth. Finally, include a well-stocked first-aid kit and a small stuff sack for personal items.

An appropriate hat protects you from sun, rain, or cold

An open-necked shirt allows air to circulate

Properly adjusted shoulder straps make a heavy backpack comfortable to carry

PUTTING IT ALL TOGETHER

The overnight hiker's ideal load is lightweight and efficiently packed. Wear the same clothes you would for a day hike – but carry extra layers.

CLOTHES FOR AN OVERNIGHT CAMP

Wear extra layers of clothes, such as long underwear made out of a moisture-wicking fabric, and a fleece jacket, when resting at the campsite.

OVERNIGHT HIKING CHECKLIST

It is easy to pack too much for an overnight hike. However, you should ensure that you have the following essential items with you:

- Clothing: shoes, socks, hat, shorts or trousers, shirt
- Navigation equipment: GPS, map, compass
- Sleeping gear: sleeping bag, sleeping mat, tent, groundsheet, stakes
- Cooking gear: stove, pot, utensils, food sack
- Foul weather and emergency gear: raingear, extra clothing layers, first-aid kit, mobile phone

NYLON STUFF SACK
Use a lightweight nylon stuff sack to keep small, essential items together in one place.

FIRST-AID KIT
A first-aid kit is a vital part of your gear – check the contents before leaving home each time you hike.

STOVE AND COOKING POT
A portable stove allows you to cook anywhere, even if camp fires are prohibited.

COMFORT AT CAMP
Your requirement for a safe and comfortable environment in which to sleep has to be set against the need to keep your pack weight down.

A tent should provide the appropriate level of shelter for the conditions you expect to encounter

A suitable sleeping bag can keep you comfortable in temperatures far below freezing

An air mat insulates you from the cold ground and enables you to sleep more comfortably

A groundsheet protects tent fabric from punctures caused by sticks and stones

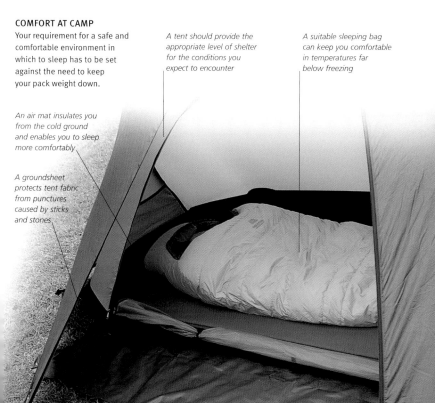

Organizing an independent trip

A hiking trip lasting several days or more will necessitate greater research and planning, and you will need to think carefully about the equipment and food you take with you. If you are hiking abroad, you may also need to organize visas and travel insurance.

Researching your destination

A hike that lasts a few days or more is a chance for a real break from your everyday routine. Such a trip will involve taking time off work and incur travel and equipment expenses, so it is important that you find an interesting trail and visit it at the right time of year. Research trail conditions, travelling to the trail (which may require visas), and any health issues.

CHOOSING A TRAIL

Once you have decided on a destination and the kind of hike you want to undertake, you can get a sense of the wide variety of hiking experiences by attending meetings at local hiking clubs, where members often give slide shows about recent trips. More experienced friends and staff at local outdoor leisure shops may be able to recommend trails. You can also find information in hiking or camping magazines. If you have decided on a particular park or reserve, call the management office to ask about their recommendations for hikes that meet your criteria. For your first few trips, look for relatively well-known trails rather than trying to devise your own routes in remote areas.

INTERNET RESEARCH

The internet is an ever-expanding source of useful information about hiking destinations. Type in the address of a recommended website or use one of the search engines to find general or specific information about a hiking location and possible trails.

USING MAPS AND GUIDEBOOKS

Try and find up-to-date material. It is worth getting in touch with land managers before you go, to check that trails described in guidebooks are open.

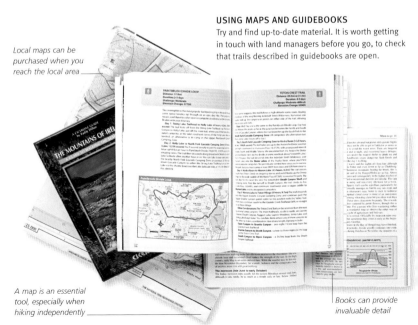

Local maps can be purchased when you reach the local area

A map is an essential tool, especially when hiking independently

Books can provide invaluable detail

INTERNET HELP

Finding the right website is a useful tool in planning a hike. It can give advice, suggest routes, and help you buy books online.

Browse the site to plan your trip

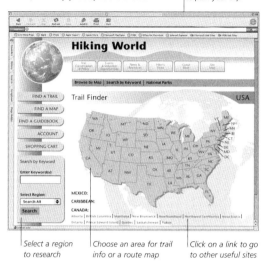

Select a region to research | *Choose an area for trail info or a route map* | *Click on a link to go to other useful sites*

CHOOSING GUIDEBOOKS

Libraries, bookshops, outdoor leisure shops, and Internet booksellers are all good sources of guidebooks. If you are travelling far from home, some internet research may yield information about guidebooks that may not be readily available in your home country. In addition to describing the actual route a trail takes, guidebooks usually provide information about nearby lodgings, campsites, water sources, trail difficulties and challenges, access to the start, local transport, seasonal conditions, and a host of other issues.

CHOOSING MAPS

Hiking maps can be very difficult to find, especially if your destination is far away. Most hiking guidebooks contain at least rudimentary maps, but these may not have the detailed topographical information that you need for navigating (*see* pp.152–3). Guidebooks usually note which maps are recommended for a hike and the contact information for buying them. Failing this, you should be able to find them in shops at or near your destination.

FINDING YOUR WAY

Having the right map, a guidebook that describes the route, and a compass, will help you to follow your chosen trail on an independent hike.

INTERNET SEARCHES

The internet can give you a great deal of information, but you need to choose your sites with care.

■ Outdoor-related sites provide useful information on all aspects of hiking. They often have chat rooms where you can compare notes with other hikers.

■ The individual websites of other hikers may give you reports and information about particular trails. However, you have no way of knowing if they have come from an experienced mountaineer or a hiking newcomer. You may be able to e-mail the author to request further information.

■ Sites may help you find relevant guidebooks or offer pages on a pay-per-download basis. The guarantee of professionally produced material may be well worth the fee.

■ *See* pp.238–48 for selected web links.

Making travel plans

Perhaps more than any other kind of travel, a hiking trip reflects the personality of the traveller. While some trips are flexible, others are carefully planned down to the smallest detail. But whatever your style, do consider transport to and from the trail, as well as your food and shelter.

PLANNING AHEAD

Most independent backpacking trips require less planning than a traditional holiday, because you do not have to rent a property, make hotel bookings, or organize your daily transport. (Your tent is your overnight accommodation and your feet are your means of travel.) But on some trips you may have to make reservations for campsites or refuges, and on longer hikes you may want to arrange for food supplies to be posted to various locations at intervals along your route. In addition, you will need to consider transport logistics, such as how you will travel to and from the start of the trail.

OPEN-AIR MEETING-POINT

Hikers meet at a cairn on a trail in the Scottish Highlands. Sharing the experience with others is one of the great pleasures of hiking.

BOOKING YOUR TRIP

Unless you are driving to your chosen destination, you will need to arrange air, train, or boat travel. These matters are simple to book on the Internet or by phone. For information on the trail itself, including details of guided trips, contact small, locally owned operators based in your destination. These are likely to be more helpful than your own local travel agent, who will probably be unfamiliar with areas away from tourist destinations, and may not have contacts in, or experience of, the remote regions often frequented by hikers.

HIKING SOLO OR IN COMPANY

Most hiking authorities recommend that you hike with a partner or in a group, because this adds an element of security in the case of accident or emergency. It is also very sensible and practical because you can share the weight of communal gear such as tents and cooking equipment. Hiking in company also allows you to share your experiences.

CONVIVIAL REFUGE
Mountain huts offer refuge in bad weather, as well as a place to meet and socialize with fellow travellers. Hut staff are usually hospitable and can be an invaluable source of local information.

Some hikers on popular trails set off alone, but are happy to join up with compatible fellow hikers. This strategy works best when you are hiking in places with well-developed trekking routes, or if you are following a route with well-established "stages" where people stop to eat, sleep, and socialize.

ARRANGING FOOD SUPPLIES

You may be able to send boxes of food on ahead to be held for you at hotels where you will be a guest, or at post offices. Alternatively, you can buy food in towns and villages en route – although it may be heavy to carry, unfamiliar, too easily perishable, or otherwise not ideal for hiking.

BUDGETING

Hiking trips are generally inexpensive, especially if you do not have the cost of hotels and restaurants.

■ Start by determining how much you can afford to spend and set a budget.

■ Remember to allow extra money for travel to and from the start of the trail, if necessary.

■ Guidebooks will provide information about the costs of campgrounds, refuges, or inns.

■ Allow enough money to treat yourself to the occasional restaurant meal.

■ Food costs vary according to the region but are almost never more expensive than eating at home.

■ On long hikes, keep an emergency budget reserve for replacing broken gear, as well as consumables such as film, insect repellent, and sunscreen.

SAFETY

Usually, hiking with people you meet on the trail is a safe way to travel. Occasionally, however, you may meet someone who wants to hike with you but makes you feel ill-at-ease.

■ Trust your instincts (women especially). Solo women hikers should be cautious about accepting male company.

■ Keep an eye on your gear, especially expensive electronic equipment.

■ Keep your options open – do not agree to pool gear such as cooking equipment or tents. You should be free to leave the partnership if you like.

Planning for the trail

The amount of planning you need to do varies according to the type and length of the trip, but drawing up an itinerary is an invaluable part of the process. In addition, you need to plan your proposed route carefully on a map, and estimate how far you will be hiking.

MAKING ITINERARIES

Itineraries are essential on longer backpacking trips because you need to calculate how much food to carry. In order to determine your food requirements, you need to know how many days it will take to get from one town to the next. Sometimes, all this means is dividing the total distance you will cover by the average daily distance you will travel. However, you may need to do more detailed planning on trails where there are few campsites or water sources, and in places where there are few opportunities to re-supply. It is important to allow extra travelling time if you are intending to hike in areas where the climate or trail conditions could slow down your progress, or require you to take a detour. It is always useful to research your route, because some parks and reserves have permit regulations that require you to stay in designated areas at night, which will affect your itinerary.

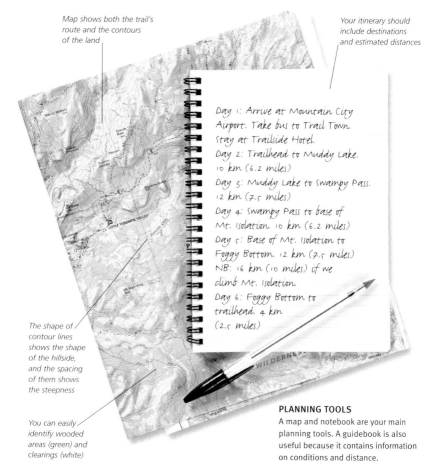

Map shows both the trail's route and the contours of the land

Your itinerary should include destinations and estimated distances

Day 1: Arrive at Mountain City Airport. Take bus to Trail Town. Stay at Trailside Hotel.
Day 2: Trailhead to Muddy Lake. 10 km (6.2 miles)
Day 3: Muddy Lake to Swampy Pass. 12 km (7.5 miles)
Day 4: Swampy Pass to base of Mt. Isolation. 10 km (6.2 miles)
Day 5: Base of Mt. Isolation to Foggy Bottom. 12 km (7.5 miles) NB: 16 km (10 miles) if we climb Mt. Isolation.
Day 6: Foggy Bottom to trailhead. 4 km (2.5 miles)

The shape of contour lines shows the shape of the hillside, and the spacing of them shows the steepness

You can easily identify wooded areas (green) and clearings (white)

PLANNING TOOLS

A map and notebook are your main planning tools. A guidebook is also useful because it contains information on conditions and distance.

MARKING ROUTE INFORMATION

If you are hiking a named trail, your map work might consist simply of finding the route of the trail on your map. But in large parks and forests, you may have a large selection of trails from which to choose. After you have read the guidebook descriptions and selected a trail to hike, highlight it on your map to make navigating in the field much easier. In addition, highlight possible campsites, any long climbs, and all water sources.

MARKING A ROUTE

Highlighting your route with a marker pen allows you to see it easily while navigating in the field, and is especially useful in bad weather.

Follow the trail on the map, which leads to a lodge and campsite

Using a transparent highligher allows you to mark the route without obscuring the map details

Note the position of the reservoir as a water source

MEASURING DISTANCE

To measure distance on a map, you can use either a map-measuring wheel or a thin piece of wire (*see below*). These kinds of measurement are at best an estimate. Small-scale maps give the least accurate result because the map cannot show all the twists and turns of the trail.

1 To measure distance on a map, simply take a thin piece of wire and try to bend it to match the route of the trail as closely as possible.

2 When you have traced the whole route, unbend the wire, measure it, and convert it, using the scale of the map (*see below*).

CALCULATING DISTANCE

When you have taken the measurement on the map, you will need to find out what distance it represents on the ground. On a scale of 1:25,000, 4 cm = 1 km (or 2 1/2 inches = 1 mile). When you place your wire against the scale on the map, you can read off the distance on the ground. When using small scale maps, you should add 10 per cent as a safety margin, because they may not show short changes of direction.

USING A MAP

A map with route information marked will help you to reach your planned destination.

Planning for destinations abroad

Hiking abroad involves research and planning. You will probably need both a passport and a visa. You will also need local currency and traveller's cheques, the correct immunizations, and travel and medical insurance. Ensure that you do not carry items that are prohibited in your destination.

VISAS AND PASSPORTS

Time frames for obtaining visas vary from country to country. For some, they take several days; for others, they can be acquired at the airport. Always check to see if you need a visa as the rules sometimes change. Transit visas may be required if you are passing through one country en route to another, and want to spend a day in the country in which you are stopping briefly.

CURRENCY AND CREDIT CARDS

Credit cards are widely accepted and reduce the need to carry traveller's cheques or, worse, large amounts of cash. Most hikers find a combination of all three serves them well, although in remote areas, where local people are not used to seeing foreign currency in any form and do not accept credit cards, you should always carry cash. This should be in small denominations, as local shops may not be able to change large notes. Choose traveller's cheques in major hard currencies – in most developing nations dollars are the easiest to change.

OTHER TRAVEL DOCUMENTS

Carry spare passport-quality photos of yourself, as these are sometimes required for permits or other paperwork. You may also need an international driver's licence if you want to rent a car while abroad.

TAKING FOOD AND EQUIPMENT ACROSS BORDERS

Border officials in some countries take extremely thorough measures to prevent agricultural diseases and pests crossing into their country. Used hiking gear is sometimes targeted because dirt clinging to boots and tent pegs may carry parasites. Clean your gear thoroughly before taking it across borders. Food items – even pre-packaged freeze-dried foods – may also be prohibited.

PASSPORT AND VISAS
Requirements for passports and visas change from time-to-time. Be sure you have enough blank pages in your passport for entry and exit stamps.

TRAVEL WALLET
A travel wallet is convenient, but if visible it can invite pick-pockets. Always keep an eye – or a hand – on your valuables when in crowded areas.

DEALING WITH AN EMERGENCY
Rescue workers evacuate an injured hiker near Seward, Alaska. Comprehensive insurance should cover these costs, but be sure you have read the fine print, as coverage may vary from country to country.

INSURANCE

If you have medical insurance, check that it covers your costs when you are travelling in another country. Even if it does, you may have to pay for any treatment on the spot and wait to be reimbursed. Check also to see if your personal insurance covers foreign travel. If not, you should buy an amendment or a separate traveller's policy in case of injury, and loss of luggage or passport, etc. Make sure your insurance will pay for emergency transport home if it is required.

INOCULATIONS

Inoculations may be necessary before you can travel to some less-developed countries. Recommendations change as diseases develop resistance to certain treatments and new drugs are introduced. Yellow fever, cholera, hepatitis, typhoid, meningitis, and rabies are all potential dangers in some parts of the world, and if you arrive at a border without the required inoculations, you may be refused entry. Check with your doctor well in advance – an immunization course may take several weeks. Not all doctors are up-to-date on tropical illnesses, so check with a specialist travel clinic if necessary. Also, check that your tetanus, measles, polio, mumps, and rubella immunizations are up-to-date.

MALARIA

PREVENTATIVE MEASURES

The female anopheles mosquito, found in many tropical and subtropical environments, transmits malaria. In some regions of the world, the malaria parasite has developed resistance to certain drugs; immunization recommendations depend on your destination. Some drugs that prevent malaria cannot be taken long-term. You will need to start taking any of these at least two weeks before departure, and continue for at least two weeks after your return.

COUNTRIES AFFECTED

Many parts of Asia, sub-Saharan Africa, and South America are affected by malaria, but you do not always need preventative drugs to travel in certain regions of some affected countries. Guidebooks and Internet resources (*see below*) can provide up-to-date information.

**FEMALE
ANOPHELES MOSQUITO**

WEB RESOURCES

■ www.fco.gov.uk/travel gives advice on all aspects of travelling abroad on a country-by-country basis.
■ www.masta.org gives information to travellers about immunization and staying healthy.

Choosing an organized trip

For many people, the prospect of planning an outdoor adventure in a far-flung region of the globe is a daunting task. As adventure travel has become more popular, hundreds of companies have emerged to offer guided trips to destinations ranging from the Arctic to the Galapagos.

Taking a guided hike

Guided hikes take much of the stress out of organizing a trip. All of the planning is taken care of, a gear list is provided, and an expert is on hand to help you deal with anything from an unexpected rainstorm to a stove that will not light. The daily cost ranges from modest to that of a luxury hotel room.

ADVANTAGES OF ORGANIZED TRIPS

In addition to trip logistics – planning, equipment, food, itineraries, travel, and emergency management – guided trips also offer a local insight into the culture and natural history of the area you are visiting. This is something you cannot get on your own, even with the best guidebook. Some companies also make an effort to take walkers off the beaten path, to see trails and terrain that you might not be able to find on your own.

Guided trips are most appropriate for people who do not have large amounts of time for planning their own trips. Many solo travellers also enjoy them because they offer a chance to socialize, and novice hikers will appreciate the opportunity to travel safely on foot in environments that they may find too intimidating to tackle alone.

CHOOSING A TOUR COMPANY

Outdoor trekking and adventure travel companies range from small, locally owned businesses to international travel agencies. Look for a company that specializes in the type of trip you are planning, whether it be a trek in the remote areas of a developing country, or for the less adventurous, a tour in a mountain range in a developed country. You can find such companies on the internet, or by looking in hiking or camping magazines. Check references by asking the company for a list of satisfied clients. Also, do an internet search. This will frequently show you independent reports from other customers, which

ORGANIZED TRIP
On a guided hike in Uganda, rangers offer protection from wild animals and poachers, while guides explain the natural history and porters carry the loads.

A DO-IT-YOURSELF GUIDED TRIP
Low budget guided tours can often be arranged on the spot. Here, a group of trekkers met in Kathmandu and hired local guides and porters for a trek of Nepal's Annapurna Circuit.

can be very revealing. Even a small independent company located in an out-of-the-way town in a developing country should have a website.

Many non-profit-making organizations also offer hiking and trekking trips. These include large environmental organizations, which publicize their offerings in their membership magazines. The cost may be lower, and the trips may be run with more stringent attention to issues such as the environmental and cultural impact of the tour group on its host country.

By using the internet, it is now possible to book trips directly with local companies in faraway places. Dealing with them direct will also be much cheaper than booking the same trip through a travel agency. Alternatively, you can usually make the same arrangements when you arrive at your destination.

COSTS AND BENEFITS

The cost of a guided tour can vary from negligible to astronomical. High-quality companies will provide trained guides fluent in several languages. They will also have reliable transport, functional gear, staff who are trained to prepare meals hygienically, and well-oiled arrangements with local service providers – important if there are complicated travel logistics such as local planes and transfers. These companies are often well worth the money if you are doing a trek requiring special skills such as mountaineering, where your safety depends on good leadership and good equipment.

FACILITIES ON A GUIDED TOUR
The type of equipment and facilities on a guided trip varies greatly according to the remoteness of the destination and the expense of the trip.

IS IT FOR YOU?

Guided trips offer great advantages in terms of planning. They suit some people well but are not for everyone. Ask yourself the following questions:
■ What are the physical demands of the trip in terms of distance, speed, and terrain? Can you meet them? How do you know?
■ Do you enjoy walking in the company of others?
■ Can you share a living space with a group of people you may not know?
■ Are you fit enough to keep up a steady pace, but flexible enough to go slowly if the group's pace is leisurely?
■ Are you willing to carry some of the group's gear?
■ How do you feel about letting someone else plan your itinerary and direct your day-to-day activities?
■ Are you willing to do your share of the chores?
■ If the trip involves challenges – such as foul weather, physically demanding terrain, and long days – have you already faced such challenges, and can you overcome them cheerfully?

Knowing what to expect

An organized trek to a remote location can be a once-in-a-lifetime experience. However, even high-end trips involve unexpected challenges.

Always remember that adventure trips are just that – "adventures" – open to the whims of nature and the inevitable surprises of foreign cultures.

CHALLENGES AND OPPORTUNITIES

Guided trips remove many of the hardships of hiking. In some, staff put up tents and cook meals; in others, porters carry your equipment, or a trailing vehicle carries your luggage. Guides make navigation skills all but unnecessary. But challenges still remain, depending on the destination, the goal of the trip, and tour company. Obviously, a walking trip through the vineyards of southern France will be far less challenging than a trek in Nepal, but in any region of the world, the weather may not co-operate, or your feet may blister. On a guided trip, if the unexpected does happen, your tour leader will help you to deal with it.

Guided trips may not provide enough of a challenge for some hikers. If you are young and fit, and want to challenge yourself – perhaps by pushing yourself to the limit – you may feel held back by the pace of the group, particularly if there are slower and weaker hikers.

On many trips, guides are well trained in local human and natural history, and will be able to identify flowers, trees, animals, and geological formations. Trips arranged through non-profit-making environmental or cultural organizations are most likely to have trained naturalists on hand to interpret what you are seeing.

Comfort and sanitation vary greatly in different parts of the world. You may encounter conditions on a hike that you find hard to deal with, or that can make you ill. Guides in developing countries are well aware of the problems that tourists often have with unhygienic conditions, and they can help you choose the right foods and find drinkable water, as well as provide adequate toilet facilities.

GUIDING YOU THROUGH DIFFICULTY

Guides will know the local area well, and can help trekkers navigate potentially dangerous spots, such as river fords and avalanche chutes.

PORTERS AND GUIDES

High-quality tours will provide guides to help you. Guides native to the region may not be fluent in your language, but their insight into local culture and traditions usually outweighs this disadvantage. In developing countries, high-quality tour companies often use expatriate guides and foreign equipment for treks that include technical activities such as mountaineering. It is traditional to tip guides in developing countries for their services. Elsewhere, check with the tour company and guide books.

Hiring porters to carry supplies and equipment is a common practice on trekking routes in many developing countries, and it will make your trek a great deal easier. Porters are often locals from nearby villages, and you may have communication difficulties if you do not speak their language. Nonetheless, interacting with porters can add to your experience.

Porters are paid very little for their work and, like guides, expect a tip. The amount will depend on the length and difficulty of the trek (ask the owner of the company what is expected). At the end of a trip some trekkers also give porters and guides their used gear, which is highly appreciated.

SHARING LOCAL KNOWLEDGE
Guides often know a great deal about the flora and fauna of a region, and can share practical information such as the medicinal uses of plants.

If your guided trek uses pack animals to carry your equipment, you will be told how much to bring and how to pack it. Usually, staff load the animals for you, drive them, and tend to them at night.

You will usually be given a list of personal gear to bring, although some companies will offer you the option of using some of their equipment, including tents. You will be charged an extra hire fee for this, usually by the item.

TREKKING WITH PACK ANIMALS
Loading your gear on to the back of a pack animal makes for easier hiking, while the necessity of taking care of the animals makes for a more tightly organized hiking day.

Preparing for hiking

Hiking on uneven ground or climbing and descending long inclines is more physically demanding than walking on pavement – especially while wearing hiking clothing and boots, and carrying a backpack. To prepare adequately you need to try out your gear and get your body in shape.

Testing your gear and clothing

However wisely you choose your gear, you should still give it a test run. Take short practice hikes close to home to make sure your pack, clothing, and boots are comfortable. You should also familiarize yourself with new pieces of equipment and check that everything you will need fits into your backpack.

WALKING WITH YOUR BACKPACK

Take a few day hikes with your backpack fully loaded to make sure it fits properly and does not chafe or rub (see pp.72–3). Does it hurt after only a short while? Have you tried all the straps to see which ones help shift the weight of the load effectively? It is better to discover any problems before you find yourself in the middle of a long hike.

Hiking with a fully loaded pack can also cause your feet to swell, which may reveal any problems with the fit of your boots. Walking on roads with a backpack is no training for walking on rough trails, so find some uneven ground on which to test your boots and strengthen your ankles for rougher conditions.

TESTING YOUR CLOTHING

On training hikes, wear the clothing you plan to wear while hiking. You will soon notice if any seams are rubbing against your skin, if your top gets rucked up under the shoulder straps of your backpack, or if the legs of your shorts ride up and cause your thighs to chafe. Note the temperature, and whether the clothes you are wearing are comfortable. Ask yourself whether they will still be comfortable at the temperatures you expect to encounter on your hike.

TAKING A TRIAL RUN

If your gear and clothing work well on a short practice hike, you're less likely to encounter problems on a longer trail.

Adjust pack straps so comfortable and not chafing

Check hat feels secure and will not blow off in a strong wind

Check that trousers do not chafe and allow enough leg mobility

After a long hike carrying a heavy load, boots should still feel comfortable

TESTING HARDWARE

Gadgets such as stoves, water filters, cameras, and GPS units take some time to learn to use. The more familiar you are with how your gear works, the more easily you will be able to use it – even in less-than-optimal conditions.

Before your hike, test your stove to be sure you have all its parts and everything is in working order. Similarly, be sure you know how your water filter works, and learn how to change or clean a water filter cartridge. Practice using a GPS unit at home and on a short hike (*see* p.157) – it will not help you to find your way if you do not know how to use it. If you are setting out with a new camera, test it first by shooting a roll of film in different lighting conditions. Finally, be sure to pack the instructions to any gear or gadgets you are not completely familiar with.

PACKING YOUR GEAR

Do not leave it until the last minute to pack your backpack. Check, for example, that your sleeping bag fits inside your backpack's sleeping bag compartment. If you have a bulky synthetic-fill sleeping bag and an ultralight small-capacity backpack, you could be in for a rude awakening. Keep size and space issues in mind when buying new gear.

Pack your backpack with everything you intend to take. Is there enough space for your tent? What about the tent poles? Where will your sleeping mat go? How much room will you need for all of your food? Is there a place for your water bottle and cooking equipment? Decide where each item goes and ensure that the pack is loaded and balanced comfortably, with no sharp objects poking against your back.

BREAKING IN YOUR HIKING BOOTS

Perhaps the most important way to prepare for a hike is to be absolutely certain that your boots and feet can co-exist in comfort and harmony. Carrying a loaded backpack puts extra stress on your feet, and at the end of a day's hiking, they may have swollen a size or more.

- Wear your boots around the house to double check the fit before breaking them in.
- Avoid blisters by going on short hikes to soften your boots and toughen your feet.

- Walk on uneven ground that forces your feet to bend in different directions.
- Wear wicking socks to remove sweat (which can exacerbate blisters).

- Wear thick, padded, woollen socks to add cushioning and avoid friction.
- Be sure to take blister treatment along, just in case your boots still rub.

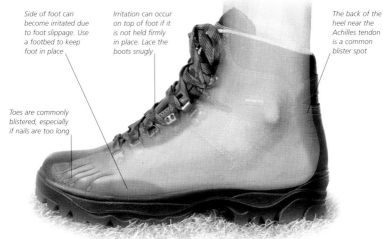

Side of foot can become irritated due to foot slippage. Use a footbed to keep foot in place

Irritation can occur on top of foot if it is not held firmly in place. Lace the boots snugly

The back of the heel near the Achilles tendon is a common blister spot

Toes are commonly blistered, especially if nails are too long

POTENTIAL PROBLEM AREAS

Conditioning your body for hiking

If you already participate in an ongoing fitness programme, you will find your introduction to hiking much smoother than your more sedentary companions. Pre-hike training should include both aerobic exercise and weight training, as well as stretches for your leg, arm, and back muscles.

EXERCISING IN THE GYM

To hike up and down mountains – or even hills – with a pack on your back requires aerobic fitness. Training in a gym in advance to strengthen your heart, lungs, and leg muscles will pay off on the trail. If you are fit, you will be better prepared for the short-term exertion of climbing hills, and have the long-term endurance to hike all day.

Arms are worked as well as legs

Screen shows level of effort and elapsed time

Adjustable weights build up leg strength

CROSS-COUNTRY SKI MACHINE

One of the most efficient ways of exercising is to use a cross-country ski machine, which works all muscle groups and provides aerobic conditioning.

WEIGHT TRAINING

Weight-bearing exercises strengthen muscles that will power you up hills. Look for exercises that work the quads, thighs, and hamstrings.

STRETCHING YOUR LEGS

Leg muscles bear the brunt of the work in hiking, and one of the chief complaints after a long day is leg stiffness. Stretching your legs regularly – both before and during your hike (*see* p.145) – can alleviate this. It can also help prevent injuries if you fall. Stretch calves, quads, thighs, and hamstrings.

HAMSTRING AND CALF

This exercise stretches the hamstring (the muscle at the back of the upper leg) and the calf (the back of the lower leg). Step one leg forward and flex the foot. Bend the other knee, lean forward and sit back into the position. Hold for a few seconds.

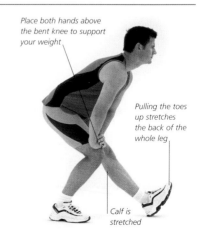

Place both hands above the bent knee to support your weight

Pulling the toes up stretches the back of the whole leg

Calf is stretched

STRETCHING YOUR UPPER BODY

The upper body may not seem to do much work in hiking, but arms and shoulders come into play when you are rock scrambling, or if you are using trekking poles. Stretching these muscles also stretches the back and neck, which can help alleviate pain and soreness.

SHOULDERS
Try to make your hands meet behind your back, and hold the position for a few seconds.

TRICEPS
Hold one elbow with the other hand and gently pull back, stretching the arm and back.

STRETCHING YOUR BACK

Back muscles can become stiff and sore from hiking with a heavy load. Stretching before your hike helps prepare your body for backpacking. When you are hiking, take time to stretch your back during rest breaks (*see* p.144) and at the end of the day.

BACK AND HAMSTRINGS
This stretch works both the back and legs. Be careful not to force any stretches, but rather gently lower yourself into a position that feels comfortable, then hold it for a few seconds.

Bend over gently and hold the stretch – do not bounce

Keep knees straight, but not rigidly locked

HIKING TIPS

ACCLIMATIZE YOURSELF

The conditions you will be hiking in may be different to those where you live. In particular, you will need time to get used to very cold or hot weather, and high altitudes.

■ Spend as much time outdoors as you can before your hike, even if the weather is poor.

■ In hot weather, be sure your first few days are slow paced with plenty of time for resting, as your feet will still be soft and prone to blistering. Drink and eat as often as possible to maintain your electrolyte balance, even if you are not thirsty or hungry.

■ At high altitudes, plan short break-in hikes before you start working hard. If hiking above 2,400 m (8,000 ft), limit elevation gain to 300 m (1,000 ft) per day. Also, try not to sleep more than 300 m (1,000 ft) higher than your previous campsite. Watch out for headaches and other symptoms of altitude sickness (*see* p.228), even at lower heights.

KNOW YOUR LIMITATIONS

It takes time to work up to long days and big climbs, so do not push yourself too far until you know what your body can do.

■ Take a rest break at least once an hour. Food, water, and rest can work miracles on drooping spirits and flagging energy.

■ Do not be afraid to slow down and alter your plans if it turns out that your original itinerary was too physically ambitious.

Deciding what food to take

On short hikes, you need food to keep your energy levels high and to refresh you during breaks. On longer hikes, you still need the energy, but also need to be concerned with overall nutrition and food spoilage. There are many different foods that fit the bill – whether fresh or dried, ready to eat, or in need of cooking – and they all taste good in the fresh air after a long hike.

FOOD FOR DAY HIKES

Unless the weather is extremely hot, most food can survive a few hours in a daypack, so your choice is wide. Select a combination of foods that provide salts (important for rehydration), sugars (which provide a quick energy boost), and proteins and fats (for longer-term energy). Examples of good hiking foods include fresh and dried fruit, wholegrain bread, cheese, peanut butter, nuts, dried meat, and energy bars.

In high temperatures, pack food such as cheese and meat in the centre of your pack to keep them cool. Avoid carrying foods that spoil easily, such as anything containing mayonnaise, sandwiches with watery ingredients such as tomatoes, or spread-type fillings, which can make bread soggy. Put foods that crumble and crush easily (such as biscuits and crisps) in plastic containers with lids.

FOOD FOR OVERNIGHT HIKES

In addition to the lunches and snacks carried by day-hikers, you will need to take dinner and breakfast. Choose meals that need the least cooking. The easiest dinners to prepare are one-pot meals such as stews or pasta dishes, or prepackaged freeze-dried foods. Foods that are somewhat soupy in texture help to replenish water and so help to prevent dehydration. For breakfast, eat hot or cold cereals, with or without dried milk and sugar, or muesli or energy bars.

DRIED FRUIT

CEREAL

SAVOURY BISCUITS

CHEESE

PASTA

POTATO GRANULES

NUTS

CHOCOLATE

PACKING FOOD

To cut down both weight and bulk, remove food from its original packaging whenever possible, but keep any wrappers that have cooking instructions on them. Repack the food in zip-locking plastic bags and store them in a waterproof stuff sack.

TEA BAGS

ELECTROLYTE REPLACEMENT DRINK

HOW MUCH FOOD TO PACK?

The amount of food required for a day hike varies according to your metabolism and how far you hike. As a rule of thumb, however, 900 g (2 lb) of mostly dried food is ample for one full day (three meals plus snacks) of hiking. On short, warm weather hikes, you may not need quite so much food. However, if you intend to cover long distances in cold weather, you may need as much as 25 per cent more.

BREAKFAST

Some hikers eat instant oatmeal, dried fruit, cereal, or nut or fruit bars for a quick no-fuss no-cook breakfast. Others like to prepare for the day ahead with a fully cooked meal, such as the dehydrated egg and pancake mixes available from outdoor retailers. Coffee and tea can be made using a camping stove, although caffeinated drinks are diuretics, so are not recommended in hot weather.

NUT BAR

LUNCH

Your midday meal should require no preparation or cooking, and should be convenient to eat even if it is raining. You may prefer not to take lunch at all but rather eat several small snacks during the day. Cheese, salami, dried meat, hummus, yeast extract, or peanut butter sandwiches, and savoury biscuits, bagels, and pitta bread are all good lunch foods.

SALAMI

BAGEL

DINNER

There are three main choices of food for an evening meal: home-cooked food that you have dehydrated and packed for the trail, prepacked freeze-dried or quick-cook foods such as mashed potato, or fresh ingredients cooked on a stove. Examples include pasta with tomato sauce, macaroni cheese, and instant rice with gravy granules and a can of meat.

CANNED MEAT

GRAVY GRANULES

SNACKS

Energy bars developed specifically for endurance athletes are popular among hikers – and so are chocolate bars containing nuts and fruit. Other choices are nuts, dried fruit, pretzels, and cereal bars. Pack several helpings of snacks, because you will enjoy having them during breaks throughout the day, as well as for dessert at lunch and dinner-time.

ENERGY BAR

DRINKS

Hot drinks are ideal for cold weather, although it is better to choose decaffeinated rather than caffeinated beverages. Tea, coffee, and hot chocolate are all popular. Also, cold electrolyte-replacement drinks can keep you going in hot weather by replacing lost sugars and salts. Carry plenty of water with you, and keep it easily accessible so you can sip it as you walk to avoid dehydration.

HOT CHOCOLATE

DRIED COFFEE

Preparing to go

Your dream hiking destination may be a very long way from your home, necessitating some complicated travel logistics. Packing a backpack for a safe commercial flight can be a challenge – as can managing the details of the local public transport when you arrive.

Packing and travelling safely

Getting all your gear, including bulky packs and tents, dangerous ice axes, and unwieldy items such as trekking poles, safely to your destination by air involves packing as carefully and securely as possible. When you arrive, you may need to organize local transport to get to the trailhead.

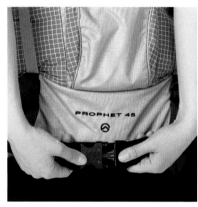

DAMAGE-PROOFING YOUR PACK
Detaching all removable straps and belts on your backpack, and tightening up any remaining straps, minimizes the chance of damage that can be done while it is in the hands of aircraft baggage handlers.

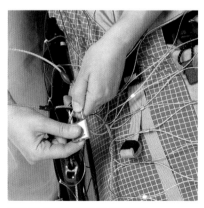

USING A STEEL NET AND PADLOCK
Enclosing your backpack in a steel net could be enough to prevent a thief from opening the pockets. Locking it with a padlock adds yet more security.

PACKING FOR AIR TRAVEL
Gear that will be stored in an aircraft's hold is liable to be damaged in transit by rough handling and airport conveyor belts. The best solution is to protect your backpack by stashing it in a large duffel bag, which you will then need to store upon arrival at your destination. Alternatively, wrap the entire pack in a bin liner held in place with sturdy duct tape. Although this is unwieldy, it does help prevent damage to the pack itself.

SECURING YOUR LUGGAGE
Locks, cables, steel nets, and other thief-foiling devices come in a variety of sizes and weights. These are useful in preventing the kinds of opportunistic thefts that occur when baggage is left unattended. A casual thief is less likely to grab a backpack if it is tied to a chair with a cable, no matter how flimsy the device may be. Alternatively, you could buy a backpack with lockable compartments. Choose a combination lock to avoid the problem of lost keys.

TRAVELLING FROM THE AIRPORT
Public transport from airports to major towns and cities is widely available in most European and some North and South American countries. In many developing nations, however, you will need to take a taxi or a hotel shuttle. Airport transport timetables and options are often described in guidebooks, and sometimes on the Internet. Check timetables in advance, if possible, because some buses and trains have

different weekend schedules, or no weekend service at all. It is worth budgeting a little extra for transport at the beginning and end of your trip, when you might most appreciate the luxury of being able to take a taxi.

REACHING THE START OF THE TRAIL
In Europe, Australia, and New Zealand, trains and regional buses go to all but the most remote regions, although services may be infrequent at the end of a line.

In the US, you may need to organize a taxi to take you to a rural location. Major trail organizations or land management agencies may be able to give you information about local public transport. Car shuttles are also sometimes available.

In developing nations, group taxis and public buses will usually take you to the town nearest to the start of the trail. If the trail is frequently used by tourists, vehicles can almost always be hired to take you from the town to the start of the trail. If the trail is less popular, you may have to hike there.

AVOIDING JET LAG
Although it is difficult to eliminate jet lag entirely, a few strategies can help. Some people find homeopathic jet lag remedies, available at health food shops, very effective. Several days ahead of the trip, go to sleep closer to your destination's time zone, and reset your watch on the day of the flight as early as is feasible. Drink plenty of water while on the flight, and avoid alcohol and caffeine. Finally, take an inflatable travel pillow and an eye mask to help you sleep on a long trip.

TO THE TRAILHEAD
Getting from your arrival point to the start of the trail may involve a journey by local bus, taxi, or train.

PACKING FOR AIRPORT SECURITY

In an age of tight security, some items of hiking gear present a problem when you are travelling by air.

STOVES
Some airlines stop passengers from travelling with stoves, even without fuel. Check with your airline in advance. You may have to send your stove ahead or buy one when you arrive.

STOVE FUEL
Fuel can never be carried on planes. Plan to buy fuel for your stove on arrival.

TREKKING POLES
These cannot usually be transported as carry-on luggage. Instead, buy collapsing poles that can fit into your hold luggage.

ICE AXES
Sharp equipment such as ice axes, crampons, or climbing hardware must be checked in at the airport for transport in the hold.

KNIVES
Penknives, scissors, and other small sharp objects must go in luggage that will travel in the hold.

Before you go: A ten-tip checklist

Planning cannot solve every potential problem or eliminate every challenge. But it can prevent many predictable annoyances, and it can set the stage for fun rather than frustration. The following tips will not prevent every mishap, nor guarantee smooth sailing, but they will certainly help.

TEN-TIP CHECKLIST

SET YOUR GOALS

■ A goal can be as specific as "hike 4 kilometres (2.5 miles) in one hour" or as vague as "walk for however long it takes to de-stress". The important thing is that you are clear about the goal you have set for yourself. Do you want to complete a certain trail, reach a mountain summit, or simply sit beside a beautiful lake and watch the sun track across the sky? Giving yourself a purpose will make it easier to plan your hike.

DISCUSS EXPECTATIONS WITH YOUR FELLOW HIKERS

■ Be sure you and your friends have the same idea about the trip. If one of you imagines lazy days of late starts, short distances, and plenty of time for sitting and reading, while the others long for physical challenge and long hiking days, you are bound to have serious conflicts.

RESEARCH TERRAIN, CLIMATE, AND CHALLENGES

■ The more you know about your destination, the less likely you are to be surprised by unforeseen problems. Knowing about challenges ahead of time means you can prepare for and face them confidently, with the right equipment and a positive attitude.

PHYSICALLY PREPARE BY WORKING OUT

■ Remember that hiking is a demanding physical activity – sometimes surprisingly so. The fitter you are, the less likely you are to suffer from aches and pains on the trail.

BREAK IN AND CHECK EQUIPMENT

■ Prevent equipment problems by ensuring it is in good condition. Check your equipment before you go – be sure that old gear is still functional and that new gear, especially boots, fits properly and is broken in. Be sure you have the "Ten Essentials" (*see* p.105).

SET REALISTIC DISTANCE GOALS

■ How far you can hike is a function of fitness, attitude, terrain, and your own personal goals. Start with conservative, comfortable distances that you know you can cover. Remember that difficult terrain and elevation gain reduce the distance you can hike per day.

BE SURE YOUR SKILLS ARE ADEQUATE

■ If you will need advanced skills, such as to cross fast-running rivers, travel cross-country, use ice axes, or make fires in the rain, be sure your skills are honed. Remember that local clubs and shops often run seminars and classes on safety and skills required in remote areas.

CHECK THE LOCAL WEATHER REPORT

■ Remember that mountains create their own weather, so where you will be hiking it will probably be colder, windier, rainier, and stormier than the weather at the nearest big town or airport, where weather reports are often compiled.

REMEMBER YOUR PERMITS AND OTHER PAPERWORK

■ Keep permits, money, credit cards, keys, and identification in a safe, dry place in your pack.

TELL A FRIEND WHERE YOU ARE GOING AND WHEN YOU WILL BE BACK

■ Leave an itinerary with a relative or a friend to let them know what your plans are – as well as instructions on what to do if you do not check in as planned. Stick to your stated itinerary, and do remember to check in when you finish your hike.

THE SUCCESSFUL HIKE
Setting realistic goals, carrying the right equipment, and being physically fit are all part of preparing for a well-planned and successful hiking trip.

ON THE
TRAIL

All about walking

Novice hikers are often surprised at how much effort it takes to hike a trail. Your lungs and heart must work harder to climb hills and carry a pack, muscles can become stiff and sore, and feet can be blistered by new boots. By taking it slowly, you can minimize these problems.

Walking with ease

It is the steep slopes and rough tracks that make trail hiking so much more arduous than walking. Uneven terrain, rocks, and mud all interfere with foot placement and rhythm, and climbing a hill requires much more effort while carrying a pack. This makes hiking both a challenge and excellent exercise. A few techniques can help you move more easily and efficiently.

PACING YOURSELF

A novice hiker may be tempted to walk too quickly, pause for breath, then set off again at the same fast speed. More experienced hikers make steady progress because they choose a pace that they can sustain all day. This pace may be much slower than they would walk on a city street, but it is one that enables them to walk steadily uphill and around obstacles while carrying a pack. The key is not to become out of breath – if you can hold a conversation while walking uphill, you have found the right pace.

TAKING REST BREAKS

Resting at regular intervals helps you to conserve energy for later in the day. Rest breaks are also opportunities to snack, drink water, check your feet for blisters, and stretch (*see* pp.144–7). At first, plan to stop once every hour for about 10 minutes. As you gain experience, you might want to alter your schedule of walking and resting.

WALKING CONTINUOUSLY

Although rest breaks are desirable, it is not always possible to stop for them. In cold or wet weather, 10-minute breaks once an hour may be dangerous, as they can increase the risk of hypothermia. In such cases, you need to adjust for the conditions so that you do not need to rest. Wear one more layer of clothing than normal, and walk a little more slowly. The extra layer will keep you warm even though you are exercising less strenuously, and the slower pace will allow you to continue longer without resting. Add or remove gloves or a hat to fine tune your body temperature without stopping.

KEEPING A STEADY PACE

A slow, steady pace is easier to maintain over a long day than short, fast bursts followed by frequent rests.

USING THE REST STEP

Sometimes a hill is so steep that you cannot climb it without constantly stopping – no matter how slowly you are hiking. In such cases, the "rest step" is an invaluable technique. At first it will seem an awkward start-and-stop motion, but, if done correctly, it will enable you to hike steeply uphill for long distances without stopping.

1 Begin the rest step from a stationary upright position. Step forward with your right leg. Keep the weight on the left (back) leg, with the knee locked. Pause before taking the next step, with the weight still on your back leg.

2 Transfer the weight to your right leg. Push yourself up with your right leg and swing your left leg forward to take the next step. Lock your right knee, so that the right leg is bearing all of your weight. Pause with your weight on your right leg.

3 Now transfer the weight to your left leg. Push yourself up with your left leg and swing your right leg forward to take the next step. Continue climbing in this fashion, and you should be walking at a slow, steady pace.

EATING AND DRINKING ON THE TRAIL

You must eat and drink regularly, and should carry a variety of snacks – both sweet and salty. High-sugar snacks give you a quick burst of energy, while dried fruits and nuts (see pp.134–5) provide longer-lasting energy release. Always have enough water on hand to drink, and know where the next source of water is.

WATER FOR DRINKING
Try to make a habit of drinking at every rest stop, even if you are not thirsty – adequate hydration is important in any kind of weather. If you are sweating frequently, electrolyte drinks help to balance your body.

CHECKLIST

SNACKS

Take along a variety of both sweet and salty snacks, such as:
- cereal bars
- nuts
- dried fruit
- chocolate
- energy bars.

DRINKS

You should have at least one of the following easily available when hiking:
- water
- powdered electrolyte replacement drinks.

You should avoid:
- caffeinated drinks such as tea, coffee, and fizzy drinks (they are diuretics, which contribute to dehydration).

Avoiding stiffness

Walking with a heavy backpack on uneven terrain for long distances means your muscles will be stressed in unfamiliar ways – even very fit people usually feel stiff after the first day's hike.

By using a few minutes of your rest breaks to stretch, you can keep yourself limber and reduce stiffness. Here are some exercises that stretch the muscles that are most likely to become stiff.

BACK AND NECK STRETCH

The back and neck can feel tight and stiff from the pressure of carrying a pack. You can use your pack's load lifters, stabilizer adjusters, chest strap, and shoulder straps to vary the pressure on your shoulders, neck, and hips while walking. However, it is still a good idea to stretch whenever you have a break.

WHAT TO STRETCH

The following muscles can become tired and sore from unaccustomed exercise and strain:
- the back from carrying a load
- the calves from climbing uphill
- the quads from uphills and downhills
- the hamstrings from hiking uphill

A towel will work as well as a t-shirt

Reach high and feel the stretch in your arms

Adopt a relaxed, comfortable stance

Feel a pull in your shoulders and chest

1 Take a piece of clothing, such as a large t-shirt. Hold each end and stretch it out in front of you.

2 Make a sweeping arc with your arms, bringing them forwards then up over your head.

3 Bend your arms and take the clothing down behind your head, holding it straight in both hands.

INNER THIGH AND QUAD STRETCH

The inner thigh and quad muscles may become exhausted from long climbs.

1 Kneel in a deep lunge. Push the knee of your back leg to the ground to stretch the quad muscle.

2 Put both hands on the ground to the inside of your front leg. Push the knee of your front leg outwards, to stretch the groin and inner thigh muscles. Repeat the exercise with the other leg in front.

Keep the neck relaxed, but do not drop your head

The back is kept straight, but not stiff

Push the leg away from the body

Keep your arms straight

HAMSTRING STRETCH

Hamstrings power much of your walking, especially uphill.

1 Sit on the ground with your legs spread wide apart, keeping the knees relaxed. Bend at the waist and reach forwards as far as you can towards one foot.

Try not to round your back too much, but stretch your chest towards your thigh

Stretch the leg only as far as it will comfortably go

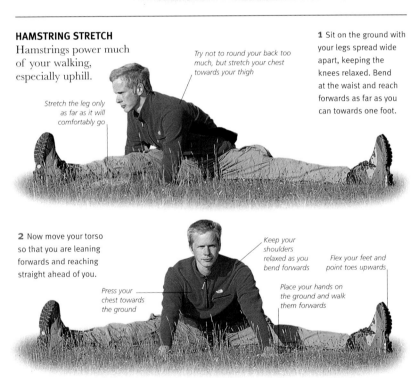

2 Now move your torso so that you are leaning forwards and reaching straight ahead of you.

Keep your shoulders relaxed as you bend forwards

Flex your feet and point toes upwards

Press your chest towards the ground

Place your hands on the ground and walk them forwards

3 Finally, stretch out over your other leg, keeping your knees relaxed.

Avoid tensing your shoulders and neck

Stretch forward as far as you can without straining

Looking after your feet

Your feet bear both your weight and the weight of your pack. Carrying this weight, wearing new boots, and ignoring "hot spots" all contribute to blisters. Keep your feet clean and dry, make sure your boots fit comfortably, and stop at the first sign of a blister. The key to an enjoyable hike is prevention.

AVOIDING BLISTERS

The first rule of foot care is to stop and check your feet as soon as you feel even a small amount of pain. It takes only a few seconds for a barely noticeable area of inflammation to turn into a fully-fledged blister, so the sooner you react the better. Even a single grain of sand lodged in a sock can cause a blister if it is not removed quickly. Hikers are often reluctant to stop for a mere feeling of discomfort, especially if this means their hiking partners must stop as well. But preventing a blister is perhaps the most important thing you can do to ensure an enjoyable hike. If a blister has already begun to form, treat the "hot spot" immediately (*see* p.222).

LOOKING FOR BLISTERS
Check feet for blisters at rest stops – look for red areas, especially at the back of the heel and on the toes where your boots are most likely to rub.

CHECKING YOUR FEET

Even if you do not feel any problems, you should check your feet during at least some of your rest stops. Do this until you are confident that you will be aware of a blister in the early stages. Taking off your socks and shoes during rest stops gives your feet a chance to dry and air, which in turn helps to prevent blisters.

WASHING YOUR FEET

A refreshing soak in cool water will remove tiny grains of dirt that could rub against your skin and cause blisters. It also rejuvenates the muscles in your feet. Make sure that you dry your feet thoroughly before putting your socks and boots back on.

CARING FOR YOUR FEET
Rinsing your feet not only feels good and cools them down, it cleans away any grains of dirt, sand, or grass seeds.

FOOT CARE TIPS

Get into the habit of taking care of your feet. A few simple routines can help keep them blister-free.

■ A thin moisture-wicking liner sock should be worn next to the skin, with a thicker cushioning sock made of wool or a wool blend over the top. If your boots feel too tight, try a lighter-weight sock (see p.63).

■ Boots come with liners already in place, but you can add to or replace them with thicker, stronger insoles to improve the fit of your boots (see pp.62–3).

■ Experiment with different ways of lacing your boots to give more room or to keep the boot more firmly in place (see below).

■ Sharp toenails can rub against adjacent toes, causing blisters, so trim your nails regularly.

■ If you know that a certain part of your foot is prone to blistering, pre-treat the area by covering it with a piece of moleskin or a sticking plaster.

■ Keep your feet and socks as clean as possible. Hikers often reuse the thick cushioning socks for two (or more) days, but rinse out the lighter, liner socks, which are worn next to the skin. This removes dirt that can contribute to blistering.

AIRING SOCKS

Keep your socks as clean as possible. If you will be reusing the same socks for several days (which is common among experienced hikers), air them whenever possible.

AIRING ON HIKING POLES

ADJUSTING YOUR BOOTS

Boot laces can be adjusted in various ways to make your feet feel more comfortable. You may have to readjust the lacing several times during the day, as your feet sweat and swell, or as they gradually work the laces loose. Tightening the lacing can keep your feet from moving around too much, and it gives more support to the bones and muscles in your feet and ankles. Loosening the laces relieves pressure.

AVOIDING TIGHT TOES
Loosen the laces to give more room in a tight toe area, but double the laces over at the arch to keep the boot from slipping.

ADJUSTING LOOSE BOOTS
Tighten the bootlaces around the forefoot if the boot feels too loose. Also tighten them if your forefoot feels unstable in any way.

SECURING LACES
To keep laces from loosening at the top, lace them across the top of the hooks first so that they cross over themselves.

Walking with others

There are many advantages to hiking with other people, or with children. You can spend hours in conversation or joint appreciation of the landscape, and even when hiking with only one partner, you can share the burden of carrying equipment and enjoy evenings at camp.

Sharing a trip

With a little planning and mutual consideration, it is possible for hikers of various speeds and abilities to go on a hiking trip together. As with any other group activity, sharing a trip means sharing responsibility and planning. Problems may arise if party members have different expectations, so good communication before the trip is important for its success.

HIKING WITH BEGINNERS

Too often, experienced hikers forget what their first days of hiking were like. If you are introducing a friend or family member to the outdoors, plan a very conservative distance, remind them to stop frequently for rest breaks, and help them to choose the right equipment and use it correctly. In this way you will ensure that they enjoy their first hike.

HIKING WITH A PARTNER

Walking in company is often more fun than being alone, but there are also other benefits to hiking with a partner. Sharing gear, for example, can lighten the load. Two of you can carry the tent, groundsheet, stove, cooking gear, first-aid kit, and miscellaneous supplies such as rope, utility knife, and emergency kit. Between you, this will cut the weight in half. It is safer with a partner, too. In an emergency, or if one of you is injured, the other one can go for help.

A partner may also see and be able to point out things that you miss, such as plants or signs of animals. And discussing what you see with a knowledgeable partner can teach you about your surroundings. You can trade useful information about gear, navigation, trails, and other hiking skills.

SHARING THE LOAD

Hiking with a partner enables you to share essential equipment, such as a stove and cooking utensils, and so halve the load for each of you.

One hiker can carry spare clothing and equipment

The other can carry pots and utensils

COMMON PROBLEMS

The two most common causes of conflict when hiking are varying levels of physical ability and differences of opinion regarding how far and how fast to hike.

If, in a pair, one hiker is stronger than the other, the stronger hiker will probably want to cover more distance more quickly than the weaker hiker can manage or enjoy. The weaker partner may then feel rushed and frustrated. And, in cold weather, it can be difficult or even dangerous for a stronger hiker to have to stop and wait repeatedly.

These issues need not be a problem if discussed in advance and possible solutions agreed on:

■ Have the stronger partner carry more weight.
■ Agree to split up for part or all of the day. The stronger partner can hike on ahead and wait for the weaker partner at a pre-arranged lunch spot.
■ The stronger hiker could walk ahead all day until reaching the campsite, then set up the tent. This does, of course, make the hike less sociable.
■ Hike together on flat and downhill stretches, and split up on the climbs.
■ If you are hiking in a group, split into slower and faster subgroups, and agree to meet at lunch and at rest spots. (If your group does split up, be sure that each party has what it needs to be safe: water, snacks, raingear, compass, map, first-aid kit, and other essentials.)

IDEAL GROUP SIZE
The ideal group size is between two and six hikers – larger groups have a disproportionately large impact on the land and on other users. Be aware of differences in physical abilities if hiking as a family group.

SHARING SKILLS IN A GROUP
Members of groups can share skills such as navigation with each other. This might include helping with compass work, map reading, and identifying relevant landmarks along the route.

HIKING WITH A GROUP

An ideal hiking party contains between two and six people. A group of more than six people becomes unwieldy when camping, and can also be difficult when making decisions. Campsite selection may also be more difficult for a large party. Be aware of your noise level and visual impact – a large group arriving at a quiet campsite can have a negative impact on other users – and behave with consideration.

Hiking in a group can be very rewarding, as each member will contribute different skills to the group and will have different interests, such as bird-watching or astronomy, which may be passed on to others. Also, if you are hiking in areas where wild animals roam, the larger your group, the less likely you are to be bothered by potentially aggressive animals, such as bears or mountain lions. However, you may see less wildlife and have fewer opportunities to photograph it.

Walking with children

Children notice things that adults have long forgotten, and many adults find that the experience of hiking with a child reawakens their own sense of wonder in the natural world. But hiking with children requires patience, planning, and attention to matters of comfort. Children have different needs from adults, and a successful family hike is one that takes these into account.

EQUIPMENT FOR CHILDREN

Children may be small and light, but their equipment is often heavy and bulky. They need extra changes of clothes, because they may suffer accidents that adults do not. Also, a very small child may spend a good part of the day riding in a child-carrying backpack. As a result, they are not generating any body heat, and so may need extra layers of clothing. Nappies for toddlers, baby supplies, food and drink, and books and games also add significantly to the weight of your backpack.

Your child's hiking equipment may be smaller than yours, but it must be every bit as weatherproof. Look carefully for children's equipment that is as functional as adult equipment. Avoid all cotton clothing, as it absorbs moisture. Instead, choose good wicking underlayers (*see* p.52), fleece layers to insulate, and waterproof, breathable raingear.

A baby should wear a sun hat and good skin protection

Adjustable straps help you carry the pack comfortably

A padded hipbelt adds comfort around the hip bones

Trekking poles help with balance and safety

CARRYING A BABY

Child-carrying backpacks are popular. Try them out in the store with your gear and your child to be sure you can manage the combined weight.

Older children can carry some of their own gear in a backpack, but they are unlikely to be able to carry all of it – which means that their parents' packs need to be large enough to hold the extra equipment.

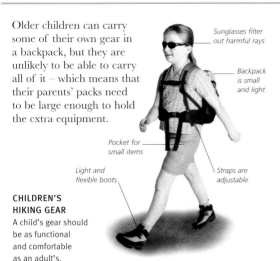

Sunglasses filter out harmful rays

Backpack is small and light

Pocket for small items

Light and flexible boots

Straps are adjustable

CHILDREN'S HIKING GEAR
A child's gear should be as functional and comfortable as an adult's.

HEALTH AND PLANNING

KEEPING CHILDREN COMFORTABLE
■ In cold weather, check repeatedly for signs of hypothermia (*see* p.229). Nappies must be changed promptly – the wetness can cause chilling. In hot weather, make sure that sufficient sunscreen is used, and that children wear sun hats and have frequent drinks to avoid dehydration.

■ Take hourly snack breaks at interesting places. A swim in a lake or river is always welcome, but be sure the water is clean.

■ Do not forget that children have shorter legs than you. A slightly rocky trail for you might be a boulder field for them, so adjust your pace as necessary.

THINKING AHEAD
■ Do not overestimate capabilities – an average child who is accustomed to walking can be expected to walk one-and-a-half times as many kilometres as his or her age in a day. For example, a five-year-old should be able to walk 7.5 km (5 miles).

■ Have a trial run – take children out on day hikes before trying overnight backpacking. Practise camping by pitching a tent in your back garden and sleeping outside.

■ Choose a hike with an appealing destination. Big rocks to climb on, waterfalls, and streams (especially with a bridge or stepping-stones) will motivate a tired child to keep walking.

■ For your first overnight hike, select a campsite that is not too far from the trailhead, where you will be able to return daily and, in case of emergency, reach civilization easily.

■ Involve children in menu-planning so that they look forward to meals. Pack some favourite snacks and treats

ACTIVITIES FOR CHILDREN

Keep children occupied and interested with a range of simple activities:
■ Devise a scavenger hunt. You can list specific items such as a piece of birch bark or a flower, or more creative items such as "something a bird could use to make a nest".
■ Lie down, look at the sky and make up stories about the different shapes you can see in the clouds.
■ Involve children in camp chores such as gathering firewood, hammering in tent pegs, carrying water, washing dishes, and putting up a clothesline.
■ Study wildlife such as frogs, bugs, and toads, and be prepared to answer a child's questions. Pack a nature book, or a local guide book with pictures.

BE PREPARED
If you overestimate your child's ability to walk, you may have to carry them, as well as your pack.

Finding your way

A map is an aerial view of the landscape. It not only tells you where you are, but also tells you what kind of terrain lies ahead. Using maps and a compass correctly will tell you what to expect on the other side of the next mountain, as well as just around the next corner.

Learning to read maps

A wide variety of maps is available to the hiker, from hand-drawn squiggles presented by fellow hikers to detailed contour maps. The wilder and more rugged the trek, the more detailed your maps need to be. Maps suitable for hiking use a much larger scale than road maps, to show sufficient detail.

CONTOUR MAPS

The most common maps used by hikers are contour maps (also known as topographic maps), which use a series of lines joining places of equal height to indicate the contours of the land.

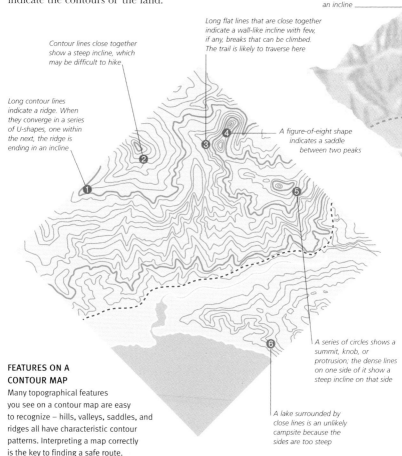

Exposed ridge ending in an incline — ❶

Long flat lines that are close together indicate a wall-like incline with few, if any, breaks that can be climbed. The trail is likely to traverse here

Contour lines close together show a steep incline, which may be difficult to hike

Long contour lines indicate a ridge. When they converge in a series of U-shapes, one within the next, the ridge is ending in an incline

A figure-of-eight shape indicates a saddle between two peaks

A series of circles shows a summit, knob, or protrusion; the dense lines on one side of it show a steep incline on that side

A lake surrounded by close lines is an unlikely campsite because the sides are too steep

FEATURES ON A CONTOUR MAP

Many topographical features you see on a contour map are easy to recognize – hills, valleys, saddles, and ridges all have characteristic contour patterns. Interpreting a map correctly is the key to finding a safe route.

HOW TO READ A CONTOUR MAP

A contour map shows information on the ground such as peaks and valleys, as well as rivers, lakes, roads, trails, buildings, and power lines. A key of symbols will tell you how to interpret the signs for natural and artificial features. Reading a contour map is just like reading any other map. The only difference is the use of contour lines to show the elevation of the land.

CHOOSING A SCALE

Look for maps that have a scale of from 1:25,000 (4 cm on the map equals 1 km on the ground, or $2\frac{1}{2}$ inches on the map equals 1 mile on the ground) to 1:50,000. The bigger the second number, the more area the map will cover, but the less detail it will show.

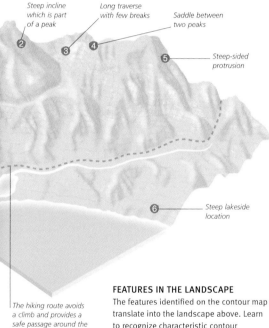

Steep incline which is part of a peak

Long traverse with few breaks

Saddle between two peaks

Steep-sided protrusion

Steep lakeside location

The hiking route avoids a climb and provides a safe passage around the peaks, following the route of the stream

FEATURES IN THE LANDSCAPE

The features identified on the contour map translate into the landscape above. Learn to recognize characteristic contour patterns on your map and visualize them as actual features in the landscape.

MAP SOFTWARE

Computerized maps for many hiking areas are available through the internet or on CD-Roms. Electronic maps frequently offer much more information than paper maps. They even allow you to compare several different routes, adding up total elevation gains and distance from campsite to campsite. When available, these programs can be an enormous help when you are planning longer hikes.

MAP ESSENTIALS

MEASURING MAP DISTANCES

Being able to look at a map and accurately gauge the distance from one point to another is an essential skill. There are two ways you can do this:

■ **Use a map wheel** – this is a tiny wheel that you trace precisely along the route you plan to take. The wheel measures the distance on the map, which can then be scaled up to an on-the-ground distance.

Distance in kilometres is shown in the window

Hold the device like a pen and roll the wheel along route on the map

MAP WHEEL

■ **Estimate distance** – split the route into sections by marking the map with a pencil each time the route turns. Measure each section with a ruler, add the figures up, then convert to kilometres.

■ **The total distance** that you calculate will probably be less than the actual distance. This is because neither method above can account for the extra distance caused by climbing and descending.

■ **The more detailed** the map, the more accurate your estimate will be. For example, switchbacks are often drawn inaccurately but add great distance. If your trail is shown as a squiggly line crossing steep contours, add 30 per cent to your estimate.

Using a map and compass

A compass is a simple instrument that points to magnetic north. With this information and a contour map, you can orientate yourself. Using a map and compass quickly and confidently takes a little practice, but it is an essential skill that will pay off time and again as you make your way through the countryside and when hiking off marked trails.

HOW A COMPASS WORKS

A compass is nothing more than a needle floating in water or oil. The end of the needle is magnetically charged, and it points to magnetic north, which is the place where the planet's magnetic lines of force converge.

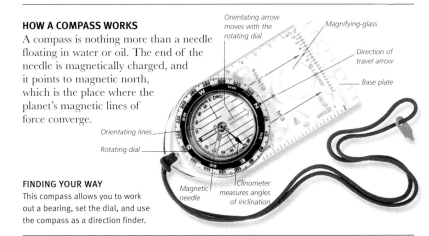

Orientating arrow moves with the rotating dial

Magnifying-glass

Direction of travel arrow

Base plate

Orientating lines

Rotating dial

Magnetic needle

Clinometer measures angles of inclination

FINDING YOUR WAY

This compass allows you to work out a bearing, set the dial, and use the compass as a direction finder.

ORIENTATING MAP AND COMPASS

To find a bearing and an exact location, you need first to orientate your map correctly with the aid of your compass.

FINDING NORTH

Align your compass with the map gridlines. Rotate map and compass until the needle is aligned with the "N" marked on the movable dial. Adjust for declination.

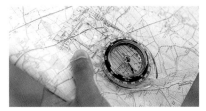

READY TO NAVIGATE

The map is now lined up with the landscape, and you can determine all other directions and find your position by triangulating (see right).

UNDERSTANDING DECLINATION

While the needle of a compass points to magnetic north, the "north" shown on maps is known as "grid north". The difference between magnetic north and grid north is known as declination, or magnetic variation. The number of degrees (east or west) should be printed on the map. You should rotate your compass dial clockwise (for west) or anticlockwise (for east) to find grid north. Without adjustment, the discrepancy between the two norths will accumulate and could put you many kilometres off route.

Magnetic north   Grid north

TURN DIAL CLOCKWISE FOR DECLINATION WEST

FINDING A BEARING

This means finding the direction between your position and a fixed identifiable object. It is best to choose something that can be easily identified on a map, such as a distinctive hill. This is a useful skill because you can use two bearings to locate your position on a map (*see below*).

Landmark
Select a landmark that is easily identifiable on your map, such as a house, church, or distinctive landform

FINDING THE BEARING TO AN OBJECT
Point the direction of travel arrow towards the object. Find north, then adjust for declination by turning the dial by the correct number of degrees west or east. The direction of travel arrow will now point to your bearing on the compass dial.

Your bearing
The degrees on your compass dial give your bearing to that object

USING TRIANGULATION

Triangulation is the practice of taking two different bearings and seeing where they intersect on the map. By identifying two features in the field and on the map, you can locate your position on the map. You will need to add or subtract the magnetic variation in order to put the correct bearing on the map. Where the two lines intersect is your location. Taking a third bearing will pinpoint your position more accurately.

FINDING YOUR POSITION

Find a bearing from your position to the first feature, remembering to adjust for declination (*see above*). Next, find the feature on your map. Without rotating the compass dial, place your compass on the map so that the direction of travel arrow points to the feature on the map. Orientate your compass to the map (*see left*). Then, using one of the long edges of the compass (these run parallel to the direction of travel arrow), draw a line from the feature back towards you. Your location is somewhere along this line. Repeat the process with a new feature, which should be at roughly a 90-degree angle to the first. The point at which the two lines intersect is your position.

Orientating the map
Let the edge of your compass touch your landmark. Turn the map and compass (together), so the magnetic needle points to true north

Draw a line along the edge of your compass from the landmark back towards yourself

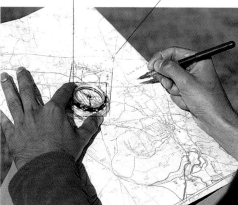

Using other navigation methods

In addition to the traditional map and compass, there are other methods that you can use to find your way when hiking. Some of these natural signposts are as old as the stars, while others are as new as satellites. In fact, both stars and satellites can be used to keep you on the right path.

NATURE SHOWS THE WAY

There are natural indicators that, if you are aware of them, can help you to find your way. By paying attention to where and how plants and vegetation grow, you can glean information to help you to determine direction. These indicators are not fail-safe, but, taken collectively, they can be used to help point you in the right direction.

Some plants, for example, lean towards the sun (to the south in the northern hemisphere; to the north in the southern hemisphere). Likewise, vegetation is thicker on the sunny side of a hill (south in the northern hemisphere, and north in the southern hemisphere). The bark of a tree will feel warmer to the touch on the sunny side, which again indicates direction depending on the hemisphere.

TREE TIP
In the northern hemisphere, moss grows on the north sides of trees in dry areas. In the southern hemisphere, the opposite effect can be observed.

PLANT POINTERS
Barrel cacti in the American Southwest are among the plants that grow tilted towards the sun. Other plants, such as sunflowers, turn to face the sun during the day.

USING THE STARS

If you are in the northern hemisphere, you can use the North Star to locate north. To find it, you first need to locate the Plough, then follow the line made by the two stars that form the front end of its "cup". These point to the North Star (Polaris), which always lies directly over north on the horizon.

In the southern hemisphere, you can use the Southern Cross to find south. Below the cross, towards the horizon, you will find two bright stars. Imagine a line running perpendicular from the mid-point between them. Draw another line from the long axis of the Southern Cross. The point where these two lines intersect lies over south on the horizon.

THE PLOUGH
This is one of the easiest constellations to identify in the northern sky. Four stars make the "cup", and three more form the "handle" of the Plough.

THE SOUTHERN CROSS
As distinctive in the southern sky as the Plough is in the northern, the Southern Cross comprises four stars that form the shape of a kite or cross.

STAYING ON COURSE

Stay focused on your route – the more monotonous the terrain, the more you need to pay attention, because lack of concentration could cause you to wander. As you travel along the trail, there are things you can do to make sure you stay on the right route. Most are pure common sense, but they are still worth noting.

Start by looking at your map before you set out, and identifying prominent features you expect to pass or see in the near distance. Mentally check them off as you spot them. If you see a landmark that you were not expecting to see, it could be an indication that you have veered off course. Stop and check your map.

Confirm your direction with your body's shadow as you walk – if you are walking north in the northern hemisphere, your shadow should be to your right in the afternoon. Keep track of the time you have been walking and your estimated pace. If you become lost, being able to accurately estimate the distance you have walked can be helpful in determining your position.

CHECKING YOUR POSITION

Pay attention to your surroundings as you hike. To be sure of your position, continually check your map for landmarks, to make sure that what you see matches what the map says you should see.

USING GPS

A Global Positioning System (GPS) receives signals from multiple satellites, which can be used to accurately calculate your position to within a few metres.

■ The GPS takes a reading of where you are. If you punch in the co-ordinates of your destination, the unit will point in the direction of travel.

■ GPS is especially valuable for navigating in thick fog or in terrain where easily identifiable topographic features are few and far between.

■ Before leaving a place to which you intend to return, note the co-ordinates. If you get lost, you can simply enter the co-ordinates and the GPS will lead you back there.

■ If the trail changes direction, you can enter the co-ordinates of intermediate stages, known as "waypoints". You can even do this before you start your trip.

■ Use GPS coordinates in an emergency to send messages to rescuers about your location.

USING A WATCH

You can use a watch in conjunction with the sun to get an accurate indication of north and south (depending on which hemisphere you are in). This technique is most reliable when you can see the sun, but if it is cloudy you can align your watch with the brightest area of sky.

NORTHERN HEMISPHERE

Look for the sun and line it up with the hour hand. South lies halfway between the hour hand and 12 o'clock.

SOUTHERN HEMISPHERE

Look for the sun and line it up with the 12 o'clock mark. North lies halfway between 12 o'clock and the hour hand.

Signal is bounced off a satellite

Multiple signals allow GPS to show your position

SATELLITE LINK

Using trail markers

Your map, compass, and GPS unit (if you have one) are tools you may use to establish your bearings and determine a route. But you can obtain a great deal of the information that you need to find your way on an established trail from trail markers, such as blazes, cairns, or signposts.

RECOGNIZING TRAIL MARKERS

Trails are marked in a variety of ways. Some, such as bright stripes of paint, are very obvious, while others, such as axe blazes (cuts in tree trunks) may be more difficult to see. In addition, each trail-maintaining organization has a different idea regarding how frequently trails should be marked, and how changes of direction should be indicated. Pay attention on each new hike and learn what the conventions are.

PAINT BLAZES
Trails are often indicated by paint blazes. Usually, a trail has its own distinctive logo, often in the shape of a rectangle, a circle, or a triangle. However, the frequency of blazing varies from trail to trail.

DIRECTIONAL SIGNS
On some trails, variations in the blazing, such as arrows or a bend in the blaze, will indicate a change of direction in the trail. These are especially useful when the trail is not clear on the ground.

ROCKS AND BOULDERS
If you cannot find the blazes, look down. Trails are often marked on boulders and large rocks, especially in the absence of trees. This is particularly true when travelling through rocky terrain.

CAIRN
A cairn is a pile of rocks. Cairns vary in size from a small grouping of three or four rocks to large piles that are intended to be visible in thick fog.

SIGNPOST
Markers made of wood, metal, or plastic, often showing the trail logo, are especially helpful in large fields where there are no trees or rocks on which to make a blaze.

FINDING AND FOLLOWING TRAIL MARKINGS

On a well-marked trail, finding and following the blazes, cairns, or signs can be very easy. But markers can wear out, be covered with vegetation, hidden under snow, or virtually invisible from certain angles. This can be particularly problematic if the trail is infrequently marked. It is therefore important to take the following precautions:

■ Note how often the trail is marked. If you go for an unusually long distance without seeing a marker, you may have wandered off the trail.

■ If you think you may be off-trail, look behind you. You may see a marker going in the opposite direction, which indicates that you are still on a trail.

■ Look down at your feet to see if you are still on an obvious pathway. You may also find trail markers on rocks at ground level.

■ Trail markers that are hard to see from one angle may be obvious from another perspective. This is especially true of cairns, which can be difficult to pick out when walking through a rock field. Try taking a few steps in several directions, or bending down to look from a lower angle. Cairns will often show up against the sky when viewed from a different perspective.

■ If you still cannot tell whether or not you are on the right trail, check your map for any obvious landmarks such as water crossings, prominent peaks, or constructions such as roads and power lines, which can help you to determine your position.

■ If none of the above methods put you back on track, trace your way back to the last marker.

MARKS ON TREES

In wooded areas, paint blazes on trees are often used as trail markers. Axe blazes on trees, which are usually one long axe mark and a shorter axe mark, are also used.

Some blazes are colour-coded. In areas where several trails cross, make sure you know which route colour to follow

Hiking in difficult terrain

Hiking could be described as the art of going around obstacles, but sometimes there is no option but to find a way across areas of difficult terrain such as boulder fields, rock scrambles, snow, and ice. As you gain experience, however, crossing these obstacles becomes easier.

Crossing rocky ground

Good balance, attention to footing, the ability to find a safe route, and confidence on steep terrain are all vital to hiking on rocky ground.

Do not be discouraged if your first foray is difficult – it will become easier with experience and by following a few basic techniques.

HIKING THROUGH LARGE BOULDERS
Look for the line of least resistance, and use your trekking poles to help you pick your way down any tricky steps and drops.

USING TREKKING POLES
Walking on rocky, uneven ground is a skill that takes practice, especially if the slope is steep or there are large boulders or loose rocks underfoot. Trekking poles will help you to keep your balance in each of these situations, whether hiking uphill or downhill. They also allow you to hike more efficiently, by transferring some of the effort of climbing on to your arms and shoulders. Using poles will also reduce the shock of each footfall on your joints when you are going downhill.

DESCENDING WITH TREKKING POLES
Trekking poles transfer weight from the legs to the arms, relieving stress on knees. They also help with balance on large downhill steps and boulders.

Walk slowly and test each rock before placing your full weight on it

On even ground, lean forward to place your bodyweight on the poles

Grip the pole securely but lightly to avoid jarring your wrist

Keep your arms bent at 90 degrees

Where possible, move one pole forward and step through with the opposite leg

SCRAMBLING

Some trails require you to use your hands and legs to scramble up rocks. Wear footwear with good traction and choose an internal frame pack that hugs the body. Transfer to your backpack items that you usually carry on your front. Pack heavier items toward the bottom, close to your back, to improve your balance, and secure your trekking poles to your pack.

Test hand- and footholds for security before committing your weight

Keep your lower body close to the rock

Use your hands to help maintain your balance

Use the large muscles in your legs to support your weight

TESTING A HANDHOLD

FINDING A SAFE FOOTHOLD

SCRAMBLING UP ROCKS

Always maintain three points of contact with the rock, and test the next hand- or foothold to be sure it will support your full bodyweight, before you move your hand or foot onto it.

ASSESSING SCRAMBLING GRADES

Use the techniques on this page to tackle terrain rated up to UK grade 2/US grade 3. Routes of UK grade 3/US grade 4 and above require specialist climbing equipment and techniques.

UK GRADES	YOSEMITE DECIMAL SYSTEM (US)
1 Occasional use of hands, minimal exposure.	**1** Normal hiking on uneven, rocky terrain.
2 Hands required for sustained sections. May involve exposure.	**2** Easy scramble with occasional use of hands.
3 Technical moves performed on steep rock. Very exposed, rope preferred.	**3** Full use of hands, with some exposure.
3s Rope and protection is necessary.	**4** Technical moves required. Rope needed, rock-climbing skills will help.

BOULDER HOPPING

When hiking through rocky terrain, you can use speed and momentum to your advantage by boulder hopping. The basic principle is to hop lightly from boulder to boulder using your arms or trekking poles to stay balanced. Practise without a pack on medium-sized, stable rocks. If you need to carry a rucksack, pack as little as possible, since the heavier the pack the more likely you are to jar your knees.

CROSSING A BOULDER FIELD

Pick your route by looking ahead for a series of evenly sized boulders. Larger boulders are more stable, but may require more effort to climb.

Look several paces ahead to plan your route

Use your hands to stay balanced

Keep your knees bent and relaxed

If you begin to lose your balance, continue forward, stepping lightly from foot to foot until you regain your equilibrium

MOVING ACROSS BOULDERS

Boulder hopping is a high-speed method of negotiating difficult terrain quickly and safely.

TRAVERSING SCREE

Scree is the mass of fine, small rocks that is often found above the treeline on mountain slopes. It slides underfoot, particularly as the angle of the slope increases. Walking on scree can be likened to trying to climb a descending escalator – for every step you take up the slope, you may slide two steps back down. But with experience, and by using the techniques shown below, hiking on scree can be exhilarating and fun.

CROSSING SCREE

Control your momentum by looking for a zig-zag path that passes over scree and consists of rocks of approximately the same size.

WALKING SIDEWAYS

Traverse scree by walking sideways step by step. This will provide more contact between the long side of your foot and the slope to give stability.

CLIMBING ON SCREE

If possible, walk near the edge of the scree slope where you are more likely to find large, stable boulders. If you are forced to walk in the middle of a scree slope, look for larger rocks that may be tightly wedged into the slope, since they are less likely to slip when you put your full weight on them. Test large rocks for stability by placing your weight on them gradually, but be particularly cautious if they are lodged in smaller scree.

Pack hoisted high on back

Arm raised to maintain balance

Leg bent at knee to support body

Foot lifted high to swing boot hard

Fine scree allows steps to be kicked

FEET SPREAD-EAGLED
Climb with your feet splayed, putting weight on the instep of each boot. Take small steps to reduce the strain on your legs and the chance of slipping.

KICKING STEPS
Keeping your bodyweight centred, kick your boots nose-first into the scree slope. Stay relaxed, but be prepared to steady yourself if you slip.

DESCENDING ON SCREE

"Screeing" is a technique where you let gravity do the work for you – by descending in a style that is part sliding and part slow-motion jogging. It is one of the most exhilarating ways to descend a mountain. Fine, deep scree is required to avoid twisting an ankle, tripping, or injuring yourself on the large rocks that sometimes poke out of mountainsides. You will find suitable scree on the upper slopes of most hills, mountains, and volcanoes. To avoid collecting small rocks in your boots, secure your trousers to your boots with strong tape, or wear gaiters that cover the top of your boots.

STARTING THE DESCENT
Launch yourself down the slope, starting with short, gentle hops as if jogging in slow motion.

SLIDING DOWNHILL
Dig your heel into the slope and use your momentum to slide a short distance with each footfall.

RIGHTING YOURSELF
Use your hands to steady yourself in case you lose your balance. Relax your knees and keep moving.

Crossing water

Water crossings can be among the most challenging obstacles you will face, especially in late spring, when mountain snow melts into streams and rivers. Water can also become an obstacle on shoreline hikes (especially during high tide), or when hiking through waterlogged ground alongside marshes and bogs. Ensure that you cross rivers, bogs, and tidal flats safely.

THE BEST TIME TO CROSS
Try to plan major crossings as early in the day as possible. During snowmelt in the spring, rivers run slower in the early morning, because the melt-off slows during the colder night-time hours.

CHOOSING A PLACE TO CROSS
The best place to cross a stream or river is usually found by following the trail to the water's edge. But in late spring and early summer, when the river is running at its highest, the situation may be entirely different – do not assume the trail is leading to the safest crossing. Avoid the turbulence that causes white water – the safest river crossings are where the water is calm and no deeper than hip-high. Look for these conditions around river bends, where the stream widens and slows to make the turn. Note that the darker (and greener) the water, the deeper it is, and there may be a powerful current. Make sure that the bank on the far side is not steep or undercut, which could make it difficult for you to climb out of the water.

SITUATIONS TO AVOID
White water is always dangerous and should never be crossed – if you trip or your feet catch on rocks while crossing, the force of the water could cause you to drown. Avoid crossing upstream of rapids or waterfalls – these should be noted on a good map.

If you are hiking with someone who is reluctant to cross, offer to carry their backpack across. If they are still unwilling, do not try to persuade them; turn back or find an easier crossing.

A SAFE CROSSING-POINT
During times of high water, evaluate the conditions. If they appear dangerous, walk upstream in search of safer options, and always cross with caution.

WADING ACROSS WITH TREKKING POLES
Trekking poles can help you to keep your balance. In a fast-running stream, face diagonally upstream, as this helps to control the effect of the river's current.

WADING ACROSS A RIVER
Wading is often the safest option when crossing moving water. Always face upstream, diagonal to the current, when crossing. If you are carrying sports sandals, wear them to protect your feet. If not, take off your socks and remove your boot liners. Put your boots back on and wade across. To help keep your balance, use trekking poles for support. It may help to unbuckle your backpack's hip belt and loosen the shoulder straps, so that you can shrug it off if you fall.

If you are crossing in a group, put the strongest hikers at the ends and link arms. Move slowly across in a line, diagonal to the river's current.

WOODEN BRIDGES
Test bridges for stability and cross carefully, one person at a time. They may be unstable and, if wet, very slippery.

ROCK HOPPING
A technique that can get you across with dry feet, rock hopping is best carried out using trekking poles for balance. Pick the route first and evaluate the steps you will take. Decide which rocks are obviously stable, and which might be slippery.

Test your steps before committing your weight. If you have already committed to a step and it turns out to be unstable, move quickly to the next step, using your poles for balance. If you start losing your balance, remember that stepping into the water is an option. It is better to step into the river and get wet feet than fall into it.

CROSSING A WOODEN BRIDGE
Wooden bridges range from well-engineered construction projects to logs placed across a stream. Always test a bridge first to see if it is fixed at either end and to assess its stability. Never cross on a log jam – it takes only a little weight to dislodge the logs. If the bridge is too narrow or unstable to walk on, try shuffling across in a sitting position.

CROSSING WITH ROPES
Unless you are trained in river rescue, do not use a hand-held rope to cross a river. However, if a rope is fixed in place, it can give added security. Hold on to it, standing on the downstream side to avoid getting tangled in the rope if you lose your balance. Do not use a karabiner (a metal clip) to attach yourself to the rope – if you fall, you could be held underwater by the force of the current.

CROSSING WATERLOGGED GROUND

Most hiking trails avoid bogs, marshland, and areas prone to quicksand. These areas are all made up of waterlogged ground, so with each step you take, you will sink further into mud or sand.

If there is no other way round, look for a route through. Wet ground is uneven, and the footsteps of previous hikers can tell you how deep and hard the soil is. Aim for natural hard spots in the soft ground. Look for trees and shrubs that grow on larger, harder pieces of ground. Large rocks are a solid place to tread, and thick tussocks of hard grass also make good footholds.

Trails that pass through waterlogged ground often rely on puncheons. These are bridges formed of short wooden posts set vertically in the ground. Bridges formed of fallen logs may also exist.

If you start to sink in mud or quicksand, try to run across, using any logs, tussocks of grass, or rocks as safe zones. If you fall in, remember it is just saturated ground. Stay afloat with a swimming motion until you work out where you can scramble out. Look for tussocks of grass, logs, or rocks to cling on to.

SAFETY IN WET GROUND
When ground becomes saturated, the suction of mud pulls at your boots. You should wear tightly laced, ankle-high boots in such conditions.

CROSSING TIDAL FLATS

You may encounter areas of mud and sand that are exposed at low tide and flooded at high tide when following coastal and estuarine trails over tidal flats. You must avoid coming across one of these areas at high tide, only to be unable to cross it until hours later. Guidebooks will tell you where you need to be concerned about tidal crossings. Use this in conjunction with a local tide table, which will tell you the times of high and low tides. Usually, you will have a safe window of several hours in which to cross both ways. Cross in bare feet or wearing sports sandals, as the damp sand will soak your boots even at low tide.

SAFETY ON TIDAL FLATS
You can only cross tidal flats at low tide, which occurs once a day. Be particularly careful of planning a crossing when the tide is rising.

Crossing snow and ice

Water in frozen form can be every bit as treacherous as flowing water. Hikers in high mountains may encounter ice and snow all summer long. Snowfields can be especially challenging in late spring and early summer, when they may be extremely slippery, especially on the northern slopes of mountains.

HIKING TRAILS AND SNOW

Snow usually lingers in the same places each year, so hiking trails are generally routed around these obstacles. However, in years of high snowfall, you may find yourself confronted by fields of late-lying snow, particularly on north-facing slopes. If these snowfields lie on steeply pitched slopes, crossing them safely may be impossible because the risk of falling is high. Turning back or taking a detour may be the only safe options.

READING THE SNOW FOR A SAFE ROUTE

Rocks underneath a blanket of snow absorb heat in the spring, causing the snow near them to melt faster than in other areas. This creates a hazard, as the soft snow may not be firm enough to hold your weight. To avoid breaking through soft snow, and perhaps injuring yourself on the rocks beneath, pick a path that avoids obvious rocky places and use trekking poles to test the snow.

CROSSING SUN CUPS
If crossing later in the day when the snow is soft, try to walk on the rims of sun cups. Keeping your balance can be tricky, but you are less likely to sink in.

Sun cups are depressions caused by snow melting unevenly during the day, making it very soft. They vary in size from that of a netball to a bath tub. Try to cross large snowfields early in the day, because the sun cups grow and soften as the day progresses. By late afternoon, you are likely to sink in as deep as your hips with every step.

BREAKING TRAIL
A climbing party walks in single file. When hiking through deep snow, take turns at the front – 10–15 minutes at a time – as breaking trail (tramping down virgin snow) can be hard work.

ASCENDING ON SNOW

A mountainside trail that can be easily ascended in the dry summer months may not be safe under snow. When walking on snow, the conditions should govern your route. You may have to create your own zigzags to ascend safely, or go straight up if that is an easier option. To climb safely, kick in several times to make a solid step on which to stand with one foot. Test your weight, then climb on to the step. Now kick in again with the other foot.

ASCENDING IN DEEP SNOW
Trekking uphill through deep snow is time-consuming and exhausting. Allow at least twice as much time for this kind of hiking.

EXTRA TRACTION
Traction devices such as 12-point step-in crampons give better purchase on icy and steep terrain.

Follow in the leader's footsteps, but be prepared to take a turn at the front

Carefully test each step before moving forward

SNOW TECHNIQUES

Travelling over snow can be challenging. Techniques for descending steep or icy slopes include boot skiing, in which you slide while hopping from foot to foot to maintain balance, and glissading, when you sit and slide, usually using an ice axe for traction and braking. Snowshoeing and backcountry skiing are options for travelling in deep snow, but skiing with a heavy pack can be difficult for beginners.

SNOWSHOEING
Snowshoes spread your weight over a large area so that you walk on top of the snow instead of sinking into it. Snowshoeing is an easy technique to learn.

CROSSING FROZEN WATER

Crossing streams, lakes, and rivers requires a great deal of caution, as a thick layer of snow may cover only a thin layer of ice. When crossing ice, use your trekking poles or ice axe to probe for holes and to test the snow. You are most likely to encounter thin ice in late spring.

FINDING A SAFE ROUTE ACROSS FROZEN WATER
Do not rely on the footsteps of previous hikers to show you a safe route. Their footsteps could be one or more days old, and the route may not be safe for you if there has been an intervening warm spell.

SAFETY

FROZEN BRIDGES

Frozen snow and ice can form a bridge over a stream, which you can usually safely cross. But do not attempt to cross a bridge during the late spring snowmelt when it could collapse under your weight. Check the snow is not dark or soft, and look for cracks. Also, test your footing before committing your weight.

GLACIER TRAVEL

Travelling on glaciers requires specialist mountaineering skills. Hidden crevasses can suddenly open underfoot, causing fatal falls. Never attempt to cross a glacier without the help of an experienced guide.

PREVENTING A FALL

The technique used for stopping a slide with an ice axe is known as "self-arrest". You should carry your ice axe in your uphill hand with the adze towards you. If you plan to travel in ice and snow, it is well worth taking a climbing class beforehand to master the technique.

SELF-ARREST TECHNIQUE

When you fall, bring the adze up to about shoulder-height. Now turn towards the adze and dig it into the snow, making sure that the axe is diagonally across your body, so the sharp point is not directly under you. Spread your weight out against the snow and dig the axe in aggressively.

Dig the ice axe in as hard as possible, and push your body into the snow

Be sure to keep crampons off the snow. Catching a point in the snow could cause you to somersault

Your face should be turned towards the snow when you dig in your ice axe

Climatic conditions

Climate is a general description of the weather patterns of a region, whereas weather refers to specific day-to-day conditions. Very few hikers truly enjoy hiking in extreme conditions such as torrential rain, scorching heat, or Arctic cold. Take time to research your destination.

Climate and planning

When planning a trip, it is important to keep in mind both the climate and the weather. It can, for example, rain in both a desert and a jungle, even though the two climates are very different. You also need to be aware of places where extreme conditions can occur and how your body might react.

CLIMATES AROUND THE WORLD

Arctic climates are cold all year round, although the summers are warm enough for outdoor activities. Summer there is characterized by 24-hour sunshine.

Desert climates are dry, but vary in temperature according to elevation and location. Some have a short rainy season.

The climate in mountain regions varies depending on the surrounding terrain and prevailing air currents, and is volatile – quick changes of weather, including fog and snow, occur even in summer. Microclimates often exist in mountain regions – the volcanoes of Mexico and East Africa are examples of mountain systems that are large enough and high enough to create a completely different climate from that experienced in the surrounding area.

Tropical coastal areas often have a seasonal climate pattern, usually a cycle of wet and dry seasons. Tropical rainforests also alternate between wet and dry seasons, whereas temperate forests can be rainy all year round, although some months may be drier than others. The climate in temperate forests ranges from extreme cold to uncomfortable heat, depending on the season. The combination of high humidity and high temperature in midsummer makes exertion difficult.

Hot, dry summers and moderate winter temperatures feature in the Mediterranean climate. Hiking can be uncomfortable in the summer.

TROPICAL BEACHES

Sunshine and torrential downpours lasting several hours are typical of tropical rainforests, such as this one in northern Queensland, Australia.

DESERT CONDITIONS
Hiking in the desert can be beautiful, especially in the cool winter or spring months.

RAINFOREST CONDITIONS
Many rainforests have dry (or drier) seasons, but at any time of year, good raingear is a must.

ARCTIC CONDITIONS
Summer in the Arctic is short but the sun shines for almost 24 hours a day. Insects can be a problem.

ADAPTING TO TEMPERATURE CHANGE

While humans can adapt to severe temperatures if they acclimatize slowly enough, quickly changing weather poses a dangerous threat. The human body is delicately calibrated to maintain a steady temperature, so be aware when changes are fast and dramatic. In high or low extremes of temperature a variation of 1–2°F (0.5–1°C) causes discomfort, 5°F (3°C) causes serious dysfunction, and more than that can be fatal.

WHAT CAN HAPPEN TO YOUR BODY IN EXTREME CONDITIONS

While hiking in extreme conditions, such as high mountains or deserts where shifts of temperature happen quickly, pay attention to changes in the weather and how your body is adapting. If necessary, take appropriate action.

Sun and snow (eyes) Snow blindness is a painful sunburn of the retina. Always wear polarized and UV-filtering sunglasses when travelling above the treeline, especially when walking on snow.

Cold and rain (core) Hypothermia lowers your core temperature, causing dangerous chilling and disorientation. Hypothermia can occur in temperatures as high as 10°C (50°F), and is especially dangerous in cool rainy weather (*see* p.229).

Cold (fingers and toes) Your extremities are vulnerable to frostbite (*see* p.228).

Sun (skin) Sunburn can be a problem almost anywhere, even on cloudy days. Always wear sunscreen of SPF (sun protection factor) 15 or higher (*see* p.223).

Heat (throat) Dehydration causes thirst, headaches, nausea, and extreme weakness (*see* p.226).

Heat (blood vessels) Heat brings blood vessels to the surface, which can cause heat exhaustion or potentially fatal heatstroke (*see* p.227).

Heat or humidity (skin) Rashes from heat can develop where sweat is not able to escape, or where skin chafes.

Heat (feet) Feet swell and sweat in hot weather, making them more prone to blistering (*see* p.222).

Heat or humidity (kidney area) Hyponatremia occurs in hot weather when a hard-working body sweats out more electrolytes than it replaces, putting stress on the kidneys and other internal organs. The condition can be fatal. The best prevention is to eat small snacks regularly, and avoid dehydration.

Understanding weather patterns

In many regions, weather patterns are fairly predictable – prevailing winds may come from one direction, certain months of the year may be rainier than others, and storms may break at certain times of day. Finding out about characteristic local weather patterns will help you to plan your hike and ensure that you have the right gear for the conditions.

WEATHER AND GEOGRAPHY

Weather is created by the movement of air currents, the moisture content of the air, and the collision between warm and cold fronts. Weather is also affected by physical geography – by features such as mountains, large lakes, seas, and oceans.

Air cools as it rises to pass over hills or mountains. Cold, moist air condenses into rain. The windward side of the mountain range receives the most rain. If you are hiking during a period of heavy rain, turn to trails on the leeward side of the range to find better weather

WEATHER PATTERNS

Nights are often clear and cold in the mountains, and many mountain hikers plan early starts to take advantage of the settled night weather. As the temperature increases towards morning, winds may build, and later clouds and storms form.

Moisture-bearing clouds are borne towards the shore by prevailing winds

NIGHT-TIME DESERT

Because there is little or no moisture in the air and no cloud cover to keep in the heat, night-time temperatures in a desert can be much colder than in the daytime.

Plants on the windward side include moisture-loving species, and they grow in more abundance than plants on the leeward side, where vegetation is sparser and water sources more sporadic

MOUNTAIN STORM
The mass of a mountain jutting into the sky interacts with the prevailing winds to cause storms. Electrical storms are dangerous, especially for hikers above the treeline, where there is no shelter.

After depositing their rainfall on the mountains, dry winds carry little or no moisture over the leeward sides, which may vary from dry grassland to genuine desert

The dry side of a mountain range may be very rocky, or may be covered with a thick scrub or dense vegetation through which it is difficult to hike

Despite their dry climate, deserts often have a short season of rainy weather. Desert storms can be fierce, but are usually short in duration and the rainfall is quickly absorbed or evaporated

Weather near the coast is milder than weather farther inland because of the warming effect of ocean currents. It can also be wet and cold in winter

EXTREME WEATHER

Mt. Washington is a relatively small mountain, only 1,917 m (6,289 ft) high. Its unique location at the intersection of three weather fronts, and the fact that it is the highest peak for 1,600 km (1,000 miles) in any direction, combine to create what has been called "the worst weather in the world". It also demonstrates the effect of colliding weather systems and the effect of altitude on temperature and precipitation.

Despite its modest elevation, Mt. Washington has the highest wind speed ever recorded on land at 372 km/h (231 mph). Hurricane-strength winds blow roughly every three days, and the average yearly rainfall is 251 cm (99 in).

Inspite of the poor weather, it is a popular hiking destination, but hikers must be well prepared for the conditions. Check with the White Mountain National Forest (www.fs.fed.us/r9/white) for current information.

MOUNT WASHINGTON
The average annual temperature recorded on the summit of Mt. Washington is only −3°C (26.5°F). The average amount of snow that falls each year is 650 cm (256 in).

Predicting the Weather

Weather forecasting is a complicated but inexact science. A forecast that is right for a big town may not be accurate for your hiking area. You can, however, forecast the weather by observing natural signs, from the smell of the forest to the colour of the sky. Many of these signs are based on scientific factors such as atmospheric pressure or moisture content of the air.

LOW AIR PRESSURE

Decreasing atmospheric pressure is a sign of bad weather. If an altimeter reading changes while you remain at the same contour, the air pressure is changing.

UNSETTLED WEATHER AHEAD

Many animals are sensitive to low air pressure. Flying insects hover closer to the ground and swallows fly low when the air pressure is dropping.

COLOUR OF THE SKY

"Red sky at night, shepherd's delight" is fairly accurate if the prevailing wind direction is a westerly. It indicates the approach of fair weather.

RAIN COMING

A red sky in the morning is caused by the sun rising in the east and reflecting on high cirrus cloud, which can mean rain is on the way in the following 12 hours.

STILL AIR

A prolonged period of still air indicates an absence of atmospheric pressure changes, caused by frontal systems, that lead to unsettled weather.

CALM WEATHER

If smoke rises straight up from a fire, you can expect good weather to continue. But how long it continues will depend on regional weather patterns.

A CORONA

This ring around the moon is a sign of impending wet weather, as is a halo around the sun. Both mean bad weather is on the way in the next 12–24 hours.

WET WEATHER TO COME

Tiny ice particles in high cirrus cloud refract, bending light from the moon in a luminous ring. This moisture is a forerunner of bad weather.

READING THE CLOUDS

Clouds are formed when moisture rises into the atmosphere and condenses on small particles of dust. The movement of clouds through the sky often foretells the arrival of a moisture-bearing frontal system. Being able to recognize the common types of cloud and noting changes in their formation can help you to predict the weather.

CIRRUS AND CIRROCUMULUS CLOUDS

"Mares' tails" and "mackerel sky" are names given to high cirrocumulus and cirrus clouds that look like wispy commas, and often occur in good weather.

BAD WEATHER TO COME
When cirrus and cirrocumulus start to gather and thicken, they indicate that a front is moving in and that bad weather will arrive in 24–48 hours.

CUMULONIMBUS CLOUDS

When white puffy cumulus clouds (*below*) darken and grow vertically into cumulonimbus (anvil-shaped) clouds, rain is likely, often occuring with storms.

LIGHTNING AND THUNDER ARRIVING
Electrical charges build up in the clouds causing lightning. The resulting shock waves become the sound waves that are heard as thunder.

CUMULUS CLOUDS

Relatively thin and white, cumulus clouds look like cottonwool balls with flat bases. Fair-weather cumulus show only a slight vertical growth.

FAIR WEATHER
Cumulus clouds that retain their shape usually foretell a period of fair weather. These clouds often have large expanses of blue sky between them.

STRATUS CLOUDS

These long, grey, shallow clouds bring long periods of drizzly, grey weather. Made up of low layers, they often cover the whole sky, blotting out the sun.

GREY, DRIZZLY PERIODS
The dark, low-lying stratus clouds usually foretell the least hiker-friendly weather – often meaning several days of continual rain.

Basic safety

With good planning, carefully chosen gear, solid skills, and common sense, most hikers are easily able to overcome the challenges of hiking in all kinds of terrain. Sometimes, however, the unforeseen does happen, and you need to be prepared for such eventualities.

Using instinct and judgement

The most important tool you have when out on a trail is your judgement. Deep down, you probably know what conditions you can handle and what you cannot. If you are torn between pressing on and turning back, stop to think about how you might tell the story of your misadventure in retrospect, and how you might justify the decision you are about to make.

DECIDING WHEN TO TURN AROUND

The best-laid plans are no match against nature. Storms, trail obstacles, and terrain that is more difficult than expected can all conspire to delay you or make a hike impossible to continue safely.

"Turn-back time" is a time that you set before climbing a mountain or undertaking any sort of out-and-back hike. Decide at what point it will be necessary to turn around in order to return safely before dark, whether or not you have reached your objective.

You should always turn around when thunderstorms are rolling in, particularly if you are above the tree line, where the bare landscape offers no place to shelter. Turn around when navigation is difficult,

EXTREME CONDITIONS
Snow and ice can slow you down, and may make your route impassible, especially if you do not have crampons and ice axes.

FORDING SHALLOW RIVERS
Boulders in shallow rivers can be used as stepping stones, but test each for stability before putting your full weight on it.

especially when hiking cross-country, on a poorly marked trail, or in fog. You should not continue if you are exhausted, if you are shivering, or if you exhibit any other signs of hypothermia.

When you are on dangerous terrain, go back if it looks too challenging. Examples include steeply pitched ice slopes and deep rivers to ford. Consider the mountaineering motto: "Better to turn back one hundred times too early, than once too late."

KNOW YOUR LIMITATIONS
In severe weather and difficult terrain, you need to evaluate whether your skills, your stamina, and your equipment are all up to the challenge.

PERSONAL SAFETY

All hikers, particularly women, should consider the following points:

■ **Whenever possible**, choose a parking area that is frequently used. Check with local trail clubs or the police whether there have been problems in the parking area. If there have, ask about alternatives in nearby towns. Some local businesses may allow you to park on their property in exchange for a fee.

■ **On the trail**, be casually friendly to hikers you meet. Do not tell others your plans or where you plan to camp.

■ **If you are hiking alone** or in a pair, and you feel uncomfortable about a person who is being overly curious or aggressive, do not be afraid to turn to fellow hikers for help. Look for a large group, tell your pursuer that you have found your friends, and wave goodbye.

■ **If sleeping** in a communal shelter, do not unpack your gear until a few other hikers have arrived and you have had time to check them out.

■ **Do not leave** expensive equipment unattended or in sight of a public road. If you are camping in a popular campsite, ask someone to keep an eye on your belongings. Alternatively, camp in a spot that is hidden from the trail.

■ **Take money** and any small, expensive gear such as cameras with you. A small lock on your tent may act as a deterrent to opportunistic thieves.

Planning ahead

To ensure a problem-free hike, it is important to to look ahead, plan carefully, and prevent any problems occurring before they happen. Learn about the area and use common sense – do not go on a trip that you are not prepared for, or one that is beyond your physical and skill capabilities.

POINTS TO CONSIDER BEFORE YOU SET OFF

MAKE A PLAN
■ At the very least, you should know which trail(s) you plan to hike, when you will be starting, and when you ideally want to finish. Also, decide on which campsites you want to use.

CHOOSE A HOME CONTACT
■ Tell someone where you are going and when you expect to be back. Ideally, you should leave them your itinerary, including information about campsites, trails, and any special plans you have, such as trying to climb a particular mountain by a particular route.

LEAVE INSTRUCTIONS
■ Give your contact at home instructions on what to do if you do not call in when arranged. Include the phone number of the relevant land management agency or warden station.

CHECK CONDITIONS
■ Before you leave, find out about recent obstructions (such as high snow-levels, ice-storm or wind damage, forest fire damage, or washed-out bridges), as well as water levels of rivers you must ford, and water availability.

BE WELL EQUIPPED
■ Carry all the essentials you will need (see pp.104–5), including extra food and clothing. Be sure you have the appropriate gear for the conditions, and one extra layer of clothing.

MAKE AN ALTERNATIVE PLAN
■ On your map, notice other trails and roads you could use to reach civilization in case an emergency forces you to shorten your trip. If you think you might be likely to use an alternative plan, make a note of it on the information sheet you leave with your home contact.

BE CAREFUL WHEN SOLO HIKING
■ Solo hiking is rarely recommended, but if you do hike alone, be especially thorough about leaving your itinerary with a home contact, checking in at warden stations, and signing trail registers and logbooks. Be especially wary about taking risks in difficult terrain.

TAKE A MOBILE PHONE
■ Whether hiking alone or in a group, take a mobile phone with the phone numbers of your contacts. Check with your phone company to see if it covers the area you are visiting. Note that mobiles will not always be able to receive a signal, especially if you are somewhere remote. Keep your mobile dry, and in cold weather keep the batteries warm.

DO NOT BE OVER-AMBITIOUS
■ Do not attempt ambitious activities if you do not have the relevant experience. If the conditions are dangerous, choose another route or re-schedule your hike.

DO NOT DEVIATE FROM YOUR ITINERARY
■ Search-and-rescue teams will have a hard time finding you if you have significantly deviated from the itinerary you filed at the warden station or left with your home contact.

KNOW THE AREA

Use maps to familiarize yourself with the trail before you go. Pay particular attention to highways, logging roads, streams, springs, and other physical features, and plan an emergency exit route in case of accident.

CAMPING

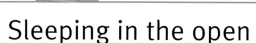

Sleeping in the open

Spending a night in the great outdoors can be a satisfying and peaceful part of your hiking trip. But whether you pitch a tent, rig a hammock, or sleep under the stars, be sure to follow minimum-impact guidelines and leave your sleeping area in the same condition as you found it.

Choosing a tent site

The places you choose to camp will all differ in degrees of comfort and amenities, but they should all offer some protection from the weather. Try to arrange to end your hiking day about two hours before sunset. This will allow enough time to pick a site that is both comfortable and safe, and it will give you enough time to make camp and cook before it is dark.

FINDING A SITE

The ideal tent site offers protection from wind and wind-driven rain. This protection could be a large boulder, or a small copse of shrubs and trees. Pitch your tent on the sheltered side of such windbreaks, with its back to the wind.

FINDING A BALANCE

A spectacular view makes sleeping in the open an enjoyable experience, but make sure the site you choose suits all your needs before pitching your tent.

A level site is essential for a good night's sleep, but avoid sites that have been compacted into hard depressions, as these will collect water if it rains. If you cannot avoid a slight gradient, place the head of the tent at the higher end. If you are unsure about the pitch, lie down to feel the direction of the slope.

Most hikers choose to camp near water. However, camping too close to a river can also be dangerous in seasons

where flooding occurs – choose a site that is at least 30 m (100 ft) away and above any evidence of a high water line. Do not camp on a dry river bed, because you could find yourself caught in a flash flood.

Avoid camping on obvious animal trails, especially near water sources in dry country. A tent site near a water source may frighten away animals that depend on it. Alternatively, an animal may decide to head for the water anyway, passing right through your tent site.

Your cooking area should be at least 30 m (100 ft) away from your tent, in order to keep food smells away from your sleeping area and prevent sparks from a fire (if you have one) from damaging your tent.

CAMPING NEAR WATER
If you pitch your tent near water, make sure you are far enough away to avoid the possibility of flooding or inadvertently contaminating a water source that could be used for drinking.

CAMPING WITH A FIRE
Choose a camping area with fire rings already in place, as making a new ring damages the environment. Pitch your tent at least 4 m (15 ft) away and upwind of a fire, to avoid cooking smells and sparks coming near your tent.

AREAS TO AVOID

Exposed, wet, or windy sites are rarely ideal for camping, but low-lying areas can also make unsuitable campsites.

TREES

Although many trees offer protection, trees with dead branches or lone trees on windswept fields, especially ones that lean at precarious angles, may be dangerous.

ROCKFALL

In high mountains, a site littered with rocks that have clearly fallen down the surrounding slopes means there is a high possibility of a rockfall.

MEADOWS

Because they are fragile environments, meadows should not be used as campsites. They may also be wet if near a river.

DRY RIVERBEDS

Riverbeds make dangerous campsites because they could be in the path of flash floods, which can occur many kilometres downstream of the storm that caused them.

VALLEY FLOORS

Cold air is heavier than warm air, which means that it sinks and pools on valley floors.

MOUNTAIN RIDGES

Such exposed areas are vulnerable to high winds and lightning.

MOUNTAIN PASSES

These act as wind tunnels, making them unsuitable for a tent site.

Camping with a tent

Putting up a tent is not difficult, but each one is different, and the process varies. Before going on a trip, pitch your tent in the garden (or living-room) to be sure you have all the parts and know which pieces fit where. Then take it down again and stow it away. Keep the instructions for future use.

PITCHING A DOME TENT

Find an area of ground that is as flat as possible. If using a groundsheet, place it down first, to protect your tent from sharp stones. Most tents come with a built-in groundsheet; however, some of these are very lightweight. A separate groundsheet can be purchased for extra protection from damp – you can also use a piece of heavyweight plastic sheeting.

1 Clear the area of rocks or sticks that might cause discomfort or damage your tent. If using a groundsheet, lay it down. Put the elastic-corded tent poles together gently (*see inset*). Avoid snapping the sections together, as this can damage them.

2 Shake out the tent until it lies flat on the groundsheet. Carefully thread the poles through the sleeves (which may be colour-coded), one at a time. Do not force the poles or you may damage the fabric. Instead, pull the fabric gently over the poles.

3 Once all the poles are in place, gently push them into their grommets. Do not put any poles into the grommets until all the poles are in place – threading a pole through the sleeve of a partially erected tent can cause it to poke through the fabric.

4 Peg the tent down. Even a freestanding tent should be pegged securely to make sure it does not blow away while you are attaching the flysheet. If the ground is too hard or rocky for pegs, tie the guy ropes around rocks or fallen trees.

TAKING DOWN A TENT

When dismantling your tent, work carefully to avoid tearing the fabric or damaging the poles.
■ Sweep away any dirt on the inside or outside of the tent. If it is a freestanding tent, shake it out after removing the tent pegs.
■ Take out the flysheet pegs. Unhook and remove the flysheet. If it is wet, shake it to remove as much of the moisture as possible.
■ Remove the pegs holding down the inner tent and disconnect the poles from the grommets.

■ Carefully remove the poles from the flysheet's sleeves in one piece (if they pull apart while in the sleeves, they will be difficult to remove).
■ Pull the pole sections apart gently, one at a time (pulling a little extra cord through each time). Fold the poles as you go.
■ Check that you have all the pegs and poles before packing up. Lay the tent flat with the flysheet on top. Fold into thirds, place the poles and pegs at one end, and roll up the tent tightly.

5 Put on the flysheet. First line it up with the inner tent so that it is in the correct position, then secure it with either grommets or buckles (depending on the model). The flysheet should not touch the fabric of the inner tent or moisture will penetrate.

6 Peg down the flysheet. While it is not always necessary to use all of the loops and eyelets, the more pegs you use, the more secure the tent will be. This is important in strong winds. If the tent has vents, keep them open to provide air circulation.

7 Tuck the edges of the groundsheet underneath the tent to prevent water from pooling on it, seeping into the tent, and getting your gear wet.

ERECTED TENT
The shape of this tent is created by curved poles that cross to form a self-supporting frame, making it stable and able to withstand strong winds.

UV-resistant nylon offers protection from intense sunlight in high altitudes

Camping without a tent

In fair weather, you may want the experience of sleeping out in the open, with nothing between you and the night sky. But for those who want plenty of fresh air, but also some degree of privacy and protection, there are simple shelters either available on the trail or that you can rig yourself.

USING A TRAIL SHELTER

Shelters, like the small, partly open-sided cabin shown here, are found on some trail systems. Most have hooks on which to hang your boots, backpack, and food bags to protect them from animals. The shelters are for communal use, so be prepared to make room for other hikers.

COMMUNAL SHELTER
Trail shelters usually operate on a first-come first-served basis, and can be busy at peak times. Always carry emergency shelter in case a trail shelter is full.

RIGGING A TARPAULIN

Tarpaulins are an excellent alternative in relatively dry climates where rain and insects are not a problem.

Tarpaulins are available pre-sewn, or can be made from rip-stop nylon or other waterproof, lightweight fabrics. A piece measuring 6 sq m (64 sq ft) is roomy for one hiker, and adequate for two, while 7 sq m (75 sq ft) allows plenty of space for two hikers and their gear.

Choose a large, flat area of hard-packed earth, and use adjustable trekking poles at the front and back to vary the height. Attach a length of cord at each end to keep the tarpaulin upright and stable.

In high winds, pitch one end of the tarpaulin perpendicular to the wind and pegged down at ground level. The side facing away from the wind can be higher, to give more air flow, a better view, and more headroom.

TARPAULIN SHELTER
A tarpaulin provides spacious shelter and some protection from the wind and rain, while still being open to the fresh air.

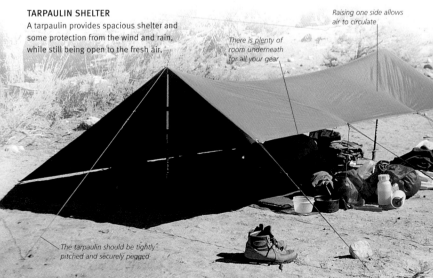

Raising one side allows air to circulate

There is plenty of room underneath for all your gear

The tarpaulin should be tightly pitched and securely pegged

SLEEPING UNDER THE STARS

Choose a comfortable flat spot for your open-air campsite. It also needs to be somewhere dry, so avoid meadows and other areas of damp ground.

Make sure you will be warm enough, but also ensure that your sleeping bag is not too warm for the conditions. A fully zipped bag can protect you from insects, as can wearing full clothing, but if your clothes and bag are too warm, you will be uncomfortable and may be unable to sleep. Place some insect-repelling coils near your sleeping area to keep insects away.

Be sure that any items that might attract animals, such as food, are hung away from your sleeping spot (see pp.99 and 219). Also, do not cook or eat in close proximity to your sleeping area, as food smells can attract animals.

SLEEPING WITHOUT A SHELTER
You will not be using mosquito netting, so choose a site on slightly elevated ground, where there will be more of a breeze to blow away insects.

Be prepared for any sudden changes in the weather during the night. Have your torch handy and a temporary shelter that can be put up fairly quickly.

SLEEPING IN A HAMMOCK

Hammocks can be rigged up at any campsite that has trees – even if the ground is sloping, muddy, and full of rocks. Because there is no impact on the earth, a well-pitched hammock will leave very little damage. Choose a hammock with wide webbing straps that will not cut into the bark of trees (see p.85).

Support ropes should be of equal length at the front and back of the hammock, and tied at the same height. A tarpaulin can be suspended over the hammock if it rains at night.

In addition to using a sleeping bag, take a sleeping mat to insulate you from the cold air below the hammock, or you may become seriously chilled even on warm nights. You can make a heat-reflective sleeping mat by wrapping a foam mat in heat-reflective material, such as a metallic space blanket. A car windscreen reflector can also be used as an insulator.

USING A HAMMOCK
Hammocks designed specifically for backpacking are lightweight and comfortable for all-night sleeping, and some come with an integrated flysheet.

Food and water

Proper sustenance is vital for hiking. Foresight and planning is needed if you are to make the most of opportunities to gather and replenish supplies of food and water during your trip. To enjoy hot food on the trail, you must know how to use your stove, or how to build a fire.

Staying hydrated

Water is essential to hikers. It prevents dehydration, maintains electrolyte balance, and can help prevent altitude sickness. On a short hike, you may be able to carry all the water you need. On a longer hike, you will need to find and purify enough water to keep yourself fully hydrated along the way.

WATER SOURCES

Hiking guidebooks and maps usually only contain a general guide to water sources, as conditions vary from year to year. For this reason, you should always check locally to find out the condition of water sources before setting off.

There are essentially two types of water source – surface water and spring water. Of the two, spring water is less likely to be contaminated. Surface water can be flowing or still, but a stream high in the mountains is likely to have cleaner water than a still pond or lake lower down, because it is closer to its source.

As you hike, take note of how well the water sources are running. If springs are bubbling and streams are flowing freely, you can assume that most of the water sources mentioned in your guidebook will

be running. If sources appear sluggish or low, be sure to drink at every opportunity, and always carry a little more water than you think you need to reach the next reliable source. If you reach a water source that is dry, or you get lost and are unable to locate the source, you may need to use your ingenuity to find another source. (*See* pp.202–3 for how to find and distill water.)

PURIFYING WATER

There are two basic ways to treat water so that it is safe to drink. The first is to filter it – a method that removes

DESERT ENVIRONMENT

You will need to carry plenty of water in the desert. Much of the surface water in Death Valley, California, is made up of saline ponds.

SURFACE WATER
Even fast-running, clear-looking streams may be contaminated – you cannot tell just by looking. Despite the temptation to drink, take the time to purify the water first. The same applies to freezing-cold water.

micro-organisms and contaminants through a filtration process. The second is purification, which kills contaminants, either with chemicals or by boiling. The major difference between the two methods is that filtering cannot remove viruses, which are too small to be trapped by a filter. While viruses are not usually a major problem in developed countries, they are a concern in less-developed parts of the world.

Water-purifying chemicals include chlorine, iodine, and potassium permanganate. Iodine tablets are the most effective and easy to use. However, it takes at least 20 minutes for iodine to kill parasites such as *Giardia lamblia* (which causes diarrhoea and is common in many parts of the world), with longer times required if the water is particularly dirty.

One solution is to use a purifier equipped with both a filtration element (which catches the large cysts that iodine takes a long time to kill) and a germicidal element (such as iodine, which kills viruses that filters cannot strain). Such filters use only tiny amounts of iodine compared to iodine tablets, making this a faster and more efficient method of water filtration.

WATER CONSUMPTION

The amount of water you need to drink depends on your body size, the temperature, the altitude, and the amount you are exercising. When you set out, carry at least 1 litre of water for one hour's hiking in cool weather. Carry more if it is hotter, you are overweight, or water resources are scarce. Use the chart below as a guide.

SEASON	ESTIMATE PER DAY (MAX)	ACTUAL CONSUMPTION PER HOUR
SUMMER	7 LITRES	1 LITRE
WINTER	4.5 LITRES	1/2– 1 LITRE

MELTING SNOW

In winter, or at higher elevations, you have an unlimited supply of water in frozen form.

■ **Do not try to** quench your thirst by eating snow – it will simply reduce your body temperature without providing enough moisture to satisfy your thirst. Always melt it first.

■ **Choose an area** with a large supply of clean-looking snow, avoiding snow heavily marked with animal tracks.

■ **Collect snow** in clean, black bin liners (which absorb heat), and leave them in the sun to melt. For quicker results, use your stove and pots.

■ **Light the stove** and heat at least a cupful of water. (If you try to melt snow directly in a hot pan, the pan will scorch.)

■ **Add the snow** slowly, one cup at a time, waiting until each cup has melted before adding more.

■ **Remove the water** from the pan and pour it into a dark fabric water bag.

■ **Place this bag** in the sun, where the dark colour will absorb heat and warm the water to a comfortable drinking temperature.

Add snow slowly

Water heated in pan

HOW TO MELT SNOW

Restocking food supplies

Whenever possible, choose foods that resist spoilage, are easy to pack, and are lightweight. However, once the supplies you brought with you have run out, you may have to restock in small towns where there is little choice. It is important to choose wisely and cook hygienically to avoid illness.

STAPLE HIKING FOODS

Hiking basics – rice, pasta, and varieties of grain – are the same the world over and are available in some form almost everywhere. These dry foods are lightweight because they contain no water, and are less subject to spoilage. Dried potatoes are a popular staple, and can be eaten mixed with a variety of foods. Choose quick-cook versions.

CHOOSING HIKING FOOD ABROAD

When you are abroad, it may be difficult to identify foods from their packaging, especially if you do not understand the language. Before you go, find out about the common staple foods you are likely to come across abroad. For example, rice and noodles are found universally and are safe staples to which you can add different meats and flavourings.

SAFE AND EASY TRAVEL FOODS

FOOD STAPLES

Non-perishable foods are safe choices that will keep for the duration of your trip, provided you keep them in dry, sealed containers. Choose foods that cook quickly to save fuel. In cool climates, certain perishable foods can be kept for several days in zip-locked bags (with the air excluded). Pack them in the centre of your bag for extra insulation.

NON-PERISHABLE		PERISHABLE	
	Rice Instant rice is less nutritious than standard rice, but it cooks quickly, saving fuel		**Salami** Hard salami lasts well, even in hot weather
	Cereals Choose instant hot cereal, or simply add hot water and dried milk to a cold cereal		**Sausages** Dried, spiced sausages last longer than soft varieties
	Sardines Tinned sardines last indefinitely. Choose cans with built-in openers		**Cheeses** Hard cheeses last longer than soft cheeses

THE NO-COOK CAMPSITE

Some hikers find that for short trips in hot weather, it is more convenient to travel without a stove and to eat only cold food. This saves the weight of cooking gear, but foods that can be eaten cold, without adding water, are generally heavier than their counterparts that need to be cooked. This strategy therefore works only for shorter trips.

- Dried fruits
- Dried meats
- Nuts
- Peanut butter
- Cheeses
- Yeast-extract spread
- Tinned meats and fish
- Tinned beans
- Just-add-cold-water food mixes
- Fresh fruit
- Whole-grain breads
- Savoury biscuits
- Cereal bars
- Raw vegetables (such as carrots, cabbage, cauliflower, broccoli, celery)

FOODS TO AVOID

Keep away from overly fatty foods, especially dairy food and meats, which can become rancid and spoil in hot weather. Though delicious and tempting, restrict your intake of fruit to avoid developing diarrhoea. Avoid lettuce because it is easily contaminated by unhygienic growing methods or washing in contaminated water.

HOUSEKEEPING

Studies have suggested that hikers are more likely to become ill from unhygienic eating and cooking practices than from contaminated water. To maintain a clean outdoor kitchen:
■ Wash hands before handling food, cooking, and eating.
■ Do not share utensils and dishes.
■ Be sure that any water used in cooking is brought to a rolling boil first. If you add cold water to a soup or stew, make sure the meal is returned to the boil for at least a minute before serving.
■ Always use bottled, boiled, or purified water to wash dishes.
■ Use biodegradable soap to wash dishes and pots. Scour dishes with a small scouring pad, or use sand or gravel to remove cooked-on food particles.
■ Periodically scour the threads of your water bottles, and rinse with treated water.

BUYING FOOD IN OTHER COUNTRIES
Although it can be bulky and heavy to carry, fruits such as oranges and bananas do not require cooking, and are usually easy to find in towns or cities. These fruits are also protected from contamination by their peels.

If possible, ask someone to explain or translate the cooking instructions for unfamiliar foods. In developed countries, look for health food shops, which often stock healthy instant meals and soups.

CHOOSING HIKING FOOD IN DEVELOPING COUNTRIES
Developing countries pose additional challenges for hikers because packaged foods suitable for hiking are difficult to find. You will also encounter different processing methods such as tinned cheeses, and unfamiliar meats and vegetables.

Fresh fruit and vegetables are often abundant in tropical countries, but avoid eating them raw unless you have washed and peeled them yourself. Buy only bottled or canned drinks, and always check that the seal on a bottle has not been tampered with, and open it yourself. Never add ice, as it could be contaminated.

EATING OUT IN DEVELOPING COUNTRIES
Residents of developing countries have built up tolerances to parasites that can make visitors very ill. In addition, food hygiene standards in some places may be poor. Try to eat food that is newly prepared and, if possible, that you have seen being cooked. Use your own utensils, cup, and plate to ensure that you avoid any contact with contaminated water.

Using a stove

A portable hiking stove takes only a few minutes to be primed, lit, and ready to cook, making it much quicker than building and lighting a fire. But stoves need to be used properly in order to work efficiently. Before you set off, test a new stove at home to be sure you understand how it works. If you do this, you will be able to start cooking a meal very quickly.

INCREASING STOVE EFFICIENCY

A few simple techniques can reduce cooking time and hence the amount of fuel you need to carry. Always use a pot lid to keep in heat – some stove sets have pot lids that can be used as frying-pans.

Lids can also be used as warmers for sauces while you cook pasta or grains inside the pot. You can also trap heat with a heat reflector or a windscreen. A heat exchanger, which attaches directly to the pot, is also very effective.

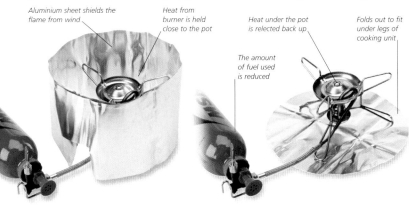

Aluminium sheet shields the flame from wind

Heat from burner is held close to the pot

Heat under the pot is relected back up

Folds out to fit under legs of cooking unit

The amount of fuel used is reduced

WINDSCREEN
To shield the stove flame from the wind, these are essential on a blustery day. Some windscreens come with a stove, but you can buy them separately.

HEAT REFLECTORS
A circular piece of aluminium placed under the burner will reflect heat back up towards the cooking pot. Heat reflectors weigh little and stow away easily.

USING A CANISTER STOVE

Make sure you buy the correct type of canister for your stove. Fix the stove to the canister and then light it. Some are self-igniting, but always carry dry matches, because flint can wear out.

1 Place the stove on a firm surface in a well-ventilated area. Turn the knob on the side that releases the fuel from the canister to the burner.

2 Holding the canister steady with your hand, flick the self-igniting flint. The flame should catch and light the fuel immediately. Adjust the flame.

USING A LIQUID FUEL STOVE

Different types of liquid fuel stoves vary slightly, but the simple mechanics of this popular model are common to many of them. Fuel flows from the container to the burner, where it is ignited to produce a steady flame.

1 Pump the fuel pump to pressurize the fuel bottle. About 20 strong strokes should result in resistance – this indicates that the fuel bottle is pressurized. If the fuel bottle is not full, you will need to pump more strokes.

2 Open the fuel control valve 1–2 turns to release the liquid fuel, and allow it to half fill the priming cup. Turn off the fuel valve. You should be able to see liquid fuel pooling in the priming cup. (Check for leaks at this stage.)

Priming cup

3 Light the liquid gas with a match or lighter. It may flare quite high. Wait for the flame to lower and start burning more strongly – the flame will be blue, and you will hear the distinctive roaring sound of combustion.

4 Open the fuel valve to let more fuel come through. The flame should settle into a steady low roar. If the combustion seems uneven, try re-pressurizing the fuel pump with a few more strokes (*see* step 1).

COOKING ESSENTIALS

For stoves that do not self-ignite, you need a lighter or matches, both of which need to be reliable in wet weather.
■ Carry windproof, waterproof matches.
■ If you use standard matches, dip the tips in paraffin or wax to make them waterproof. Scrape off the wax before lighting.
■ If your matches are wet, in an emergency you can use a magnifying glass to focus sunlight on the tinder to light a fire. Many compasses contain magnifying glass.

STOVE SAFETY

Portable stoves are safe to use if handled carefully. The following steps will ensure safe operation:
■ **Inspect your stove** before taking it on a trip, and always use, maintain, and clean the stove according to the manufacturer's instructions.
■ **Never cook inside** a tent. Risks include flare-ups (flames out of control), fire, and asphyxiation from carbon monoxide fumes.
■ **Always set the stove** securely on a firm surface before putting a pot on top of it. Do not use an over-sized pot – a 2 litre (3½ pt) pot is about the maximum size that can be safely used on most small camp stoves.
■ **Use only the type** of fuel recommended for your stove.
■ **Be sure to mark** your fuel bottle so that it cannot be confused with a water bottle.
■ **Make sure your** fuel bottle does not leak.
■ **Do not fill** a liquid fuel bottle to the top. Liquid fuel stoves burn fuel more efficiently when the bottles are about three-quarters full, because when the pump is pressurized, the air in the container puts pressure on the fuel and helps it to flow smoothly.
■ **Flare-ups** and incomplete combustion (evident by an orange rather than a blue flame) are signs of malfunction.
■ **Wait until a hot** stove cools before you relight it.
■ **Wait for a hot stove** to cool before you clean it.

Making a fire

The advent of portable stoves means that fewer hikers use fires for cooking. Indeed, in some ecologically fragile or heavily used areas, fires may not be permitted. But a fire can still be an invaluable source of heat and a method of signalling. The ability to build and light a fire is essential.

BUILDING A FIRE

A successful fire needs plenty of dry material, from tiny pieces of tinder to thick sticks and even small branches. Collect your wood first and organize it into piles according to size. Resist the temptation to load too much fuel on the fire too quickly – add sticks gradually.

1 Never make a new fire-ring if you can use an existing one. However, if you must make a fire in a new place, first clear the ground of flammable debris. If making a fire in a grassy area, use a knife to cut out turf about 30 cm (1 ft) in diameter, and set it aside to replace when you have finished. Surround the fire area with a ring of stones and build a small pile of tinder.

2 Over the tinder pile, build a small teepee using sticks about the size of a pencil. Start with a couple of forked sticks, which will balance more easily against each other and provide a stable frame on which to lean others to form the shape. The advantage of this construction is that if the sticks are slightly wet, the heat from the burning tinder will dry them before they catch light.

3 Around the outside of the teepee, place three medium-sized stones (about the size of a grapefruit). These can be used to support your pot. Never use stones from a riverbed, as they may have absorbed water and could explode when they are heated. If you have extra tinder or flammable material such as bark or pine needles, sprinkle a little more around the teepee.

FUEL TYPES

Tinder is the smallest building block of your fire and can be any small material that ignites quickly – bark, pine needles, dry twigs, moss, grass, and paper are ideal. These will burn long enough to light other larger pieces of fuel. Kindling is small bits of wood and tiny twigs that will ignite easily. Small twigs no bigger than a pencil should be used to form the foundation of your teepee. Logs and branches will provide sustaining heat.

TINDER　　　　KINDLING　　　　TWIGS　　　　BRANCHES

FIRELIGHTERS

In addition to windproof, waterproof matches and a lighter, carry a small amount of material that ignites very quickly and burns long enough to help a sluggish fire get going.

- Crumpled-up pages of an old guidebook
- Waxed milk cartons, cut into slivers
- Birthday candles
- Paraffin firelighters
- Homemade balls of sawdust and wax
- Lint from the pockets of your clothing
- A cotton bud coated with petroleum jelly

4 Add more sticks to the teepee, building it up gradually. Ideally the largest stick should be no thicker than your thumb, and no more than about 30 cm (1 ft) long. Leave a space at one side, so that you can reach inside the teepee to add more tinder if necessary.

5 Reach into the teepee and light the tinder. Once the tinder is burning, add pieces of fuel such as kindling and twigs, one piece at a time. When the heat builds up so that the teepee collapses, place the pot on the stones over the burning embers and start cooking.

USING A FIRE RING

Try to use existing fire rings. Fire rings help to contain the fire, but too many rings in popular areas has an unsightly visual impact.

LIGHTING TIPS

Fires can be difficult to make in high winds, or after long periods of rain.

- Choose a site protected from the wind.
- Look for dry wood inside hollow tree stumps, or close to the trunks of trees.
- Whittle away wet bark to find dry wood, which can be shaved into tinder.
- Collect more tinder than you think you will need.

FIRE SAFETY

Forest fires are sometimes caused by camp fires that burn out of control.

- Dry, windy conditions are extremely dangerous. A fire should only be made in such conditions in an emergency. Build the fire on the leeward side (the side sheltered from the wind) of a rock wall, and keep it as small as possible.
- Build the fire on dirt, sand, or gravel and clear the area of flammable material, such as pine needles and twigs.
- Overhanging trees can accidentally catch fire from errant sparks.
- Keep fires small – pieces of wood should be no larger than your forearm.
- Sparks from some types of wood can fly long distances. Keep your fire at a safe distance from tents and sleeping bags.
- Keep a pan of water near the fire at all times, and never leave a fire unattended.
- When you have finished with the fire, extinguish it thoroughly by covering with sand, dirt, and water.

Stones are stacked in a ring around the fire area to protect the surrounding ground

Finding food in the wild

For most hikers, wild foods are an interesting experiment, but not a reliable source of nourishment. Finding edible wild foods requires knowledge of their habitat, and being able to identify them is vital. If you do gather food in the wild, be sure not to over-harvest any one area.

EDIBLE PLANTS

A host of familiar berries grow in fields and forests during the summer. Collect berries in a water bottle and use them to flavour breakfast cereals.

Many plants are entirely or partially edible. Chives (a wild member of the onion family), can be used to flavour sauces. Tender green shoots from young plants such as bamboo and coconut palms can be boiled or mixed into sauces.

Edible mushrooms are also a tasty addition to homemade sauces, but make sure you learn to identify them. Morels, field varieties, and ink caps are common and fairly easy to identify, but if you are in any doubt, do not eat them. As a rule, do not eat anything that you cannot positively identify as safe to eat.

YOUNG PLANTS

Young shoots and leaves are less fibrous and tough than old ones, and contain more goodness.

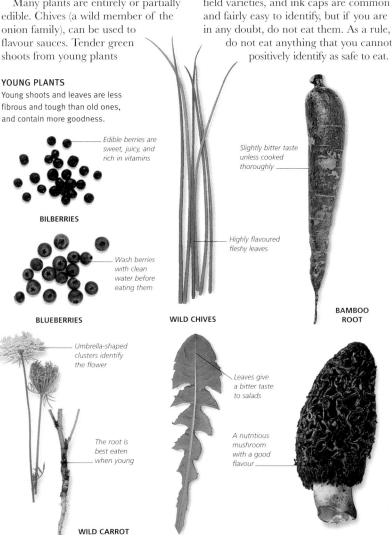

Edible berries are sweet, juicy, and rich in vitamins

BILBERRIES

Wash berries with clean water before eating them

BLUEBERRIES

Slightly bitter taste unless cooked thoroughly

Highly flavoured fleshy leaves

WILD CHIVES

BAMBOO ROOT

Umbrella-shaped clusters identify the flower

The root is best eaten when young

WILD CARROT ROOT AND FLOWERS

Leaves give a bitter taste to salads

A nutritious mushroom with a good flavour

DANDELION LEAF

MOREL

TESTING FOR EDIBILITY

The "universal edibility test" is for survival emergencies only. The test requires a minimum of 24 hours. All parts of the plant to be eaten must be tested.

1 Smell for strong or acid odours. **2** Place food against your skin and wait 15 minutes to see if a rash develops. **3** Abstain from eating for 8 hours. **4** Test for a burning sensation by placing food on the lips (3 minutes), then on the tongue (15 minutes). **5** Chew a pinch of the plant and hold it in the mouth for 15 minutes. **6** If no burning or irritation follows, swallow and wait 8 hours. **7** If no adverse reaction, ingest a little of the plant; wait another 8 hours. **8** If there is no adverse reaction, the food is probably safe to eat by the person who tested it.

Break open the plant and sniff

EDIBILITY TEST

INEDIBLE PLANTS

Never eat a wild food you have not learned to identify positively, and remember that some plants are edible only at certain stages of their growth. Never eat white berries – almost all of them are poisonous.

If you plan to eat wild plants, memorize their distinguishing features and habitats, along with any poisonous lookalikes for which they could be mistaken. Edible and poisonous mushrooms can be easily confused, with sometimes fatal results. Do not eat what looks like a field mushroom but grows in a forest. Edible field mushrooms grow in fields, while the deadly poisonous death cap, which looks very similar, grows in forests.

There are some poisonous varieties of this plant

FIDDLEHEAD

Totally toxic. Do not touch under any circumstances

DEATH CAP MUSHROOM

POISONOUS PLANTS

Many poisonous plants in temperate regions resemble edible ones, so avoid all plants unless you are sure.

Most white berries are poisonous, so should never be eaten

WHITE BERRIES

Lakes, rivers, and seas can yield some delicious outdoor dinners. If you want to dine on fresh fish, plan your hiking days so that you can be casting your line when the fish are biting. Foraging along the coast may also yield buckets of mussels or other shellfish. However, before eating any shellfish or fish, be sure you have any necessary licences or permits, and check that fish and shellfish from the local waters are safe to eat. In some regions, the waters may be contaminated.

MUSSELS

These are not viable options for the hiker. Hunting follows its own timetable, which does not fit easily with that of a hiker. You cannot follow your quarry while you are carrying a backpack and hoping to reach the next campsite. And, after a full day's hiking, most people do not have the energy to set off with a gun in search of wild rabbits or other animals, always assuming that this is permitted. As for trapping, this is feasible only if you are staying at a site for more than one night, and it, too, may not be allowed.

No-trace camping

As hiking has become more popular worldwide, it has had an impact on the environment. In some cases, the landscape has been scarred from overuse, and water sources have been contaminated. Some common-sense precautions can help ensure that your stay leaves no trace.

Using no-trace techniques

The basic concept of "leave no trace" is quite simple – leave things as pristine as you found them, if not a little better. Areas of particular concern are sanitation, hygiene, and campsite degradation. Overuse of fires is also damaging, especially in regions where wood is very scarce.

BEING ENVIRONMENTALLY CONSCIOUS

In order to make the least impact on the environment, read about your destination in advance. Find out which times of year attract the most tourists, and consider whether hiking in a nearby area would offer the same terrain and a similar experience without the crowds. Visit in a small group, so that you have a minimal impact on the environment.

When walking, stay on the trail – in particular, do not cut switchbacks, as this leads to erosion. On marshy or boggy ground, try to stay in the middle of the trail, rather than edging around it, because this can cause the trail to widen into an unsightly bog. Always pitch your tent on a firm, stable surface.

Find out what the regulations are, especially rules about permits and fires. Always obey campfire regulations, use stoves rather than campfires to cook on,

LOW-IMPACT CAMPSITE
Hard ground without any vegetation will not be damaged by a tent.

STICKING TO MARKED PATHS
In very popular areas, such as the Lake District in the UK, large numbers of tourists have a huge impact on the landscape. Keep to public footpaths across farmland and do not take shortcuts.

and avoid making fires in fragile regions such as deserts and alpine tundra. Do not make fires in arid climates when high winds are blowing. Take away with you everything that you have brought in, including all your rubbish – any hidden rubbish will be found by animals and may be scattered around the area.

Avoid bringing home cultural souvenirs such as ancient arrowheads, pottery shards, or other items you might find. Such archaeological remains should be left for others to enjoy or study. The remote area you are visiting is home to a community of animals, so avoid camping on game trails, or close to water sources used by them (especially in arid country). Never feed wild animals because those that depend on human food can become dangerous or destructive pests at campsites. They can also be made ill by an unnatural diet or even starve once the visitor season is over.

LOCAL CUSTOMS AND ETIQUETTE

In foreign countries, try to learn enough about local customs and etiquette to avoid giving inadvertent offence, especially at religious sites. When hiking across private property, respect landowners, stay on trails, and leave gates as you found them. Be aware of your impact – both visual and aural – on other hikers, and follow the no trace adage: "Take only photographs, leave only footprints".

CLEANING UP A CAMPSITE

Areas that are popular with campers can deteriorate. Try to leave each site cleaner than you found it and carry out all your litter. If you made a fire ring, replace the grass sod and restore the area to its original condition. If you used an existing fire ring, clean out any rubbish, be sure no food remains on the ground, and leave the area around the fire ring tidy.

HIKING ESSENTIALS

KEEPING WATER CLEAN

Keeping yourself clean without polluting the environment can be a challenge on a long hike.
■ Use biodegradable soap.
■ Take advantage of natural baths – streams and lakes – but do not bathe in springs from which others will draw water. Try not to swallow any water, just in case it is contaminated.
■ When using soap, carry water away from the source in a container and use it to wash, so that soap does not enter the source. Scatter used wash water over a large area for minimal impact.

LATRINES AND SANITATION

A few simple procedures can help to preserve an area's cleanliness.
■ When travelling in small groups, each member of the party should dig a small hole about 15 cm (6 in) deep with their toilet trowel. The hole can be re-covered with dirt once it has been used. Site the hole at least 90 m (295 ft) from any water source.
■ Larger groups can share a latrine. Dig a deep pit out of view, at least 90 m (295 ft) from a water source, and downwind from the tents. Screen it with some vegetation to provide privacy. Scatter earth into it after each use to avoid bad smells, which attract flies.
■ Soiled personal hygiene products should be stored in sealed zip-locking bags and taken away when you leave, or burned on site.

OVERCOMING CHALLENGES

Improvizing in the field

How you choose to respond to situations you encounter in the field is a matter of flexibility and skill – the ability to apply your knowledge and your equipment to the unexpected. And as you gain experience, you will also acquire the confidence you need to be able to cope.

Spending the night outside

A sudden violent storm, illness, injury, or the rare event of being so thoroughly lost that you cannot find your way back to the start of the trail, are just a few reasons why you may need to spend an unexpected night outside.

Knowing how to find or improvize a quick, secure shelter means that you will have a safe place to spend the night while waiting for help or daylight. If you are injured and cannot walk, you may need to signal for help.

USING NATURAL FEATURES

The simplest way to spend a night in the open is to lay your sleeping bag and mat in a dry, sheltered spot. If you are on an open hillside, descend. Look for trees or large rocks or a wall of stones (a "redoubt") to break the wind. Look out too for trail shelters and shepherd's huts.

SHELTERING UNDER A TREE
Evergreen trees give the best protection from the rain. Look for thick groves of evergreens but make sure your sleeping bag is protected from wet ground.

MAKING AN EMERGENCY LEAN-TO

You can construct an emergency lean-to using pieces of dead wood and foliage. If possible, use a large fallen log as the main structural component of your shelter. Lean large branches and sticks against the log to form a lean-to under which you can crawl. Cover these large sticks with a layer of branches that have leaves, interweaving the branches among the sticks, or holding them in place with twine or rope. The thicker the layer of

leaves, the more the protection offered. Build the lean-to in a sheltered area because it will have little integral strength against the force of the wind.

Emergency gear such as bin liners and space blankets can be draped over your lean-to to add extra protection. Any discarded materials you find, such as pieces of cardboard, plastic sheeting, or corrugated iron, can also be used. Wear your rain jacket to retain heat and keep water away from your clothes.

A large fallen log supports the lean-to

Long branches and sticks propped against the log form the roof

CONSTRUCTING A LEAN-TO
An emergency lean-to may not be luxurious but it can provide effective shelter.

Layers of small leafy branches, interweaved among the larger branches, keep out wind and rain

MAKING A SNOW SHELTER

In an emergency, time and energy are in short supply and conditions are, by definition, difficult, so it is practical to choose a simple design for a shelter. To shelter from the wind first make snow bricks and form them into a wall. This wall can be used in conjunction with a tent or as part of an emergency shelter. To make a shelter, pitch a tarpaulin or a space blanket to the lee side of the wall, and secure it in place with a layer of snow. Body heat is lost through contact with the ground, so in any snow shelter, be sure to place as much insulation (clothing, stuff sacks, a bin liner, a backpack, sticks, branches from evergreen trees – anything you have or can find) between your body and the ground. Here are some other types of snow shelter:

MAKE A ROOFED TRENCH

Dig a trench in the snow, then use a blanket or bin liner to form the roof (be sure to make an air hole). This will protect you from wind on a clear, cold night, but should not be used if snowing because the roof could collapse.

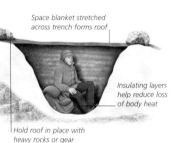

Space blanket stretched across trench forms roof

Insulating layers help reduce loss of body heat

Hold roof in place with heavy rocks or gear

USE A TREE HOLLOW

A natural hollow is often found under a tree, especially a large conifer. Lower branches overhanging the hollow may form a kind of roof to block out wind and snow, which makes this a good natural shelter.

Low leafy branches form roof

Hollow beneath tree provides shelter

DIG A SNOW CAVE

A snow cave can be dug into the side of a large snowdrift. Make an entry hole at the low side of the drift, and dig up from the entrance to carve out a sleeping shelf. Block the entry hole behind you with snow. Poke ventilation holes in the ceiling to provide plenty of fresh air. This will also stop snow from the roof dripping on you as the air that you,breathe out causes it to melt.

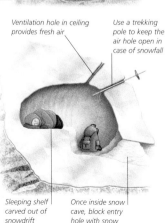

Ventilation hole in ceiling provides fresh air

Use a trekking pole to keep the air hole open in case of snowfall

Sleeping shelf carved out of snowdrift

Once inside snow cave, block entry hole with snow

SIGNALLING FOR HELP

Ensure there is a clear line of sight from your signal to any potential rescuers. Ideally, mark the way to your shelter with a trail of brightly coloured gear.

LIGHT A FIRE

Smoke from a fire is highly visible if lit in an open area. Put damp wood or vegetation on the fire to increase the smoke.

USE A MIRROR

Point the mirror towards the sun, then move it back and forth so that the light it reflects can be seen from different vantage points. If an aircraft is within range, catch the light on the mirror, angled towards the plane.

DISPLAY ORANGE GEAR

The colour orange and number three are both signs for help. Pile orange gear together in a visible place, or make three highly visible piles.

MAKE GROUND SYMBOLS

Make outlines on the ground, using brightly coloured gear, branches, or rocks. Symbols that are internationally recognized by pilots are: "I" to indicate a serious injury; "F" means you need food and water.

SOUND WHISTLE BLASTS

Signal SOS with three short blasts, three long, then three short. Repeat this frequently.

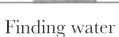

Finding water

A ready supply of fresh drinking water is essential for your health – indeed, for your survival. Always check on the reliability and cleanliness of water sources before hiking in a new area.

When hiking, you should drink freely at every opportunity, even if you are not thirsty. Carry a little more water than you think you will need, so there is no danger of running short.

CARRYING WATER

Water weighs 1 kg per litre (1 lb per pint). How much you need will depend on the weather and terrain, but 1 litre (1¾ pt) is only sufficient for a day hike of an hour or two, making it impractical, if not impossible, to carry enough for a longer hike. This means that you must find water sources along your route. Note that any water you find should be purified before you drink it.

NATURAL WATER SOURCES

Seasonal waterways will be lined with vegetation, and the thicker and greener it is, the better the chance of finding water. In arid country, a strip of green running along a depression generally indicates a seasonal watercourse. Willows and cottonwoods are thirsty plants that need a fairly reliable supply, so a large grove of cottonwoods is almost always a sure sign of water. Digging in the cool sand or soil under willows can also sometimes yield water.

If you find a seasonal source that is dry, do not assume that it will be dry throughout its course. Walk downstream a little to see if the vegetation appears more lush. Look for puddles and search

under large rocks, which provide shade and delay evaporation. If the ground looks as though it has recently been wet, try digging – you may find water just a few centimetres below the surface.

Water can be found in shaded rock crevices, especially if they are on the north side of a hill, and springs are often marked on maps. Animals also depend on water, so look for animal tracks – in a dry country they may lead to a source.

MAN-MADE WATER SOURCES

In addition to signs of natural sources, you can look for evidence of structures such as wells or water mills. Humans cannot survive in settlements without a water source, so a cluster of buildings shown on a map may indicate a source, even if the area is currently uninhabited. Note, however, that wells found in a deserted settlement may be capped or broken. There is also the possibility that the source has become polluted.

FINDING A SOURCE

Lush vegetation is a good indicator of water in dry regions. Trees such as cottonwoods, willows, and alders need plenty of water and generally grow close to perennial sources.

DISTILLING WATER

This method of obtaining water using a still (a device for distilling) is based on two scientific facts. First, a plant transpires (gives off water vapour) through its leaves. Second, the difference in temperature between two surfaces causes water vapour to condense.

1 Dig a deep hole that is wider than your container. Choose soft sandy ground, if possible. For digging harder ground, use a toilet trowel to loosen the soil.

2 When the hole is deep enough – 60 cm (2 ft) is ideal – sit a suitable container at the bottom. You can use a cup, bowl, plastic container, or billy can.

3 Surround the container with vegetation. The more dense you make the layer of vegetation (and the bigger the hole), the more effective your still will be and the more water it will yield.

4 Cover the hole with a piece of plastic and weigh it down around its edges with rocks. Put a small rock in the centre to indent the plastic and act as a funnel on the underside of the plastic.

HOW A STILL WORKS

A simple solar still such as this produces water using vegetation, the sun's rays, and simple physics.

The condensed water vapour runs down the underside of the plastic and drips into the container beneath

Water vapour from the vegetation condenses on the underside of the plastic

COLLECTING TIPS

USE A WIDE-MOUTHED BOTTLE

A wide-mouthed bottle can be used to collect water from all kinds of sources, including shallow pools and streams.

USE A NATURAL CONTAINER

Large leaves and tubes from hollow grasses such as bamboo can be used to collect and funnel water from small springs. This takes some patience, but allows you to collect water from a slow source.

USE A HANDKERCHIEF

If the water source is so shallow that you simply cannot use a bottle, spread a clean handkerchief on the surface (to avoid stirring up dirt). When it has absorbed as much as possible, wring it out into your cup.

COLLECT RAINWATER

Lay out a waterproof tarpaulin, bin liner, or groundsheet on a sloping piece of land, and fix it tightly in place with tent pegs. Place a rock in the middle to help funnel the water to the centre of the material so it can flow downhill into a waiting container.

FIND PLANT SOURCES

Some cacti can provide liquid. The leaves of the prickly pear can be chewed (remove the thorns first), while the pulp of a barrel cactus can be mashed to produce a liquid. Be sure you can identify these, as other varieties can be toxic.

Severe weather

The best advice regarding severe weather is to avoid it. Of course, this may not always be possible, especially if you have travelled a long distance to your destination, or if you are on a long hike in high mountains or other regions where the weather is unpredictable.

Hiking in storms and heat

While prolonged periods of bad weather can spoil the enjoyment of a hike, several strategies can help you prevent the trip becoming a disaster. Torrential rain may soak you to the skin, lightning may scare you, a heat wave may bake you, and humidity may sap your energy. But knowing how best to shelter from or cope with the elements will ensure your safety.

TORRENTIAL RAIN

If you are hiking in a region where torrential rain falls in short showers, you can dry out your gear during dry or sunny periods. However, in some regions you can expect long periods of heavy rain. Guidebooks and local land management agencies will tell you whether the area where you plan to hike is subject to unpredictable storms or long periods of rain. Be aware that one side of a mountain range can be very wet while another is quite dry. Be prepared to detour to a different trail in search of drier conditions.

You will need extra gear to cope with rain. You should carry more warm layers (packed securely in a waterproof bag) than in drier climates, a rain hat, a protective case for your maps, and a tent with full flysheet protection. To make sure you have a warm, dry place to sleep at night, pack your sleeping bag in a waterproof stuff sack. Carry ready meals that you can cook quickly and easily under the rainfly.

SHELTERING FROM A STORM
Dense, low tree foliage provides safe natural shelter from rain and lightning. Insulate yourself from wet ground and to keep your gear as dry as possible.

LIGHTNING

It is dangerous to be in a lightning storm on a mountain above the treeline where there is no shelter. Act immediately and descend from high ground as quickly as you can, looking for cover. A grove of trees is the best natural shelter – the thicker the tree cover, the greater the level of protection.

Avoid standing under a solitary tree, as it can act as a lightning conductor. Also, never shelter in a shallow cave, on a ledge, or in a depression, because these can all attract ground lightning. Finally, avoid areas of wetness, as these too attract lightning. Sit on your pack to insulate yourself from wet ground.

If no shelter is in sight and the lightning is dangerously near, crouch down as low to the ground as you can, while minimizing your contact with the earth. Use your arms to shield your head.

HEAT WAVES

Intense heat can cause exhaustion, dehydration, and heatstroke (*see* pp. 226–7), particularly in dry places or on rigorous trails with steep climbs.

Slow your walking pace and take breaks whenever possible, especially in the middle of the day. Put on a light-coloured, reflective or vented hat that allows air to circulate: this will protect your head, and also help to keep bugs away. You should also avoid sunburn by wearing protective loose-fitting, well-ventilated clothes that cover your arms and legs, and by applying a high-factor sunscreen at regular intervals.

Your water requirement will increase, and you may need 3 litres (5 pt) or more a day. Take frequent small sips, and never walk past a water source without having a drink and filling your bottle.

If you find a fresh stream or lake, take the opportunity to bathe in it. This gives instant relief from the heat and also removes sweat from your skin, helping to prevent heat rashes. Pay attention to your feet. Feet sweat and swell in hot weather making them larger, wetter and more prone to blistering.

COOLING OFF
In hot weather, use every opportunity to cool off. A few minutes in a cold pool of water can refresh your body, and your spirits, on a sweltering day.

SEVERE HUMIDITY

Humidity is common in hot climates, but may also occur in temperate regions in the summer. It is more comfortable to walk in sparsely forested uplands where the air is drier and cooler than in low-lying forests. Choose a trail that includes rest places or destinations near waterfalls, lakes, or streams. Wear wicking, ventilated clothing to avoid heat rashes and wash yourself and your clothing frequently to avoid a build-up of sweat. Drink regularly and eat easily digestible snacks to replenish the salts and sugars you are losing through sweat and exertion.

AVOID EXPOSED AREAS
Lightning can strike from a thunderstorm at any time of year. Avoid projecting above the surrounding landscape, as you would in an open field.

Hiking in fog, snow, and extreme cold

Fog, snow, and extreme cold are not conditions reserved for winter hikers. In many high mountain ranges, a summer's day can produce four seasons' worth of weather. Hikers should be prepared for cold and wet conditions, and should be particularly on guard against hypothermia.

BANKS OF FOG

Fog usually occurs in unsettled weather, and it is a particular problem in high mountains, on moorland, and along some coastlines. A bank of fog can roll in very quickly – more quickly than a hiker can move – and can be particularly dangerous when travelling cross-country as it obscures the landscape. You will not be able to see landmarks that would normally help to orientate you, making map reading difficult and using a compass impossible. Navigation will be much easier if you use a GPS receiver, which gives you an exact position.

Inside a bank of fog, it is cold, wet, and often windy. If you see a fog bank rolling towards you, add a warm layer and put on a waterproof jacket and trousers straight away. If you need to stop frequently to navigate, you may have to add more layers. In a group, stay in close contact, ensuring that you are always within calling distance of other people. It is a good idea to use a whistle – the sound carries further than a shout.

UNEXPECTED SNOWFALL

Mountain weather is unpredictable and snow storms can occur at any time of the year in most of the world's highest mountain ranges, even at the height of summer. Such snow may fall in brief flurries or for more prolonged periods, covering trails. Your progress may be slowed down, but summer snows usually melt quite quickly, so you will have time to catch up on your schedule.

Summer trails are not usually designed with snow in mind, and even a thin layer of snow can make traversing rocky, uneven terrain hazardous – use trekking poles for balance if you need to.

Route-finding can be difficult when the trail is covered in snow. It may be easier to navigate to the next visible destination rather than trying to follow a trail buried under snow.

LOW VISIBILITY
Even in summer, sudden fog can obscure the trail, making navigation difficult. If the fog is thick, you may have to wait for it to clear before continuing.

Fifty per cent of body heat is lost through the head. A hat will prevent much of this heat from escaping

Wear socks over gloves for an extra layer of warmth for hands

Drink a cup of hot, instant soup to reduce the chills

SURVIVING THE COLD
Staying dry and warm is vital. Wear wicking layers to remove sweat from your body, protect your extremities, and change out of any wet clothing.

EXTREME COLD
Sudden, extreme cold is always a possibility in mountainous areas. In the summer there is an increased likelihood that cold weather will be accompanied by rain. This is a dangerous combination that can lead to hypothermia (*see* p.229), so it is important to stay dry. If you do get wet, it is vital to warm up quickly.

AVOIDING AVALANCHE DANGER

Avalanches are most likely to occur in winter, but hikers in high mountains in late spring may encounter them too. They are most common on sunward slopes (south-facing in the northern hemisphere, north-facing in the southern hemisphere) and on the leeward side of a ridge. Avalanches tend to follow the same paths year after year, so slopes with sheared-off trees are a sure sign of danger, as is a clear chute below a cornice. Most avalanches occur on slopes with an angle of 30–45 degrees, and they are most likely in the 24 hours after a heavy snowfall.

■ **In avalanche conditions,** carry an avalanche beacon, avalanche probes (which can be trekking poles), and a shovel.

■ **Cross avalanche slopes** in the early morning. The risk of avalanche increases as the temperature rises during the day.

■ **Step cautiously and check** that the snow is solid. Avalanches can be set off by loud noises or the pressure of a person's steps, so move carefully. If you are in a group, cross the slope one at a time.

■ **Unbuckle your pack belt** before crossing the slope, so that you can drop your pack easily in case of an avalanche. Loosen hiking-pole straps, and zip up clothing (to keep out the snow). If you have a GPS receiver, set it to the "transmit" position.

■ **If you see an avalanche** coming, attempt to run downhill and away from it.

■ **If you become trapped** under snow, move your hands in front of your face to clear an air hole. Push a pole or stick upward through the snow so that rescuers can find you.

HEAD FOR THE SURFACE
If an avalanche knocks you down, lie on your front and try to "swim" your way towards the surface and out of the snow.

Avoiding natural disasters

Tornadoes, hurricanes, and floods are natural disasters that often follow seasonal patterns, which means that you can time your hike to avoid them. However, along with forest fires, they can also occur unexpectedly, so you need to know how to react. Also, although a volcano causes disaster only when it erupts, you must take great care in volcanic country.

FOREST FIRES

Forest fires are started accidentally (by lightning strike or naked flame), or deliberately (as a controlled burn to remove vegetation, or an act of arson).

Although a potential danger in any dry, wooded area, forest fires are especially likely in areas forested with conifers, which are highly flammable. The likelihood of fire is even greater if the region has a built-up supply of dead and fallen wood, or if there has been a period of drought. In many areas, land managers will post information about the current level of fire danger. During periods of drought or high fire danger, campfires may be prohibited by the authorities.

Smelling or seeing smoke, hearing rumours from other hikers, and meeting a warden on patrol are all ways that you might find out about a fire. Wardens may post notices about controlled burns or wildfires at trailhead junctions. It is essential that you read these notices, as they may include instructions and information about escape routes.

MONSOONS AND FLASH FLOODS

Monsoons follow predictable seasonal patterns so are easily avoided. However, flash floods, caused by monsoon storms many kilometres away, can take hikers by surprise. The floods follow previously etched courses through dry streambeds, which, as a result, can quickly become raging torrents.

The same danger exists in arid areas adjacent to high mountains – a rainstorm in a nearby range may produce run-off that cannot be absorbed quickly by the dry, hard ground, and the resulting flood can be extremely powerful. For this reason, never camp in a dry streambed in semi-arid and arid areas, even if the sky is clear and rain is not predicted. Choose a campsite on higher ground.

FIRE ALERT

Forest fires are a danger in dry country – always carry maps that show other trails and roads, which can be used as ways out of the area if necessary.

HOW TO SURVIVE A FOREST FIRE

Leave the area if you can, and go as far away from the fire as possible. If you cannot leave, look for the safest place to shelter.

■ If there is a natural fire break, such as a road or river, cross to the other side of it.
■ Look for a vegetation-free zone, such as a rock field or lake. The larger the area, the less smoke you will have to inhale.
■ Never descend into a valley where a fire is burning – the more ridges between you and the fire, the safer you are.
■ After the fire, watch out for burning, overhanging branches and ground fires, which can flare up suddenly.
■ If you are in a flammable area, lie face down on the barest patch of ground and cover yourself with soil. Put your mouth against the soil and breathe through it.

Lie face down and breathe through the soil

FOREST FIRE SURVIVAL

CAMPING ON HIGH GROUND
To avoid the possibility of getting caught in the path of a flash flood, camp in an area that is higher than nearby drainages or valleys. You can identify high campsites using a contour map of the region.

TORNADOES AND HURRICANES

While a tornado is relatively small and ephemeral, a hurricane is a much larger system that may last for a day or more. Both, however, have the power to damage and destroy, so are extremely dangerous. The good news for hikers is that they follow seasonal patterns and rarely arrive unannounced. A small radio (or a dedicated weather radio) can provide up-to-date forecasts.

A tornado can form suddenly, so you need to be alert. They are often accompanied by violent storms. Radio stations report "tornado watches" (when the conditions are right for a tornado) and "tornado warnings" (when a tornado has been spotted). As soon as you hear a tornado warning, leave the area. If you are unlucky enough to be caught in a tornado, seek shelter in a cave or ravine, or – as a last resort – a ditch.

A hurricane is formed at sea and may travel great distances before reaching land, so you usually have several days' warning of its arrival. During this time, you can decide upon an alternative route back to shelter. Once a hurricane hits land, strong winds and heavy rain can cause great destruction, and may be accompanied by tidal waves and flooding. Stay away from areas that are likely to be affected by flash floods.

VOLCANOES

Active volcanic areas are dangerous. Take the recommended precautions:

■ **If you hike in** an active volcanic zone, always check with the land management agency for up-to-date information. This should tell you the level of danger based on seismic readings. Find out which trails are safe and the location of recommended escape routes from the area.

■ **In an active zone,** local knowledge is your best defence – a reputable guide can lead you to the safest viewpoints. Never approach the vent of an active volcano – this is the so-called "death zone", where the risk to yourself is extremely high. Avoid breathing fumes and gases from a vent, bearing in mind that these can drift some distance. On a windless day, or if the fumes cannot escape, these toxic gases can be extremely dangerous.

■ **Safe zones near** an active lava flow change on a daily, even hourly, basis. Lava flows both on the surface and under it, and frequently changes direction. The ground near a lava flow may be unstable, and breaking through and falling into an underground lava tube would be fatal. Follow directions from wardens, and obey off-limits signs.

■ **Hot springs,** geysers, and mud pools are found in volcanic areas. Stay on marked trails through such areas, as the ground may be unstable.

Getting back on route

Being lost eventually happens to many hikers who venture off well-worn trails. It can also happen on marked trails in foggy weather, in snow, if trails are only sporadically marked, or if you simply take a wrong turn. Often, reviewing your journey reveals where you are.

Using a map to find your way

Becoming lost happens slowly, over a period of time. Realizing you are lost happens very suddenly. Because it is so unexpected, you may feel disorientated. To remedy the situation, you need to work out where you deviated from your route, how long ago, and how to get back to the trail.

LOCATING YOUR POSITION

To work out where you should go, you first need to find out where you are now. Comfort yourself with the fact that, since you have probably been travelling at no more than 3–5 km (2–3 miles) per hour, it is unlikely that you are as lost as you fear you might be. However, resist the temptation to keep walking, as this may make your situation worse.

LOOKING FOR FEATURES

Stop and think through the route you have been taking. Identify on your map the last point at which you were sure of your location. Try to remember landmarks since your last known position and look for identifiable features. The view will be better from a ridge or a summit, so climb a little to reconnoitre, but go no further than you have to.

FINDING YOUR BEARINGS

Taking notice of obvious landmarks can help you locate your position if you become disorientated. In foggy weather, pay close attention to where you are.

USING YOUR MAP

When you have thought through your route and examined the terrain, take a close look at your map. Often, after a short rest and a little bit of thought, your location will become clear to you. If not, you will need to do some detective work. Apply the following steps, calmly and methodically, to help you pinpoint your position.

1 Find your last-known position on the map as accurately as possible, and circle it.
2 Estimate the length of time you have walked since your last-known position. Multiply your estimated travel time by your average speed to determine your maximum distance from your last-known position. Draw a circle with a radius of that distance. You are somewhere within this circle.
3 Estimate a general direction of travel (if you have been walking towards the sun all evening, you can reasonably guess that you have travelled west). Draw a pie-shape area from your last known position out to the location circle in the general direction of travel.
4 Look for features (such as a lake or a meadow) within the pie-shape section on your map that match features you remember passing earlier on your route.

5 Find your likely position by looking for features on the map that match the current terrain. If you can identify surrounding landmarks on the map, you can triangulate your position (see p.155).
6 If you have an altimeter, remember that your elevation is also a clue to where you are. Your location will be along one of the contour lines that matches the elevation shown by the altimeter.
7 Look on your map for a large identifiable feature that you can easily walk to from your likely position. An example might be that by walking northwest for a short distance you will reach a road. Then look for a prominent landmark along the road (such as a junction) that will pinpoint your location exactly.
8 When you reach the landmark, work out how to return to your original route and continue as planned.

FINDING YOUR POSITION ON THE MAP

Establish your likely position by estimating the distance and direction of travel. Confirm your location by walking to a known point on the map.

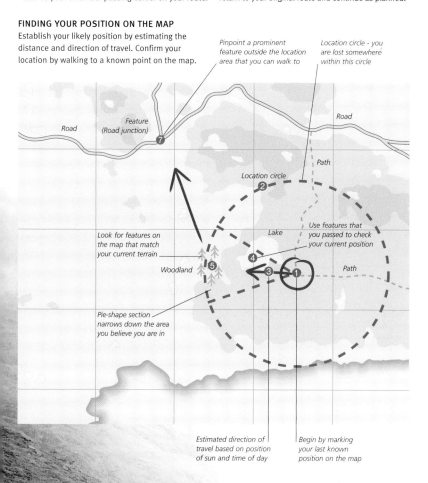

Pinpoint a prominent feature outside the location area that you can walk to

Location circle - you are lost somewhere within this circle

Road

Feature (Road junction)

Road

Path

Location circle

Look for features on the map that match your current terrain

Lake

Use features that you passed to check your current position

Woodland

Path

Pie-shape section narrows down the area you believe you are in

Estimated direction of travel based on position of sun and time of day

Begin by marking your last known position on the map

Using the terrain to find your way

It is much easier to pinpoint your position on a warm, sunny day in high mountains where the topography is obvious and dramatic, than when you are lost in thick fog on a wet day on featureless moorland. If you cannot locate your position by comparing your surroundings to a map, start walking until you get your bearings, letting the terrain be your guide.

CHECKING YOUR MAP

If you are unsure of your position, stop and take a good look at your map. Note an obvious feature (such as a river or road), which if you stumble upon it, will help you to work out where you are. If you do reach it, look for an intersecting landmark to pinpoint your exact position.

FOLLOWING A BEARING

Some types of terrain, such as grassland, are easy cross-country walking. You should be able to take a bearing (*see* p.155) and follow it directly to your destination. However, tangled jungle undergrowth can be difficult to cross without a path. In these conditions, you may be forced to take a circuitous route.

USING ROADS

Unless an area is reserved for walking exclusively, roads are likely to cross it at frequent intervals. Roads usually lead to civilization, and there is always the chance that a motorist will come by and offer help. Be aware, however, that a road might lead you considerably out of your way, or to a dead end. In mountains, following roads downhill will usually lead you out of the wilderness. If you note the features you pass, you may have enough information to identify your location on your map.

FOLLOWING WATER

An oft-repeated theory tells hikers to follow streams downhill when lost, the theory being that streams will eventually converge with other streams, become rivers, and lead to habitation. In practice, however, following a stream may not be the best choice. Streams often take precipitous plunges; they can be choked with vegetation or boulders; and, while they certainly lead downhill, they may not follow the quickest route. So before choosing a stream as your route, look at your map to see in which direction the streams flow, and if their routes are steep. In hot areas, following a dry stream bed may lead to habitation.

ACQUIRE SOME PERSPECTIVE

Climb a ridge from which you can get a good view of the surrounding terrain and identify prominent landmarks from which to triangulate. If you can identify two features, you can use your map and compass to figure out precisely where you are in relation to them (*see* p.155).

USE THE LANDSCAPE

These hikers have a great deal of information to help them identify their position on a map: the lake, the bare rock, the steep hill, and the forested areas.

FOLLOW ROADS TO INHABITED AREAS
Take roads leading downhill out of mountains. Even in remote areas, you will often find farms or homes where you can ask for help and identify your location.

FINDING YOUR ROUTE AGAIN

If you lose your path in dense terrain, try to retrace your steps until you reach a familiar place, such as the turn-off you missed or the trail you were supposed to take. If you can see your destination, do not be tempted to go straight towards it – unless you are in a flat area. In wilderness areas, a straight line is rarely the best or shortest route and may take

you over mountain-tops, into ravines, or across raging rivers. Check your route on a map carefully before setting off.

CONTOURING AND DETOURING

Contouring is the practice of following a contour line around any hills or ridges between you and your destination, rather than climbing and descending them. Detouring avoids obstacles (such as hills, swamps, or thick vegetation) by going round them. Watch your compass to see how far off-course you are going as you detour around the obstacle – for example, if you walk a kilometre west to go around a hill, compensate by walking a kilometre east once you get past it.

CONSIDERING YOUR WATER SUPPLY

In arid lands, finding water is even more important than finding your way. Following a dry streambed downhill will lead you to both water and habitation. Travel cross-country to signs of human habitation, such as wells, stock tanks, electrical lines and pylons, and shacks, which will be located near a road.

AIMING OFF-COURSE

Following a compass bearing is never totally accurate, especially when travelling cross-country over rough terrain or through dense vegetation. Instead of arriving at the crossroads you expected, for example, you

might arrive at just a stretch of road, with no way of knowing which side of the junction you are. To avoid this situation, deliberately aim for a large feature on your map that is to one side or the other of your less-visible target.

1 Determine a bearing from your location to the spring. Then search your map for a bigger feature nearby – in this case a large copse.

2 Adjust your bearing by a few degrees so that you are actually aiming for the more visible copse to the right of the spring.

3 When you arrive at the copse, you know that you need to turn left, and continue walking, to reach the spring.

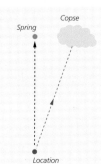

Animal encounters

While predators such as lions and bears can be dangerous, animals such as deer, moose, and buffalo are responsible for many human injuries, especially in parks. Most animal encounters, however, are benign and you are likely to see only startled animals dashing for cover.

Meeting wild animals on the trail

For most hikers, seeing wildlife is often the highlight of a hiking trip. However, even small animals such as mice and marmots can do quite a bit of damage to expensive hiking gear, as well as eating your food supply. Preventing these kinds of encounters, and knowing what to do when you are close to wild animals, is important for both you and the animals.

WILD ANIMALS IN NORTH AMERICA

In North America hikers may see bears, mountain lions, wolves, coyotes, buffalo, moose, and deer, along with a host of other large and medium-sized mammals.

Contrary to popular belief, wolves – a highly endangered and reclusive species – are not a danger to hikers. However, mountain lions are now approaching inhabited areas, and attacks on humans, though very rare, do occur. The North American mountain lion (also known as a puma, panther, or cougar) is a shy, solitary creature. If you come across one, give it time and space to retreat. Usually, it will do so. Otherwise cluster together with your hiking companions and try and present a big, noisy group. If you are alone, make sure the lion can see your pack, which will help you to look bigger. If the lion approaches you, wave trekking poles and shout. Never run or bend down, as this makes you a smaller target. Call any children to stand next to you, but do not bend down to them.

Deer, moose, bison (American buffalo), and elk are all large, wild animals that can potentially harm you. If they are cornered, or protecting their young, their hooves, antlers, and horns can be used as lethal weapons. Retreat if you see an animal becoming agitated, and give it plenty of room to leave the area.

WILD ANIMALS IN EUROPE

There is less chance of encountering large wild animals in Europe than in North America, since the continent has been settled for longer and is more densely populated. Deer are fairly common, but do not pose great risk. Wild boar are also common in more

BISON/AMERICAN BUFFALO

You are most likely to come across herds of bison on flat grasslands in parks and reserves. Although they are herbivores, they are still wild animals and dangerous if provoked. Always keep your distance.

remote forests and woodlands, but they tend to be shy and will usually run away from people. A small remnant population of European brown bears is thought to exist in western Europe, located in the Pyrenees mountains along the border between France and Spain.

WILD ANIMALS IN AFRICA AND ASIA

The big cats of Africa and Asia – lions, tigers, and leopards – are fearsome and dangerous, but you are unlikely to encounter them by accident. Most live in national parks and protected wildlife areas, where travel on foot is either limited or prohibited. However, if you do plan to travel in big-cat country, join a guided group, which will usually be accompanied by local guides and armed rangers who understand animal behaviour.

Large herbivores, particularly hippopotami and buffalo, actually cause far more injury to hikers than big cats. Never camp or walk between a hippo and water, because if frightened it will charge for water, flattening anything in its path. Solitary male buffalo are among the most dangerous animals you can encounter. They are notoriously bad-tempered, so keep your distance, or take a detour.

GROUPED WILDLIFE TOURS
The safest way to see the big cats of Africa is with a guided safari, usually conducted using vehicles. Walking tours, accompanied by rangers and armed guards, are available in some parks.

PHOTOGRAPHING WILD ANIMALS

■ Go on a safari, or, better still, join a specialized photo safari where you can approach the animals closely in a car.
■ If you are not in the safety of a vehicle, keep your distance from wild animals, and use a telephoto or zoom lens.
■ Never approach within touching distance of a large animal, as you may annoy or frighten it. This is especially true of a mother with her young – the mother may attack you, or even abandon her infant until you leave.
■ Choose dawn and dusk for your photography sessions, when animals are more likely to be out and about.

ANIMAL VISITORS

Animals quickly learn that hikers carry food and leave crumbs in cooking areas.
■ **Camp away from** obvious animal paths, water sources, and animal signs (indicated by droppings, claw marks on trees, tracks, etc.).
■ **Avoid popular campsites,** where animals are used to finding food.
■ **Food smells linger,** so try to cook as far away from your sleeping area as possible.
■ **Never sleep with food** in your tent. Store it in a waterproof stuff sack, a bear-proof canister, or a bear-proof stuff sack, and suspend it from a tree branch (*see* pp.99 and 219)
■ **Resist the temptation** to feed wild animals begging at a campsite. Giving food to animals can be fatal for them. They become dependent on human food and may stop feeding themselves or neglect their migratory instinct. When people leave the area out of season, the animals could starve.
■ **Begging also quickly** becomes stealing. An animal can become aggressive, damaging gear and injuring people when it comes to the campsite. Even normally shy and docile large animals such as deer can become dangerous. Small animals such as mice and marmots can damage your gear and food supply.
■ **Report any aggressive** animal encounters to the local authorities. More dangerous animals, such as bears, may have to be killed if they injure humans in their quest for food.

Dealing with bears

Though the idea of seeing a "cuddly bear" close up may have a certain appeal, it is important to remember that bears are wild animals, and if threatened, afraid, or hungry will react as such. In North America in particular, you must take certain precautions, and you need to respect their presence.

MEETING BEARS ON THE TRAIL

Bears are remarkably adaptable animals, and can be found worldwide in many environments, ranging from mountain tundra to Arctic ice floes, wet temperate forests to chaparral drylands, and deep wilderness to suburban lawns. But it is the hiker in North America who is most likely to encounter bears in the wild – either the common black bear, which ranges virtually all over the North American continent, or the relatively rare grizzly bear. Polar bears mainly inhabit the southern tundra regions of the north pole, and are rarely seen by hikers.

Most bears will quickly retreat from humans, but if you surprise a mother bear with cubs, she may send them up a tree and then watch you cautiously from a safe distance. Do not step between the mother and the tree, or approach the cubs. A large detour, however far off the track, is preferable to an attack from a bear protecting her young.

Black bears are not usually predatory (to humans), but they can become dangerous if they are surprised, feel cornered, or if they are protecting their young. If a black bear exhibits signs of predatory behaviour, your best defence is to become as aggressive as possible. Stay with your hiking partner (to present a bigger threat to the bear), yell, and wave your hiking sticks. As a last resort, throw rocks to scare the bear away.

Technically, the North American grizzly bear and the European brown bear are the same species, although the American

BLACK BEARS IN NORTH AMERICA

The North American black bear is highly adaptable, intelligent – and hungry! When camping in known bear country, always store your food safely.

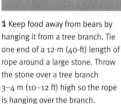

1 Keep food away from bears by hanging it from a tree branch. Tie one end of a 12-m (40-ft) length of rope around a large stone. Throw the stone over a tree branch 3–4 m (10–12 ft) high so the rope is hanging over the branch.

2 Untie the stone and attach your food bag to the rope. Hoist it into the air and tie a weight (such as a rock) to the other end of the rope. Use a trekking pole or long stick to push the weight up so that it is hanging even with the bag.

variety is larger and more fearsome. In western Europe, the shy brown bear is extremely rare and occupies only remote corners of the Pyrenean mountains. In North America, the grizzly is found in the northern Rockies, Canada, and Alaska. While attacks by grizzly bears on humans are rare, they do occur. When hiking in grizzly country, always ask the local land managers for advice.

PROTECTING FOOD

In some American national parks, bears have learned to associate people with food. The usual way to keep food away from bears is to hang it in a tree out of their reach (*see above*). Choose a branch strong enough to hold your stores, and at least 30 m (100 ft) from your sleeping area. However, in some regions, bears are skilled at finding food in trees, which means that you have to use other methods (*see p.99*). These include storing food in a bear box (a metal locker provided at the campsite), a bear-proof canister (available at some campsites and outdoor shops), or a bear-proof stuff sack (which bears usually cannot tear or chew through). In addition, some parks provide bear poles for hanging food. A karabiner is a useful piece of equipment for attaching food to the cables or ropes on bear poles.

If you are camping in the wild, cook your meals before stopping for the evening, then hike several kilometres further on to set up camp to avoid any food smells attracting bears to your sleeping area. Once at camp, hang food from a strong tree branch.

GRIZZLY BEAR PRECAUTIONS

Grizzly bears are potentially more dangerous to hikers than other bears, so take these precautions if hiking in areas where they live.

AVOIDING GRIZZLIES

- Stay in a group – bears do not usually attack groups of more than four people.
- Avoid areas where you find signs of bears – fresh claw marks on trees, the smell of carrion, smashed vegetation, decimated berry bushes, droppings, and disturbed earth.
- Be especially alert near water, which masks sounds and smells. You may surprise a grizzly that has not seen, heard, or smelt you.
- Make a noise so that the grizzly can hear you and leave the area before you have to confront it.
- Carry pepper spray that is specially formulated to deter an attacking bear.

ENCOUNTERING GRIZZLIES

- Look for trees that you can climb (adult grizzlies cannot climb trees).
- Talk quietly, do not make direct eye contact, and give it plenty of time to leave.
- Discharge your pepper spray, but only if the bear comes within 5 m (15 ft).
- If you are attacked, do not run. Play dead instead. Bring your legs up to your chest (to protect your vital organs), tuck in your head, and protect the back of your neck with your hands. Most grizzly attacks are defensive, and playing dead shows the bear that you are not a threat.

FIRST AID

Common ailments

While beginner hikers often worry about major accidents, encounters with dangerous animals, or dramatic storms, the fact is that most hikers are far more likely to be affected by common ailments. Sometimes these can escalate into major problems if not appropriately treated.

Treating basic conditions

Minor injuries can result when a hiker over-exerts (i.e. muscle cramps) or spends too long in hot conditions (i.e. sunburn). Blisters, cuts, and scrapes are also common, but easily treated. If hiking alone, you should aim to be self-sufficient by carrying a first-aid kit for the treatment of basic injuries.

BLISTERS

Blisters are a primary cause of discomfort when hiking, and occur when the skin is rubbed repeatedly against a surface. A blister starts as a small, almost imperceptible irritation and may first appear as a red spot.

1 Clean the area with sterile water and dry gently.
2 If possible, pop the blister with a sterile needle. While not recommended normally, this is advisable for hikers, because the continued friction from walking will pop the blister sooner or later.
3 When you pop the blister, be sure to clean, dry, and protect the area properly to lessen the risk of infection.

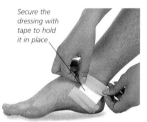

Secure the dressing with tape to hold it in place

4 Apply a protective covering. Plasters, padded moleskin, or gel-like dressings can all be used.

BRUISING

Bruising results when an injury breaks the blood vessels under the skin. When hiking, this can be caused by falling against a rock or other obstruction.

Reduce swelling and pain with a cold compress

1 To reduce the swelling, if you have access to cold running water, ice, or snow, soak a cloth and apply it to the injured area. Hold it in place for at least five minutes. Re-apply frequently.
2 If possible, elevate the bruised area to reduce the blood flow to it.

CUTS AND GRAZES

Cuts and grazes can occur on a hike as a result of falls, bashing through vegetation, or scraping against rocks. Any break in the skin needs to be cleaned and covered to prevent germs entering and causing infection.

QUICK TIPS

AIMS

■ Apply pressure to stop any bleeding
■ Keep wound clean by washing and bandaging

IMPORTANT

Scrapes from falls on rock may be full of gravel, sand, or dirt that needs to be rinsed off.

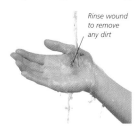

Rinse wound to remove any dirt

1 Clean the wound by rinsing it in cold running water (if possible), and drying it throughly.
2 Apply an antibiotic ointment and bandage with an appropriate dressing. Plasters may be sufficient for small wounds. For larger scrapes, cover with a gauze dressing and hold in place with adhesive bandages.

CRAMP

Cramp is common, especially in the early stages of a hike, and the pain can occur suddenly. It happens when a muscle is stressed repeatedly, particularly if the muscle is not receiving enough oxygen.

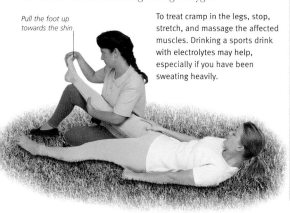

Pull the foot up towards the shin

To treat cramp in the legs, stop, stretch, and massage the affected muscles. Drinking a sports drink with electrolytes may help, especially if you have been sweating heavily.

QUICK TIPS

SYMPTOMS

■ Pain in muscle
■ Muscle may feel as if tightening uncontrollably

HOW TO PREVENT

■ Condition your body with pre-hike fitness training and stretching
■ Monitor exertion and rest regularly
■ Drink plenty of water to avoid dehydration
■ To lessen a cramp or stitch in your side, slow your walking pace and breathe slowly and deeply through your nose

SUNBURN

Sunburn is a constant outdoor hazard, and can contribute to dehydration, sunstroke, and skin cancer. It can occur even on cloudy days, especially at high altitudes, where the thinner air provides less protection against UV rays. Reflection by snow increases the risk.

1 Move the sufferer out of the sun into a cool, shaded spot.
2 Give the victim water to sip. It is important to drink frequently, as sunburn is a dehydrating condition.
3 Soothe mild burns by applying sun cream or calamine lotion. Cold water sponged onto the skin with a soft cloth can relieve pain and discomfort.

IMPORTANT

Monitor exposure to the sun, and continue to re-apply sun protection lotion. If exposure is extended or there are signs of sunburn, wear clothes that cover the affected area.

QUICK TIPS

SYMPTOMS

■ Reddish colouring and skin that is hot to the touch
■ Blistering indicates a second-degree burn, which should be treated by a professional

AIMS

■ Take victim out of sun
■ Treat a mild burn for pain and discomfort
■ Ensure victim drinks water frequently to avoid dehydration

Stings, bites, and plant poisons

While much of the natural world is not harmful to humans, some plants and animals have developed toxins that can cause severe reactions, especially in those who are allergic.

Stinging insects, venomous snakes, and poisonous plants are easily avoided most of the time – but, unfortunately, not always. Snake bites in particular require prompt attention.

INSECT STINGS

Insect stings rarely cause more than temporary discomfort unless you are highly allergic. If you are, you should carry a bee sting kit to treat anaphylactic shock and instruct your hiking partners in its use.

1 The sting may be embedded in the skin. It can usually be scraped away (using the edge of a credit card, or a fingernail).
2 Place a cloth soaked in cold water on the injured skin.
3 The casualty should rest with the injured part elevated until swelling ceases.
4 If the casualty suffers a severe allergic reaction (anaphylactic shock), seek medical attention.

If you can see it, carefully scrape away the sting

IMPORTANT

A sting in the mouth or throat can cause swelling that blocks the airway. Treat with cold water, ice, or snow, and seek medical attention if swelling develops. Also note that severe local responses to stings or a reaction, such as a rash all over the body, indicate that you are becoming more sensitized and should carry a bee sting kit on future hikes.

TICKS

Ticks are tiny creatures that attach themselves to humans and bite into the skin to suck blood. They carry disease and can cause infection, so should be removed as soon as possible. Lyme Disease is of most concern because it is increasingly common worldwide.

1 Watch for ticks by checking skin. Ticks swell to the size of a pea. Check warm, moist places such as under the arms.

2 Ticks are best removed with tweezers. You should try to pull a tick out whole by encouraging it to let go of your skin. Grasp the tick as close to the skin as possible, and pull it out gently.
3 Wash the area thoroughly with water or a disinfectant and keep it clean.
4 Put the tick in a small container, so that it can be checked for Lyme Disease.
5 If symptoms occur, contact a doctor for tests and antibiotics.

Grasp the head close to the skin and pull gently

SNAKE BITE

The danger of venomous snakes varies greatly worldwide. Suctioning with a snake-bite venom extractor may be of benefit if far from a hospital, but should not be attempted by an untrained person.

1 Try to identify the snake to facilitate later treatment.
2 Lay the casualty down. Reassure them and make sure they are comfortable. Not all bites from venomous snakes inject venom, and many inject only a small amount.

The amount of venom is not necessarily in proportion to the size of the snake.
3 Immobilize the bite area. Put on a light compression bandage above the bite. This can slow the spread of venom.
4 Go for help, or assist the casualty in walking out, if necessary and possible.

Raise the level of the heart above the level of bite

Secure padding around injured limb to immobilize

COMMON VENOMOUS SNAKES

SNAKE	COUNTRY	TOXICITY
European adder	Europe, parts of Asia	moderately venomous (causes internal bleeding)
Viper	worldwide except Australia	moderately venomous (causes internal bleeding)
Cottonmouth (pit viper)	southeast USA	very venomous (clots the blood)
Cobra	south Asia and Africa	very venomous (causes paralysis)
Diamondback (rattlesnake)	North America	extremely venomous (can kill within one hour)

STINGING PLANTS

There are many stinging plant varieties, but poison ivy and stinging nettles are two of the most common. Poison ivy is found worldwide and causes rashes that vary in severity – some may need medical treatment. Stinging nettles are found in many countries, but cause only a temporary stinging sensation. After contact with stinging nettles, apply a cold compress to the site to soothe the pain. Watch for an itchy red rash that indicates an allergic reaction.

1 After contact with poison ivy, immediately wash the area with cold water and apply an anti-poison ivy cream as soon as possible.
2 Get medical help as soon as you can.

POISON IVY

Medical emergencies

In the wilderness, a medical emergency can happen with devastating suddenness, and professional help may be far away. Steps can be taken to avoid minor ailments, but for a serious condition such as hypothermia, or a bad fall, practical first-aid skills are essential.

Dehydration and heat maladies

One of the biggest challenges you face when hiking is maintaining your body's balance of water, electrolytes, and temperature, while undertaking strenuous activity and sweating excessively. This can be difficult in hot or humid weather, or when exposed to extreme conditions such as very dry air or high altitude. Make sure you drink water at every rest stop.

DEHYDRATION

Dehydration is commonly associated with strenuous exercise, particularly in hot weather. It is exacerbated by high altitude, heat, sun exposure, and by both extreme humidity and extreme dryness. Dehydration is dangerous in itself, but it can also contribute to heat exhaustion, heatstroke, and even hypothermia.

1 Find shade if possible, or make shade using a tarp.
2 Make the casualty comfortable and encourage them to slowly drink small amounts of water. Dilute an electrolyte-replacement drink to half the original strength and administer it in small amounts. Or you can make a solution by adding a tablespoon of sugar and a teaspoon of salt to a litre of water.
3 To prevent a relapse, identify causes. Common causes include diarrhoea or vomiting (from adverse food reactions or altitude sickness), over-exertion (especially at high altitude and in dry air), and sun exposure.
4 Encourage rest until the casualty is fully recovered.

Support the casualty while they sip slowly

ELECTROLYTES

Electrolytes are mineral salts in the body that move between body cells. One function of the kidneys is to keep these salts in balance. This balance is essential for the functioning of body processes such as heart and nerve function, muscle co-ordination, and bone health. When you are on a hard hike you lose electrolytes as you sweat. To help replace this loss, some drinks have electrolytes (such as sodium and potassium) added to them to help the kidneys keep the electrolyte concentrations in your body fluids constant.

HEATSTROKE

Heatstroke can develop suddenly. The body's heat-regulating mechanisms break down completely and the body is unable to cool itself by sweating, so it becomes dangerously overheated. The skin will feel hot and may be either damp from perspiration (if the victim was exercising), or dry. A heatstroke victim should be cooled down and taken to a hospital quickly.

1 Move the casualty to as cool a place as possible and protect them from the sun.
2 Maintain an open airway if the casualty is unconscious.
3 Do anything possible to reduce the temperature quickly. Sponge the body with cool or cold water and try to fan the casualty, using clothing or equipment to help move air. An unconscious victim can be covered with clothing soaked in cold water. Immersion in cool or cold water is recommended for conscious victims.
4 Massage extremities to encourage blood circulation. Once temperature has dropped, replace the wet clothes with dry ones.
5 Monitor the level of response, pulse and breathing.

Fan the casualty to lower temperature

QUICK TIPS

SYMPTOMS
■ Confusion and impaired mental function
■ Headache or dizziness
■ High body temperature – above 40°C (104°F)
■ Flushed, very hot skin
■ Fast, strong pulse

AIMS
■ Stabilize victim – cool them as quickly as possible
■ Seek medical attention

Under no circumstances should a victim of heatstroke resume activity until they have been medically evaluated. Severe organ damage is possible, and relapse is common, even after several hours.

HEAT EXHAUSTION

Heat exhaustion occurs in heat and humidity, especially when hikers are not used to such conditions. Blood vessels in the skin dilate and the blood supply to the brain lessens, causing dizziness and possibly fainting. Heat exhaustion can sometimes develop into heatstroke.

1 Help the casualty to sit or lie down, preferably in a cool or shaded place. Make them comfortable and raise the legs to improve blood flow to the brain.
2 Give plenty of water or non-fizzy drinks to replace lost fluids. Include diluted electrolyte-replacement drinks, if available.
3 Reduce the body temperature with a cool compress (such as a handkerchief soaked in water), and by fanning.
4 Make sure the casualty rests until body temperature and urine output are normal.
5 Monitor the casualty's condition because heat exhaustion can turn into potentially lethal heatstroke. If it does not improve, seek medical attention. Immediate medical attention should always be sought for those who have chronic conditions such as heart or kidney disease, which could be exacerbated by heat exhaustion.

QUICK TIPS

SYMPTOMS
■ Cramp-like pains
■ Damp, pale skin
■ Headache and confusion
■ Decreased urine output
■ Nausea and fainting
■ Raised body temperature
■ Fast, weak pulse

AIMS
■ Cool the casualty
■ Make them comfortable
■ Encourage rest
■ Replace lost body fluids
■ Obtain medical help, if necessary

Altitude sickness, frostbite, and hypothermia

Although ailments caused by cold are more common in winter, they are a possibility at any time of year in high mountains, where both the elevation and cold climate can stress the human body. Treatment is necessary to restore normal body temperature and breathing as rapidly as possible.

ALTITUDE SICKNESS

Everyone responds to altitude differently, but one thing is consistent – the higher you go, the more likely you are to be affected by the lack of oxygen in the thinner air. Many hikers feel symptoms of altitude sickness above 3,000 m (10,000 ft). Once you reach this height avoid gaining more than 300 m (1,000 ft) a day. Most hikers feel some effects above 3,600 m (12,000 ft). Acute Mountain Sickness (AMS), can result in cerebral or pulmonary oedema (waterlogged brain or lungs).

1 Treat mild symptoms by resting at the same altitude for a day or two.
2 If symptoms persist, go downhill to the last altitude where the casualty felt well.
3 Hikers with serious symptoms should descend immediately and seek medical treatment, which usually includes extra oxygen.

IMPORTANT

If mild symptoms persist for more than a day or two, or become worse, it is important to descend immediately – even 500 m (1,500 ft) can help.

FROSTBITE

Frostbite is usually a winter injury. The tissues of the extremities – such as fingers and toes – freeze because of low temperatures. Trekkers in high mountains may be at risk if under-equipped during a summer snowstorm.

1 If possible, take the casualty to a warm place and remove wet or constricting clothing.
2 Use body heat to warm the area. Frostbitten fingers can be warmed by putting them under the arms or against the stomach. Or, if toes or feet are frostbitten, a hiking partner's armpits or stomach can be used to warm them. Do not, however, thaw a frostbitten foot if the casualty needs to walk further.
3 Do not use anything hot such as heating pads, a stove, or hot water because the casualty may not be able to feel burning sensations.
4 Avoid rubbing or massaging the affected area as this can further damage the skin.

5 After warming, loosely bandage the area to protect it. Keep the area bandaged until feeling returns to the skin

Tuck frostbitten hands in armpits to generate body heat

HYPOTHERMIA

Hypothermia is sometimes called the "killer of the unprepared". Cold is not just a winter problem – a hiker on a cool rainy day can be even more susceptible than a winter skier if he or she does not have the appropriate rain and wind protection. Rain and dampness exacerbate the danger, because wet, cold air takes warmth away from the skin much faster than dry, cold air. Hunger and fatigue can also contribute.

1 Remove the casualty from wind or rain by choosing a sheltered spot or erecting a shelter such as a tent. Make them comfortable, using clothing, backpacks, or sleeping mats to insulate them from the cold ground and to prevent further heat loss.
2 Warm the casualty slowly – remove wet or damp clothing (cut it away to avoid jostling the casualty). Replace with dry, insulated clothing or sleeping bags.
3 Administer warm drinks slowly to a conscious victim.

4 Ensure the casualty rests.
5 For casualties with severe hypothermia, seek medical help.

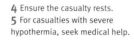

Give warm liquids, but not alcohol

Provide reassurance and comfort

A hat gives extra warmth

Protect from rain and wind with a survival bag

PREVENTING HYPOTHERMIA

It is very important to dress correctly for cool conditions. You should be able to add or remove layers according to your activity level and the outside temperature. Wearing clothing in multiple layers means that you can control your temperature and avoid heavy sweating. Carry warm hats, extra socks, scarves, raingear, gloves, and a survival blanket. Nibble high-energy foods, such as energy bars and nuts, and carry enough fluid. The warning sign of hypothermia is prolonged and uncontrolled shivering. You must act immediately to prevent severe hypothermia, which can be fatal.

Injury

It only takes a moment's lack of attention to slip on a wet rock or fall off a boulder that unexpectedly shifts underfoot. The result can be a nasty cut, or a more serious fall or jolt can lead to a broken bone or dislocation. Whatever the outcome, you will need to carry out some form of first aid.

SPRAINS AND STRAINS

Sprains and strains are much less likely to occur if you stretch regularly as part of your exercise regime. Flexible joints are more likely to be able to absorb the sudden twists, jolts, and falls that can happen to a hiker on tricky terrain. A strain is a torn muscle or tendon, and is caused when the muscle is overstretched. A sprain occurs when the ligament that supports the joint is stretched or torn. Ankles are especially prone to this happening, which is one reason that heavily laden hikers wear boots with strong ankle support. Sprains and strains can be extremely painful and indistinguishable from fractures without an x-ray. If in doubt, they should be treated as a fracture.

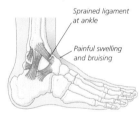

Sprained ligament at ankle

Painful swelling and bruising

SPRAINED ANKLE

IMPORTANT

Treat sprains and strains initially with the RICE (rest, ice, compression, and elevation) procedure, explained below. If you are unsure about the severity of the injury, treat it as a fracture instead, and immobilize the injury. If one leg is injured, bandage this leg to the sound one, using triangular bandages above and below the sprain or fracture site.

1 Rest – For complete healing, the injured part needs to rest. In an isolated area, the casualty may have to leave on foot. Assist by carrying as much of their backpacking load as possible. When at rest, steady and support the injured part.

2 Ice – Cool the area to reduce pain and swelling by applying ice or snow if available. If it is not, use a cloth soaked in cold water, lightly applied around the injured area.

3 Compress – Apply gentle pressure to the injured joint. Surround the area with a layer of thick, soft padding, then secure with an elastic bandage. Wrap in a figure-of-eight pattern (around the forefoot, then the ankle, then looping back again) to support the joint. Check there is adequate circulation in the toes.

4 Elevate – Raise the injury, if possible above the heart. This helps reduce swelling and bruising by helping the body to absorb blood and body fluids.

Reduce swelling at the ankle with ice or a cold cloth

2 Ice

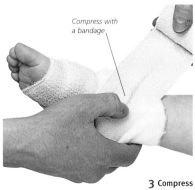

Compress with a bandage

3 Compress

DISLOCATION

Dislocation occurs when a bone is forced out of its normal position by a wrenching jolt. It is an extremely painful injury that may also affect the surrounding nerves. Commonly affected areas of the body are shoulders, fingers (especially the thumb), and jaw.

Dislocation can have serious consequences. Dislocations of the hip or shoulder may damage the large nerves to the arm or leg, resulting in paralysis. Any dislocation may also be accompanied by a fracture of the adjacent bone.

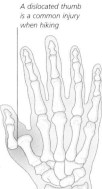

A dislocated thumb is a common injury when hiking

DISLOCATED JOINT

1 Advise the casualty to keep still, and support the joint in as comfortable a position as possible.
2 Immobilize the injured joint using padding, bandages, and slings. Do not move the casualty until the injured part is secured

and supported, unless the casualty is in danger.
3 If it is a shoulder dislocation, secure the arm against the chest using a bandage.
4 Treat the casualty for shock, if necessary (*see* p.231), and seek medical help.

QUICK TIPS

SYMPTOMS

- Contorted limbs
- Possible swelling around the joint
- Pain aggravated by motion
- Bruising

AIMS

- Immobilize the joint to reduce pain
- Arrange for transport with comfortable support to hospital, if possible

WARNING

Do not attempt to reposition a dislocated bone into its socket. This may cause further injury, especially if there is also a fracture or nerve damage. Seek medical help.

BROKEN BONES

Fractures and breaks are traumatic injuries to the bones. In some cases, pieces of bone may break through skin; in others, an x-ray may be required to identify the injury as a fracture. If an injury is severe enough to cause fracture-like symptoms, it should be assumed to be a fracture for first-aid purposes.

1 First, immobilize the bone by splinting the joint. This helps to decrease pain, reduce shock and bleeding, and prevent further damage. Almost anything can be used as a splint, from part of a foam pad or a trekking pole, to a stick or a rolled-up magazine.
2 The limb may need to be straightened before being splinted – this should be done as soon as possible after the accident. Protect protruding bones such as an elbow or knee with cloth or bandages.

3 Support the injured part with a sling or by bandaging it to an unaffected part of the body. Check periodically for feeling in the extremities, to be sure the splint or bandage is not too tight.

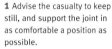
Use a bandage or sling to immobilize the injured part and keep the splint in place

QUICK TIPS

SYMPTOMS

- Pain
- Inability to move, or difficulty in moving, the limb
- Swelling and discolouration
- Shortening, bending, or twisting of a limb
- Visible deformity of bones or bones breaking through skin
- Signs of shock (*see* p.233)

AIMS

- Immobilize joint to prevent movement in the area of injury
- Protect protruding bones
- Reduce pain
- Control bleeding from wounds by elevation
- Arrange for removal to hospital, with comfortable support during transport

BLEEDING

Bleeding often looks drastic and dramatic. Except in the case of highly unusual and severe injuries, it can usually be slowed or stopped by a combination of elevation and direct pressure. Do not use a tourniquet as this can be dangerous. In remote areas, an additional challenge is keeping the injured area and any dressings as clean as possible. Victims of severe bleeding injuries should also be treated for shock.

1 If the skin is torn, place your hands on either side and push the edges together, while placing direct pressure on the wound. Most wounds are of capillaries and veins, and will clot after several minutes of direct pressure. Arterial bleeding takes longer because the arteries are under more pressure. However, arterial injuries are less common.
2 If the bone is not broken and the patient can be moved, lie them down comfortably and raise the affected limb. Direct pressure on the wound should be maintained. Use a gauze pad to absorb the blood. Even if the wound does not completely stop bleeding, it can still be bandaged and wrapped.

Push the edges of the wound together to stop the bleeding

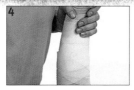

Elevate the legs above the level of the heart

Raise the limb, maintaining direct pressure on the injury

3 Apply a sterile dressing. Place a gauze pad over the wound, and hold it in place by wrapping bandages around the limb. If blood seeps through the dressing, add another pad.
4 Continue to apply pressure, if necessary, and keep the wounded area elevated. Support the injured limb in a raised position with a sling or bandage.

5 The dressing should not be so tight that it restricts circulation. Check frequently that there is adequate circulation below the bandage. Check for a pulse, and look at fingernail and skin colour (bluish skin indicates lack of circulation). Ask about tingling sensations, pain, or numbness.
6 If the dressing is too tight, take off the bandage, then re-apply.

7 Remove the bandage after the bleeding has stopped. Dress the wound in clean bandages, which should be changed daily.
8 Movement of the wounded area should be restricted, even after bleeding has stopped, because excessive movement and jostling can cause the wound to open. If the casualty must leave, splint the wounded area.

Shock

Shock occurs when the circulatory system fails, and as a result, vital organs such as the heart and the brain are deprived of oxygen. Shock can be life-threatening. It requires emergency treatment to prevent organ damage, and casualties must be referred to a medical professional for follow-up care.

TREATING SHOCK

The underlying cause of the shock should be treated first. Shock is commonly caused by severe blood loss. It can also be a result of fluid loss caused by severe burns, fractures, heatstroke, or hypothermia. Symptoms do not always appear immediately, so you should treat for shock regardless of symptoms in cases of major blood loss, unconsciousness, and severe heat- and cold-related disorders.

1 Lie the casualty down. The head should be at the same level as the body or lower, and the feet raised 25–30 cm (10–12 in). If possible, lie the casualty on a camping mat to prevent loss of heat, and provide shelter from wind and cold, either with natural windbreaks or by erecting a tarp or tent.
2 Maintain the body temperature of the casualty. Sleeping bags and extra clothing may not be enough – an external source of heat such as a fire or another person's body heat may be required. Loosen any restrictive clothing around the body.
3 Keep the casualty calm. Panic, fear, and pain can increase the severity of shock. Do not move the casualty until the the cause of shock has been treated and it has been controlled. Monitor the casualty's breathing, pulse rate, and level of consciousness. If possible, also monitor their heart rate, temperature, urine output, and blood pressure.

QUICK TIPS

SYMPTOMS

- Fast, weak pulse
- Pallor
- Cool skin
- Chills
- Lack of urination
- Mental confusion

AIMS

- Stabilize condition
- Keep casualty warm and comfortable
- Monitor condition
- Keep notes
- Seek medical attention

IMPORTANT

It is vital to seek urgent medical treatment. Shock victims will need to be monitored until help arrives, as their condition can deteriorate quickly.

Monitor the casualty's pulse rate

Raise legs to improve blood supply to vital organs

Keep the casualty warm

Keep legs elevated above the level of the heart

Dealing with unconsciousness

Unconsciousness can result from a number of disorders, including illness such as heart attack, diabetes, and seizures, trauma, hypothermia, altitude sickness, and the later stage of heatstroke. If you are in a very remote area, medical help may be far away and difficult to contact. The victim's survival can depend on your ability to perform life-saving techniques, summon emergency help, and arrange an evacuation.

QUICK TIPS

SYMPTOMS

- The victim does not respond to stimuli
- Breathing and pulse may have ceased

AIMS

- Get help
- Assess the victim's response
- Establish and maintain an open, clear airway
- Check for breathing and give rescue breaths (*see* p.235) if necessary
- Check for signs of circulation and give chest compressions (*see* p.236) if necessary
- Stabilize the victim: deal with severe injuries or medical conditions, then place in the recovery position (*see* p.237). Monitor and keep a record, if possible, of the victim's pulse, breathing, and level of response
- Protect the victim from extremes of weather

REVIVING AN UNCONSCIOUS PERSON

A person who is unconscious is in danger of their airway being blocked, especially if the tongue falls into the back of the throat. If the airway is blocked, the person is unable to breathe, so opening it up quickly is a vitally important early action.

1 Look for any danger to yourself or the victim, such as loose rocks, as you approach the scene and deal with it if necessary.
2 Check for a response by speaking loudly and clearly to the victim and gently shaking the shoulders. Use the person's name if you know it.
3 Shout for help – there may be someone else hiking in the area.
4 Open the airway by placing one hand on the forehead and tilting the head back, removing any obvious obstruction from the mouth and lifting the chin. Check for breathing by looking along the victim's chest for movement, listening for breath sounds, and feeling for breath on your cheek. Do this for ten seconds.
5 If the victim is not breathing, send for emergency help if possible, and start rescue breathing (*see* p.235).
6 If the victim is breathing, stablize them by dealing with any severe injuries or known medical conditions. Place them in the recovery position (*see* p.237).
7 Monitor pulse, breathing, and level of response until help arrives. Protect the victim from weather by erecting a shelter. Do not leave the victim unless there is no other way of getting help.

Speak to the victim and shake gently to assess whether they are conscious or unconscious

Check for signs of circulation – breathing, coughing, or movement

RESCUE BREATHING

If the victim is not breathing it is very important to send for emergency help if possible and then start rescue breathing. The organs of the body – especially the brain – start to suffer damage from lack of oxygen very quickly. Rescue breathing is an effective way of giving some oxygen to a victim who is not breathing. Your exhaled breath contains about 16 per cent oxygen – 5 per cent less than air but still a very useful amount for someone who is not breathing. Rescue breaths force air into the lungs of the victim, from where it is carried around the body to organs, including the brain.

1 Open the airway. Place one hand on the victim's forehead and gently tilt the head back. Remove any obstructions, such as vomit or false teeth, from the mouth and lift the chin.

2 Keeping the airway open, pinch the nose closed with the fingers of the hand on the forehead. This prevents air from escaping through the nostrils.

3 Take a deep breath and seal your mouth over the victim's mouth.

4 To start, give two rescue breaths. If the chest does not rise, adjust the airway and try again. Make five attempts to give two effective breaths (the chest should rise and fall fully). This takes around six seconds.

5 After each breath, take your mouth off the victim's mouth to allow air to escape.

6 After giving two initial breaths, check for signs of circulation – breathing, coughing, and movement. If signs are apparent, go to step 7. If no signs are apparent, go to step 10.

7 Continue giving long, slow rescue breaths at a rate of ten breaths per minute.

8 Check circulation after every minute. If circulation ceases at any point, administer cardio-pulmonary resuscitation, or CPR (see p.236). CPR combines rescue breathing with chest compressions.

9 If the victim begins to breathe again, stabilize them and – if the victim can be moved – place in the recovery position (see p.237).

10 If there are no signs of circulation, begin CPR immediately (see p.236).

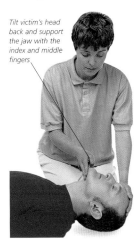

Tilt victim's head back and support the jaw with the index and middle fingers

Seal lips over victim's mouth while pinching their nose

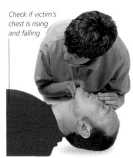

Check if victim's chest is rising and falling

CPR

Cardiopulmonary resuscitation (CPR) is a combination of chest compressions and rescue breathing (*see* p.235). The procedure is applied to a victim who is not breathing and has no circulation. CPR stimulates blood flow to the brain and ventilates the lungs. This procedure is taught worldwide in courses offered by many organizations, including the Red Cross. The specific procedures vary depending on the age of the victim (*see* Child Technique, *below*) and the number of people involved in the rescue. If two rescuers are present, one can administer the rescue breathing while the other does the chest compressions. If only one rescuer is present, he or she must alternate between rescue breathing and chest compressions.

Place middle and index fingers on breastbone

1 Find the point on the chest where the lowermost rib meets the breastbone. Place the middle finger and index finger of one hand there.

Position heel of other hand above fingers

2 Put the heel of the second hand next to the two fingers that are on the breastbone. This is where you will apply pressure during the compressions.

Lock fingers firmly together

3 Place the first hand on top of the second hand and interlock the fingers.

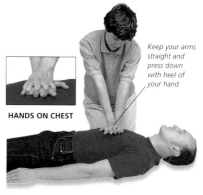

Keep your arms straight and press down with heel of your hand

HANDS ON CHEST

4 Give 15 chest compressions by pushing down 4–5 cm (1 1/2–2 inches) at a rate of 100 per minute.

CHILD TECHNIQUE

The procedure is slightly different for a child.
■ Administer five chest compressions with one hand only, then one rescue breath.
■ Continue the cycle of five compressions to one breath.

5 Give two rescue breaths.
6 Continue cycle of 15 compressions and two rescue breaths until the victim recovers, help arrives, or it becomes impossible to continue. If you are in a very remote area, professional medical assistance may not be available. Therefore, it is very important that you carry on with the cycle of chest compressions and rescue breaths until you are exhausted, so that you give the victim the best chance of survival.

Pinch nose and seal lips over mouth

RECOVERY POSITION

If breathing and heartbeat are present, the unconscious person will need to be stabilized (*see* p.234), until evacuation can be arranged. If you are hiking in a group, one or two members of the party can go for help, while others stay with the victim. Do not hesitate to seek help from other hikers in the area.

Once the victim has been stabilized, he or she should be put in the recovery position (*see below*), which promotes clear breathing, good blood circulation, and keeps the victim resting comfortably until help arrives. The position, however, should be used only with victims who can be moved safely.

1 Kneel beside the victim and straighten the victim's legs. Remove any bulky items from the victim's pockets.
2 Place the victim's arm that is closest to you at a right angle to the body, with the hand facing upward (as if the victim was waving at someone).
3 Put the arm farthest from you across the victim's chest and hold the hand palm outwards against the victim's cheek nearest to you.
4 Grasping the thigh of the leg that is farthest from you, pull the leg up until the foot is flat on the floor. Pull the leg towards you and roll the victim onto their side.
5 At the end of the manoeuvre, the victim should be lying on one side, with the bottom leg extended and the top leg bent at the hip and the knee in a comfortable position. Be sure that the victim is stable and cannot roll onto their back.
6 Check that the victim is breathing evenly, and that the airway is not obstructed.

SEEKING HELP

■ Use a mobile phone to call emergency services, if possible. Climb to a high ridge, or try in several locations, as reception in hiking areas may be bad.
■ If you have to walk out to find help, check your map to find the quickest route.
■ Take notes with you that list the victim's vital signs (breathing and pulse), any evident injuries, and what first aid procedures you have performed.
■ Mark your location precisely on a map and take it with you so rescuers do not have to waste time searching for the victim.

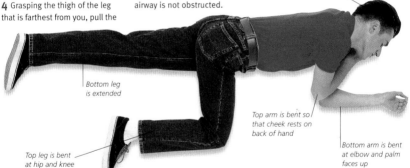

Hand under cheek helps to keep head tilted and airway open

Bottom leg is extended

Top arm is bent so that cheek rests on back of hand

Bottom arm is bent at elbow and palm faces up

Top leg is bent at hip and knee

WARNING

There are certain situations when placing a victim in the recovery position is not recommended.
■ If head, neck, or spinal trauma is suspected, the victim's body should not be moved, but the jaw can be pulled forward to position the tongue so it is less likely to obstruct the airway.
■ If a victim is in the late stages of hypothermia, movement could cause heart fibrillation (a life-threatening rhythm disturbance in the heart), but you should make sure the airway is not blocked.

In both cases, you must pay close and continual attention to the victim's breathing, because the tongue of an unconscious person can fall back into the airway and block the passage of air.
■ If, however, you have no choice but to leave the victim unattended while you go for help, you should use the recovery position to reduce the chance of airway obstruction. Move the victim as gently as possible. In the case of head, neck, and spinal injuries, try to keep the victim's spine completely straight and supported during the manoeuvre.

Resources

Whether you are planning your first overnight hike or making preparations for a multi-week overseas expedition, this section provides you with a selection of phone numbers, addresses, and web links to help you find the information you will need.

USEFUL WEBLINKS

WALKING ROUTES

www.go4awalk.com
Searchable archive of walks in the UK, with printable route maps.

www.ordnancesurvey.co.uk
Website of the UK's official mapping organization. Includes a searchable map archive.

www.walking-routes.co.uk
Portal site containing links to other sites with walking routes in Britain.

www.walkingworld.com
Website containing over 2,000 walks in the UK. Some sample walks are free to download but most require subscription to the site.

WEATHER RESOURCES

www.metoffice.com/weather
Forecasts and climate records for locations all over the world.

www.onlineweather.com
Worldwide weather forecasts and climate records.

www.accuweather.com
Weather forecasts for the US.

OUTDOOR WEB DIRECTORIES

www.gorp.com
Contains information on hiking, covering attractions, outdoor gear, adventure travel, and national parks and wilderness areas.

www.thebmc.co.uk/links.asp
Directory of the British Mountaineering Council, with links to websites containing worldwide travel advice, trekking companies, and access and conservation bodies.

TRAVEL INFORMATION

www.fco.gov.uk
UK Foreign and Commonwealth office website that gives advice for overseas travel.

http://travel.his.com/travel
US Department of State web page containing advice for overseas travel.

www.masta.org
Offers advice and products on the medical risks of overseas travel. Also includes a jetlag calculator.

www.timeanddate.com
Contains international time zones.

www.oanda.com
Includes an online currency converter.

www.convert-me.com
Website containing conversion charts for length, weight, volume, area, and temperature.

MEASUREMENT CONVERSIONS

Length

10 mm = 0.39 in = 0.05 ft
1 m = 3.28 ft = 1.09 yd
1 km = 0.62 mile

Mass

1g = 0.01kg = 0.03 oz = 0.002 lb
1kg = 36.27 oz = 2.20 lb

Volume

1 ml = 0.03 US fluid oz
1 cm3 = 0.06 in3 = 0.002 pint
1 litre = 2.11 pint = 1.06 quart = 0.26 gallon

Temperature

To convert °C to °F = x 9, ÷ 5, + 32
To convert °F to °C = − 32, x 5, ÷ 9

UK ADDRESSES

MEMBERSHIP ORGANIZATIONS

British Mountaineering Council
177-179 Burton Road,
Manchester, M20 2BB
0870 010 4878
office@thebmc.co.uk
www.thebmc.co.uk
Membership body that promotes interests of climbers, hillwalkers, and mountaineers.

The Ramblers' Association
2nd Floor, Camelford House,
87-90 Albert Embankment,
London, SE1 7TW
020 7339 8500
ramblers@london.ramblers.org.uk
www.ramblers.org.uk
Registered charity and membership body. Protects rights of way and campaigns for the right to roam over uncultivated, open country.

The Long-Distance Walkers' Society
Secretary@ldwa.org.uk
www.ldwa.org.uk
Association of long-distance walking clubs. Website contains details of local clubs and long-distance paths.

ACCESS AND CONSERVATION ORGANIZATIONS

Access and Conservation Trust
c/o British Mountaineering Council
Info@accesstrust.org.uk
www.accesstrust.org.uk
Charitable trust that protects access to the countryside by supporting rural access and conservation projects.

The John Muir Trust
41 Commercial Street
Edinburgh EH6 6JD

0131 554 0114
admin@jmt.org
www.jmt.org
Aims to protect and conserve wild places by working closely with local communities.

Open Spaces Society
25a Bell Street, Henley-on-Thames,
Oxfordshire, RG9 2BA
01491 573535
hq@oss.org.uk
www.oss.org.uk/main.htm
The oldest conservation body in the UK campaigns for access over open lands and for keeping public rights of way open.

HIKING AREAS

Brecon Beacons National Park
Plas y Ffynnon, Cambrian Way,
Brecon, Powys, LD3 7HP
01874 624437
enquiries@breconbeacons.org
www.breconbeacons.org
1,347 sq km (520 sq miles) in size, the park is located on the England/Wales border.

Broads National Park
18 Colegate, Norwich,
Norfolk, NR3 1BQ
01603 610734
broads@broads-authority.gov.uk
www.broads-authority.gov.uk
The largest protected wetland in the UK, the Broads is a unique habitat for a huge range of rare animal species.

Cairngorms National Park
14 The Square, Grantown-on-Spey,
Morayshire, PH26 3HG
01479 873535
www.cairngorms.co.uk
The largest national park in the UK, the Cairngorms contains a quarter of Scotland's native woodland.

Dartmoor National Park
Parke, Bovey Tracey,
Devon, TQ13 9JQ
01626 832093
hq@dartmoor-npa.gov.uk
www.dartmoor-npa.gov.uk

368 sq miles (953 sq km) in area, the park contains moorland, wooded valleys, and wind-swept tors.

Eryri (Snowdonia) National Park
Penrhyndeudraeth,
Gwynedd, LL48 6LF
01766 770274
parc@eryri-npa.gov.uk
www.eryri-npa.gov.uk
Located in north Wales, the park contains Snowdon, the second-highest mountain in the UK.

Exmoor National Park
Exmoor House, Dulverton,
Somerset, TA22 9HL
01398 323665
nfo@exmoor-nationalpark.gov.uk
www.exmoor-nationalpark.gov.uk
Located in north Devon, the park contains rolling moorland and a dramatic coastline.

Lake District National Park
Murley Moss, Oxenholme Road,
Kendal, Cumbria, LA9 7RL
01539 724555
hq@lake-district.gov.uk
www.lake-district.gov.uk
With open fells, rocky crags, wooded valleys, and tidal estuaries, the park also contains Scafell Pike, the highest mountain in England.

Loch Lomond & The Trossachs National Park
The Old Station, Balloch Road
Balloch, Alexandria, G83 8SS
01389 722600
info@lochlomond-trossachs.org
www.lochlomond-trossachs.org
Less than an hour from Glasgow, the park contains rolling hills, high mountains, and deep lochs.

North York Moors National Park
The Old Vicarage, Bondgate,
Helmsley, York, YO62 5BP
01439 770657
info@northyorkmoors-npa.gov.uk
www.moors.uk.net
Located in the north of England, the park contains open moors, dales, and a stunning coastline.

Northumberland National Park
Eastburn, South Park,
Hexham, Northumberland, NE4 1BS
01434 605555
admin@nnpa.org.uk
www.nnpa.org.uk
Located in the northeast of England, the park contains the rolling Cheviot hills and Hadrian's Wall.

Peak District National Park
Aldern House, Baslow Road,
Bakewell, Derbyshire, DE45 1AE
01629 816200
aldern@peakdistrict-npa.gov.uk
www.peakdistrict-npa.gov.uk
The park contains two distinct areas: the "White peak" with limestone hills, and the "Dark peak" with gritstone hills and outcrops.

Pembrokeshire Coast National Park
Llanion Park, Pembroke Dock,
Pembrokeshire, SA72 6DF
0845 3457275
pcnp@pembrokeshirecoast.org.uk
www.pembrokeshirecoast.org.uk
Located in southwest Wales, the park features rugged cliffs, islands, tree-lined estuaries, and open moorland.

Yorkshire Dales National Park
Yorebridge House, Bainbridge,
Leyburn, North Yorkshire, DL8 3EE
01969 650456
info@yorkshiredales.org.uk
www.yorkshiredales.org.uk
Located in the north of England, the park covers a diverse area of gritstone outcrops, dry-stone walls, limestone cliffs, and waterfalls.

New Forest National Park
The New Forest Committee,
4 High Street, Lyndhurst,
Hampshire, SO43 7BD
023 80 284144
office@newforestcommittee.org.uk
www.newforestcommittee.org.uk
Until the area gains full national park status, information is available from the New Forest Committee.

Forestry Commission
Silvan House, 231 Corstorphine
Road, Edinburgh, EH12 7AT
0131 334 0303
www.forestry.gov.uk
*Protects the UK's forests and
woodlands through sustainable
forest management. Website
contains a searchable directory of
forests that can be walked in the UK.*

INTERNATIONAL
ADDRESSES

www.chamois.org.uk/world
*Comprehensive list of hiking and
mountaineering club websites in
countries across the world.*

www.hejoly.demon.nl/countries
*Web portal containing links to clubs,
organizations, hiking areas, and
routes in countries across the world.*

FRANCE
**Fédération des Parcs Naturels
Régionaux de France**
9 rue Christiani, 75018 Paris
+0033 1 44 90 86 20
info@parcs-naturels-regionaux.tm.fr
www.parcs-naturels-regionaux.tm.fr/
lesparcs/index_en.html
*Contains maps and web links to
French regional nature parks.*

www.gr-infos.com/gr-an.htm
*Contains maps of the Grands
Randonnees and details of
accommodation en route.*

www.franceonfoot.com
*Includes a useful explanation of the
French network of national, regional,
and local paths.*

SPAIN
www.mma.es/en
*Spanish government website
containing maps and links to
national parks in Spain.*

ITALY
www.cai.it
Website of the Italian Alpine Club.

www.parks.it/eindex.html
*Contains links to national and
regional parks in Italy.*

GERMANY
www.alpinweb.de/frame/s9e.htm
*Contains links to German hiking and
mountaineering clubs.*

www.spotlightgermany.com/links/
Transport/walking_hiking.htm
*Web portal containing links to hiking
routes in Germany.*

SWITZERLAND
www.swisshiking.ch
*French-language website of the
Swiss Hiking Federation.*

www.noth.ch/hiking_e.html
*Website containing details of day-
hikes in Switzerland.*

USA
American Hiking Society
1422 Fenwick Lane
Silver Spring, MD 20910, USA
+001 301 565 6704
www.americanhiking.org
*Membership body that represents
the interests of hikers. Website
contains details of local clubs, trails,
and conservation projects.*

National Park Service (USA)
Director NPS, 1849 C Street NW,
Washington DC 20240, USA
+001 202 208 6843
www.nps.gov
*Contains listings and information on
all the national parks in the USA.*

USDA Forest Service
1400 Independence Ave, SW
Washington DC 20250-0003, USA
+001 202 205 8333
www.fs.fed.us
*Contains information such as permits
required for hiking in national forests.*

CANADA
Alpine Club of Canada
PO Box 8040, Indian Flats Road
Canmore, AB T1W 2T8, Canada

+001 403 678 3200
alpclub@telusplanet.net
www.alpineclubofcanada.ca
*Contains details of hiking and
mountaineering clubs and huts.*

National Parks of Canada
Parks Canada National Office,
25 Eddy Street, Gatineau, Quebec
Canada, K1A 0M5
information@pc.gc.ca
www.pc.gc.ca
*Contains details of Canada's
national parks.*

SOUTH AFRICA
South African National Parks
PO Box 787, Pretoria 0001,
Republic of South Africa
+0027 012 428 9111
reservations@parks-sa.co.za
www.parks-sa.co.za
*Contains details of South Africa's
national parks.*

The Mountain Club of South Africa
97 Hatfield Street, Cape Town 8001,
Republic of South Africa
+0027 21 4 653 412
mcsacc@iafrica.com
www.mcsa.org.za
*The MCSA is an umbrella
organisation with 13 sections that
organise hiking and climbing trips.*

AUSTRALIA
www.bushwalkingaustralia.org
*Website containing information on
bushwalking in Australia and links to
clubs and organizations.*

www.atn.com.au/parks
*Guide to the national parks of
Australia.*

NEW ZEALAND
New Zealand Tramper
www.tramper.co.nz
*A comprehensive online guide to
hiking routes, national parks, and
forest reserves in New Zealand. Also
includes a messageboard for finding
hiking companions.*

Trails directory

Long-distance paths criss-cross the continent of Europe, ranging from the arid plains of Spain to the frosty tundra of Alpine peaks. Shorter trails, national parks, and nature reserves are also found in most European countries – you will find details of each below.

E-TRAILS

The European Ramblers Association works to connect thousands of kilometres of trans-European trails, which are identified by the letter "E" and a number. Many are already in place; some are still in the planning stages. Although rarely hiked in their entirety, the trails offer a wide range of opportunities for hikes of any duration. In many cases, hikers stay in B&Bs, inns, gites, or refuges along the way. Wild camping is permitted in some areas.

A 1:3,500,000 map and a booklet with more route details is available from Freitag & Berndt (Vienna), ISBN 3 7079 0100 9. Route information is currently only available in German, as are the three recently publishsed books on the E-trails:
Auf Tour in Europa, Hans Jürgen Gorges, ISBN 3 8134 0338 6
Europäische Fernwanderwege, Frank Auerbach, ISBN 3 8965 2177 2
Auf Europa's Grossen Wegen: Wandern und Kultur, Robert Wurst, ISBN 3 2221 2346 2.

E1 NORTH–SOUTH
www.era-ewv-ferp.org/index.php?E1
Distance: *4,900 km (3,038 miles)*
Highlights: *Gothenburg, Sweden; Arhus (Denmark); Hamburg, Frankfurt, Black Forest (Germany); St Gotthard (Switzerland); Apennines, Lazio/Molise border (Italy).*

E2 ATLANTIC–MEDITERRANEAN
www.era-ewv-ferp.org/index.php?E2
Distance: *4,850 km (3,007 miles)*
Highlights: *Stranraer (Scotland) to Antwerp via eastern England and the Netherlands or central and southern England and Flanders. The Ardennes (Belgium); Luxembourg; the Vosges and Jura mountains, the Grande Traversée des Alpes (GR5) and Nice (France).*

E3 BLACK SEA–IBERIA
www.era-ewv-ferp.org/index.php?E3
Distance: *6,950 km (4,309 miles)*
Highlights: *Black Sea coast (Bulgaria), Balkan Travers; Ártánd (Hungarian/Romanian border); western Carpathian mountains (Poland, Slovakia, and Czech Republic); Thüringen and Rheingau (Germany); the Ardennes (Belgium); Morvan, Le Puy, the medieval pilgrim route via Cahors, the Pyrenees (France); Burgos, Leon, Santiago de Compostela (Spain).*

E4 MEDITERRANEAN ARC
www.era-ewv-ferp.org/index.php?E4
Distance: *10,450 km (6,479 miles)*
Highlights: *Tarifa on the Strait of Gibraltar, Montserrat, the Pyrenees (Spain); Carcassonne and Grenoble (France); the Jura mountains and Lake Constance (Switzerland); to Vienna via two options: a mountain route through Austria or a low-level route through Bavaria and Salzburg; Lake Balaton and Budapest (Hungary); Ártánd on the Hungary/Romania border; western Bulgaria and Sofia; Florina, Olympos, Delphi, and the Peloponnese (Greece); Kato Zakros (Crete).*

E5 ATLANTIC–ADRIATIC
www.era-ewv-ferp.org/index.php?E5
Distance: *3,050 km (1,891 miles)*
Highlights: *Western tip of Brittany, Brest, Mont St-Michel, Fontainebleau, Ballon d'Alsace (France); Lake Constance (Switzerland); Bolzano, Verona (Italy).*

E6 SCANDINAVIA–DARDANELLES
www.era-ewv-ferp.org/index.php?E6
Distance: *5,200 km (3,224 miles)*
Highlights: *Eastern Sweden, Stockholm, Malmö; Copenhagen (Denmark); Lübeck, Bayerischer Wald mountains (Germany); Mariazell (Austria); Slovenian Karst caves; Alexandropouli (Greece).*

E7 ATLANTIC–BLACK SEA
www.era-ewv-ferp.org/index.php?E7
Distance: *4,330 km (2,685 miles)*
Highlights: *Lisbon (Portugal); El Escorial and Sierra de Guadarrama, Vivel, eastern coastal mountains (Spain); Andorra; Cévennes, Tarascon, and Provence (France); Ligurian Alps and Piacenza (Italy); Ljubljana (Slovenia); Baja (Hungary); Nagylak (Romania).*

E8 ATLANTIC–ISTANBUL
www.era-ewv-ferp.org/index.php?E8
Distance: *4,390 km (2,722 miles)*
Highlights: *Western Cork, southern Ireland; Trans-Pennine Trail (Britain); Rotterdam (Netherlands); Aachen, Bonn, Rhine Valley, Regensburg, and Passau (Germany); Vienna (Austria); Bratislava, Carpathians (Slovakia); Beskid Pass on the Poland/Ukraine border. Detached leg through Rhodope Mountains in southern Bulgaria to Mezek near Svilengrad by the Turkish border.*

E9 EUROPEAN COAST PATH
www.era-ewv-ferp.org/
index.php?E9

Distance: *5,000 km (3,100 miles)*
Highlights: *Brest, Cherbourg, Le
Havre, Calais (France); Ostend
(Belgium); Rotterdam (Netherlands);
Wilhelmshaven, Hamburg, Rostock
(Germany); Gdansk (Poland);
Estonia to Russian border.*

E10 NE–SW
www.era-ewv-ferp.org/
index.php?E10

Distance: *2,880 km (1,786 miles)*
Highlights: *Helsinki (Finland);
Potsdam, Oberlausitz (Germany);
Prague, Budweis (Czech Republic);
Salzburg (Austria); Bolzano, Lake
Maggiore, Ligurian Alps and the
Grande Traversata dei Alpi (Italy);
Menton (France); Catalan Coast Path
to Ulldecona (Spain).*

E11 NW–NE
www.era-ewv-ferp.org/
index.php?E11

Distance: *2,070 km (1,283 miles)*
Highlights: *The Hague, Leiden
(Netherlands); Osnabrück, Harz,
Potsdam, Frankfurt (Germany);
Poznan, Torun, Masuria (Poland) to
Lithuanian border.*

ENGLAND

England is rich in walking paths, and
you are never more than 50 miles
from a National Trail. These are
designated and waymarked by the
Countryside Agency, while other
long-distance paths exist that may or
may not be marked. Accommodation
can be found in B&Bs, hostels, or
pubs, so there is usually no need to
carry a tent. Terrain varies from
country paths through farmers' fields
to the wild and rugged moors and
fells of the Lake District.

CLEVELAND WAY
www.nationaltrail.co.uk/
factfile.asp?trailCode=cl

*177 km (110 miles) long, this trail
runs through northeast England and*

*takes about nine days. It takes a
semi-circular route around the North
York Moors National Park – the
largest area of open moorland in
England, then follows the Heritage
Coast on top of rugged cliffs.*

THE COTSWOLD WAY
www.nationaltrail.co.uk/
factfile.asp?trailCode=cw

*This trail is 163 km (101 miles) long
and runs through west-central
England, taking about seven days. It
follows the escarpment of the
Cotswold hills, which give excellent
views, and almost all of the trail is
within the Cotswalds Area of
Outstanding Natural Beauty.
Landscape includes beech woods,
open pastures, dry stone walls, and
villages with limestone cottages.*

HADRIAN'S WALL
www.nationaltrail.co.uk/
factfile.asp?trailCode=hd

*130 km (80 miles) long, this trail runs
from Bowness to Newcastle in
northern England and takes about
nine days. Terrain includes a riveside
route along the Tyne, farmland and
grazing uplands, and the open salt
marsh of the Solway Estuary.
Highlights include Roman ruins
including forts and earthworks.*

THE NORTH DOWNS WAY
www.nationaltrail.co.uk/
factfile.asp?trailCode=nd

*This trail runs for 227 km (141 miles)
in southeast England and takes
about 14 days. Following the chalk
escarpment of the North Downs,
terrain includes woodland, open
fields, and natural chalk grassland.
Most of the path is within the Kent
Downs and Surrey Hills designated
Areas of Outstanding Natural Beauty.*

THE PEDDARS WAY AND
NORFOLK COAST PATH
www.nationaltrail.co.uk/
factfile.asp?trailCode=pd

*150 km (93 miles) long, this trail is in
East Anglia and takes 8 days. The*

*Peddars Way follows a 2,000-year old
Roman road, and the coastal path
passes over cliffs, sandy beaches, and
dunes. Half of the route lies in the
Norfolk Coast Area of Natural Scenic
Beauty, and a quarter lies in the Breck's
Environmentally Sensitive Area.*

THE PENNINE
BRIDLEWAY
www.nationaltrail.co.uk/
factfile.asp?trailCode=pb

*When complete, this trail will run 330
km (205 miles) from Derbyshire to
Cumbria and will take about a month
to walk. Terrain includes farms and
fields with dry-stone-walls, the Peak
District and Yorkshire Dales National
Parks, heather moors, lakes, and
sweeping valleys. 120 km (75 miles)
of the route is currently open through
Derbyshire to the South Pennines.*

THE PENNINE WAY
www.nationaltrail.co.uk/
factfile.asp?trailCode=pn

*A 16-day traverse of the "Backbone
of England", this trail runs for 402
km (250 miles) through central and
northern England. It is a classic, but
crowded, walk. The majority of the
trail lies within three national parks:
the Peak District, Yorkshire Dales,
and Northumberland National Parks.*

THE RIDGEWAY
www.nationaltrail.co.uk/
factfile.asp?trailCode=rd

*This trail runs for 136 km (85 miles)
through central and southern
England and takes about five days.
The trail is entirely located within
two Areas of Outstanding Natural
Beauty, varying from chalk hills to
beech forests, and views of rolling
downs and the Thames Valley.*

SOUTH WEST COAST PATH
www.nationaltrail.co.uk/
factfile.asp?trailCode=sw

*Approximately 965 km (600 miles)
long, this trail runs through
southwest England. It is the longest
national trail and takes about two
months to walk in its entirety. The*

walk offers a wide range of experiences and landscapes, from busy harbours and resorts to moorlands, plateaus, coastal valleys, intimate coves, and long pebble and sand beaches. Two-thirds of the route passes through Areas of Outstanding Natural Beauty. The path also passes through England's first World Heritage Site, a UNESCO designated Biosphere reserve at the Braunton Burrows Sand Dunes, World War II historic sites, and archaeological features from the Iron Age.

THE THAMES PATH
www.nationaltrail.co.uk/factfile.asp?trailCode=tp
Running for 288 km (179 miles) through southern England, this trail takes about 14 days. It follows the Thames from its source in the Cotswolds, through London, and to the Thames Barrier near Greenwich.

THE SOUTH DOWNS WAY
www.nationaltrail.co.uk/factfile.asp?trailCode=sd
This trail runs for 171 km (106 miles) through southeast England and takes about eight days. All of the route is within the Sussex Downs and East Hampshire designated Areas of Outstanding Natural Beauty, soon to become a National Park. The landscape ranges from rolling farmland to steep, wooded hillsides, open grassland, and sea cliffs.

THE YORKSHIRE WOLDS WAY
www.nationaltrail.co.uk/factfile.asp?trailCode=wl
This trail is 127 km (79 miles) long and runs through northern England. This five-day hike features rolling chalk wolds and dramatic dry valleys.

THE COAST-TO-COAST PATH
www.coast2coast.co.uk
Running for 306 km (190 miles) from St. Bee's Head on the Irish Sea to Robin Hood's Bay on the North Sea, this trail passes through the Lake District, the Yorkshire Dales, and the North York Moors.

WALES
THE PEMBROKESHIRE COAST PATH
www.nationaltrail.co.uk/factfile.asp?trailCode=ps
Running for 268 km (166 miles) through southwest Wales, this trail takes about 15 days. It features a spectacular coast with rugged cliffs and long beach arcs. Almost all of the trail is in a national park, with about a quarter in designated conservation sites.

OFFA'S DYKE PATH
www.nationaltrail.co.uk/factfile.asp?trailCode=of
270 km (168 miles) long, this trail follows the Wales/England border and takes about 15 days to hike. The landscape ranges from mountains and hills to river valleys and pastures. About a third of the trail lies in Areas of Outstanding Natural Beauty. Two-thirds of the trail is in Wales, the remaining third in England.

THE GLYNDWR WAY
www.nationaltrail.co.uk/factfile.asp?trailCode=gd
This 213-km (130-mile) path takes about nine days. The landscape ranges from open moorland and rolling farmland to woodland and forests. Highlights include views over the Cambrian Mountains.

SCOTLAND
THE SOUTHERN UPLAND WAY
www.dumgal.gov.uk/southernuplandway
This trail runs for 341 km (212 miles) across southern Scotland, from Portpatrick in the west to Cockburnspath on the east coast. The scenery is varied, passing from gentle valleys to open moorland and plantations to forests. Some sections are quite remote and may require the use of a tent due to the distances between villages. The walk takes about two weeks.

THE SPEYSIDE WAY
www.moray.org/area/speyway/webpages/swhome.htm
This trail is a 68-km (42-mile) path starting at the Spey Bay on the Moray Firth, and following the river Spey south to Tomintoul. It takes about four days to walk.

THE WEST HIGHLAND WAY
www.west-highland-way.co.uk
Scotland's most famous walk (see p.23) passes some of the country's finest scenery, including Loch Lomond, Glencoe, Rannoch Moor, and Glen Nevis. It is 153 km (95 miles) long.

ST CUTHBERT'S WAY
www.st-cuthberts-way.co.uk
This trail is 101 km (63 miles) long and takes around 7 days to hike. Established in 1996, it runs from Melrose in the Scottish Borders to Holy Island in Northumberland, northeastern England.

THE FIFE COASTAL WALK
www.fifecoastalpath.co.uk
Running for 151 km (94 miles) from Newburgh to Inverkeithing, this walk is still under development. It passes fishing villages, beaches, and wild headlands.

FRANCE
The French word for trail is "randonnee", and trails are divided into three categories – the "grandes randonnees" (GR), which are long-distance trails marked with red and white paint blazes; "randonnees de pays", which are regional routes marked in red and yellow; and "promenades" or "randonnees", which are local trails marked in yellow. The long-distance system of GRs, in which routes are given internationally recognized numbers, has spread into nearby countries such as Holland, Belgium, and Spain;

some of the routes cross international borders. In all, France boasts 60,000 kilometres of long distance paths and another 80,000 kilometres of regional and local footpaths.

The *Federation Francaise de Randonees Pedestres* (FFRP, www.ffrp.asso.fr) produces guidebooks called "Topoguides", which contain detailed maps and descriptive text. Topoguides are available from Stanfords bookshop (www.stanfords.co.uk).

GR-5 NORTH SEA TO MEDITERRANEAN
Topoguides: 502, 504, 507, 511, 530, 531, FFRP
Although the GR-5 is not solely a French trail, it spends most of its time in France. It begins near Rotterdam in the Netherlands and crosses Belgium, Luxembourg, and part of Switzerland. The most spectacular section is the "Grand Traverse des Alps", which starts at Lake Geneva and climbs into the Alps before heading south along the Swiss and Italian borders to the Mediterranean Sea.

GR-10 ATLANTIC TO MEDITERRANEAN
The GR10 Trail: Through the French Pyrenees, by Paul Lucia, 2002, Cicerone; **Topoguides: 1086, 1090, 1091, 1092,** FFRP
The GR-10 is a six-week walk from the Atlantic Ocean to the Mediterranean along the French side of the Franco-Spanish border, in the Pyrenees. This rugged, highly serrated mountain range offers extremely challenging walking, with thousands of metres of descent and ascent. Accommodation is in gites or refuges, although wild camping is possible in some areas.

PYRENEAN HAUTE ROUTE
Pyrenees: High Level Route, by Georges Veron, 1998, West Col Productions ; **Pyrenean Haute Route,** by Ton Joosten, 2004, Cicerone
Roughly parallel to (and sometimes

contiguous with) the GR-10, the route stays close to the France/Spain border, meandering between the countries, and crossing through Andorra. It is remote and requires advanced map and compass skills. Wild camping (with a tent) is required in some of the more remote regions (see p.21).

GR-20 CORSICA
GR20 Corsica: The High Level Route, by Paddy Dillon, 2001, Cicerone; **Topoguide: 067,** FFRP
This 125-mile (200-km) trail through the middle of Corsica is considered one of the most difficult but scenic in France. The mountains of this rugged Mediterranean island can be sweltering and hot one minute and snow-covered the next (even in summer), but this trail enjoys a reputation among serious hikers as one of the finest in France.

GR-65 FRANCE AND SPAIN
Topoguides: 651, 652, 653, 698, FFRP
Historically, the Camino de Santiago de Compostela brought pilgrims from all over Europe to the Spanish shrine of St. James. Pilgrims would begin walking from their homes, and as they got closer and closer to their destination in northern Spain, the paths converged into several well-trod pilgrim routes. In France, there are still several branches from various parts of the country, most of which merge on one side or the other of the Spanish border. Starting in Le Puys, the GR-65 is a favourite among contemporary pilgrims.

TOUR DE MONT BLANC
Tour of Mont Blanc, by Kev Reynolds, 2004, Cicerone
This 167-km (104-mile) high mountain tour takes 11 to 14 days around Western Europe's highest peak, and passes through three countries. Accommodation in refuges is possible, but should be booked in advance. This is a popular hike, so expect lots of company. The French-language Office de Haute Montagne

(www.ohm-chamonix.com) *has a list of accommodation.*

VANOISE NATIONAL PARK
www.vanoise.com/indexgb.htm
France's first national park features glaciers, alpine meadows, a true sense of wilderness, and less crowds than many other alpine areas. Its trails include a spectacular section of the GR-5 and the 59-km (37-mile) Vanoise Glacier Tour, which lasts 4 to 5 days and circumambulates the mountain massif. You are likely to see the endangered ibex.

QUEYRAS TRAVERSE
www.parcduqueyras.com
Topoguide: 505, FFRP
This linear hike follows a section of the GR-58 through the Parc Naturel Regional de Queyras. Located close to Mont Viso and the Italian border, the route is 47 km (29 miles) long and takes about four days. The park offers exceptional birdwatching, over 2,000 species of flowering plants, more than a dozen summits above 3,000 metres, and 300 days of sunshine a year.

PARC NATIONAL DE MERCANTOUR
www.parc-mercantour.fr
This stunning park in the Maritime Alps combines the dry Mediterranean climate with a high mountain landscape, featuring glacially cut valleys and soaring peaks. It is less popular with hikers than many of France's other walking areas. Wild camping is permitted. The GR-52 traverses the park, taking about a week.

PARC NATIONAL DES ECRINS
www.les-ecrins-parc-national.fr
The challenging Tour d'Oisans (GR-54) is 200 km (124 miles) long and includes 18,290 m (60,000 ft) of ascent through the rugged Ecrins massif. These are the southernmost glaciers in the Alps. Accommodation is in refuges, gites, and wild camping.

PARC NATIONAL DES PYRENEES

www.parc-pyrenees.com/index_english.htm

Nestled in the central Pyrenees, this popular park draws hikers from all over the world to the heart of this serrated and dramatic mountain range. Sections of the GR-5 and Pyrenean Haute Route cross the park, but there are dozens of other trails of varying lengths.

SPAIN

Although not as renowned among hikers as the Alpine countries, Spain arguably boasts more variety for hikers than any other European country. It offers dramatic and spectacular high peaks, Mediterranean scrub, and stark arid valley expanses. Most hikers contemplating a long-distance hike in Spain opt for the famous and historic *Camino de Santiago de Compostela*, but there are many hiking options in the Pyrenees and a host of national parks to choose from as well.

CAMINO DE SANTIAGO DE COMPOSTELA

The Way of St James: Pyrenees–Santiago–Finisterre, by Alison Raju, 2003, Cicerone

This ancient pilgrimage route is really a network of several trail branches that converge in northern Spain and then follow the medieval pilgrimage route to the city of Santiago de Compostela. You are considered an "official" pilgrim if you hike at least 100 km (62 miles) to reach the Cathedral at Santiago de Compostela, once the third- holiest shrine in the Christian world. Pilgrimage rituals abound on this trail, such as carrying emblematic scallop shells, ruminating over the meaning of the journey, and the hospitality of trailside "refugios" and "hospitales". In addition to the French Route (see p.244), a "silver route" brings pilgrims from southern Spain, and a Portuguese Route brings pilgrims from Portugal.

GR-11 ATLANTIC TO MEDITERRANEAN

GR11: Senda Pirenaica, Senderos de Gran Reccorido

Running roughly parallel to France's GR-10, the GR-11 stays on the Spanish side of the border, and is sometimes contiguous with, or an alternative to, parts of the Pyrenean Haute Route. This is one of the wilder, more remote trails in Europe. In places it is difficult to locate – it is less consistently marked than the GR-10 and at times follows a number of secondary and country roads.

COSTA DA MORTE

Walking in Spain, 2003, Lonely Planet

The Costa del Morte in Galicia, northwestern Spain, is named in memory of the countless shipwrecked sailors who drowned offshore. The route passes dramatic granite headlands, rarely-visited beaches, and small ports, where you can sate your appetite on fresh seafood and local wine. It takes five to seven days to complete. Sparse accommodation makes carrying a tent necessary.

COVADONGA NATIONAL PARK

www.picoseuropa.net

Covodonga was originally set aside as a national park to commemorate its historic role as the site where the Spanish first held back the Moors in AD 722. The park is now more than 250,000 acres in size, including much of the Picos de Europa, and is the largest national park in Europe. The Picos de Europa is a limestone mountain range located along the Atlantic coast of northwestern Spain. Proximity to moist Atlantic winds make the range misty all year long. Water from constant precipitation and glaciation has carved the range into a labyrinth of cirques, tarns, and caves. The four-day Macizo Circuit and the nine-day Lago de la Ercina hike offer trekkers a chance to escape the crowds (the higher you climb, the sparser the company). Huts in the mountains and inns in

the valleys offer accommodation. Camping is allowed with a permit.

ORDESA NATIONAL PARK

www.ordesa.net

Located in the central Pyrenees, Ordesa's popularity matches it's scenic beauty, but in August, the hordes of hikers can be such that you have to take your turn on the trails. Highlights are Monte Perdido (the lost mountain) and the namesake Ordesa Valley, carved by glaciers. Sections of the GR-11 and the Pyrenean Haute Route run through the park, but there are dozens of other trails of varying lengths, many of which lead far above the treeline to wildflower meadows. Wildlife is abundant, with more than 170 species of birds and 30 mammals, including the chamoise deer and the Pyrennean mountain goat. The village of Torla makes a good starting point for exploring the region.

GARAJONAY NATIONAL PARK

www.garajonay.com

For a completely different hiking experience, try the Garajonay National Park, located on the island of La Gomera in the Canary Islands, just off the coast of Africa. The island contains remnants of the temperate rainforest that covered the Mediterranean basin before the ice age. It boasts the challenge of Alto de Garajonay, a 1,500-m (5,000-ft) peak.

SWITZERLAND

Perhaps no nation is as synonymous with mountains as Switzerland. Packed with one scenic range after another, the nation is criss-crossed by hiking trails and dotted with mountain refuges, not to mention some of the highest peaks, deepest valleys, and largest glaciers in the Alps. Most of these hikes are not described on dedicated websites, although web links are given where relevant. For planning information, the best resources are local guidebooks to each region. Also, each of the routes are described in **Walking in Switzerland** by Clem Lindenmayer, 2001, Lonely Planet.

www.swisstopo.com/en/INDEX.htm
Maps from *Bundesamt fur Landestopographie* are available at scales of 1:25,000 and 1:50,000.

TOUR DE MUVERANS
www.tourdesmuverans.ch
This is a four-day 52-km (32-mile) circuit. From the Muverans Massif in French-speaking western Switzerland, the Alps stretch like an unbroken sea of glinting white peaks, with Mont Blanc shouldering above the rest like a burly big brother. This is a strenuous route through some of Switzerland's wilder areas, with elevations ranging from 1,100 m (3,600 ft) to 2,600 m (8,500 ft).

WILDSTRUBEL TRAVERSE
This 24-km (15-mile) traverse takes three days to complete. The Wildstrubel divides the central and western Bernese Oberland regions, and this wild, high hike requires some high-altitude experience. Parts can remain snow covered through the summer, the climbs are demanding, and loose rock and exposure can be unnerving. Not for those who suffer from a fear of heights!

SURENENPASS
This 28-km (17-mile) walk is occasionally done in one day, although perhaps not enjoyably – it requires a 1,800-m (5,900-ft) ascent and a long 1,200-m (3,900-ft) descent. A better idea is to take two days and enjoy what some have called the most spectacular walk in central Switzerland. The pass has been a trade route for 700 years.

VANIL NOIR
This 2-day 20-km (12 mile) walk in northwestern Switzerland is protected by a nature reserve. The route stays on the north side of the mountain, offering spectacular views in one of

the wilder parts of the region. The trail passes close to the 2,389-m (7,838-ft) summit, and a strenuous side-trip to the top is possible.

SWISS NATIONAL PARK
www.nationalpark.ch/snp.html
A wide variety of trails leads hikers of all levels of fitness and ability through the national park. What was once one of Switzerland's most environmentally damaged regions is now among its wildest, thanks to the establishment of the national park in 1914. Wild camping is not permitted in the park, but there are several long day-hikes, some of which can be divided by staying at mountain huts (reservations are necessary).

SWISS HAUTE ROUTE
Chamonix to Zermatt: A Walker's Haute Route, by Kev Reynolds, 2001, Cicerone; Haute Route Chamonix–Zermatt: A Guide for Skiers and Mountain Walkers, Peter Cliff, 1993
This trail runs from Chamonix (France) to Zermatt. (see p.22).

ITALY
The best walking in Italy is located in the Alps, where there are scores of excellent hikes ranging in duration from a few hours to a week or more. While spectacular mountains such as Mont Blanc and the Matterhorn lie in France and Switzerland, both are partly in Italy – Italy's peaks, while less famous, are just as big and dramatic as the peaks of its neighbours. Some hikers consider the Dolomites to be the best Alpine scenery anywhere. If you have an interest in climbing, try the "*via ferrate*" (iron path) routes that use walkways, ladders, and iron supports bolted to the rocks for protection. Alternatively, coastal walks offer an experience of the Mediterranean landscape.

For information on "*via ferrate*", see Via Ferratas of the Italian Dolomites: Volumes 1 and 2, by Graham Fletcher and John Smith.

For maps, refer to the *Touring Club Italiano* 1:200,000 maps, which are available for the Dolomites, western Alps, and Maritime Alps. *Istituto Geografico Centrale* in Turin publishes 1:25,000 and 1:50,000 maps suitable for hiking.

MARITIME ALPS
MARGUARREIS CIRCUIT
www.parks.it/parchi.cuneesi/Eser.html
This is an extremely challenging two-day hike of 35 km (21 miles), largely in the Parco Naturale Alta Valle Pesio e Tanaro *near Italy's border with France. The region offers dramatic limestone cliffs, caves, spectacular waterfalls, and a wide variety of vegetation.*

TERME DI VALDIERI TO ENTRACQUE
www.parks.it/parco.alpi.marittime/Eindex.html
This is a challenging four-day walk that covers 45 km (28 miles) and five high passes through the Parco Naturale delle Alpi Marittime *along the French border. Accommodation is available in refuges; no wild camping is permitted. Ascending a 3,000-m (9,800-ft) side-peak provides an extra challenge.*

WESTERN ALPS
VALMONTEY TO RHEMES NOTRE DAME
www.parks.it/parco.nazionale.gran.paradiso/Eindex.html
Located in and around the Parco Nazionale del Gran Paradiso, *this is a route that might unnerve those with a fear of heights. It has steep ascents and descents and friable rock – but the pay-off is outstanding scenery in Italy's oldest national park, which was founded to preserve the ibex. The 31-km (19-mile) walk takes two days.*

MATTERHORN AND MONTE ROSA
Walking in Italy, 2003, Lonely Planet
The Matterhorn and Monte Rosa give two of the most compelling

mountain vistas in the Alps, and they frame this three-day 50-km (31-mile) walk, which links four contrasting mountain valleys. It starts in the Valley of Valtournenche, which sits at the base of the Matterhorn on the Italian side. This is a challenging hike for fit and experienced hikers; trail markings are inconsistent, so a good map and compass are necessary, and the total amount of ascent works out to an average elevation gain of about 1,250 m (4,100 ft) per day.

VAL DE RABBI TO MARTELLTAL
www.parks.it/parco.nazionale.
stelvio/Eindex.html
This is a challenging and highly scenic mountain walk covering 55 km (34 miles), and taking about four days to complete. The hike passes through the southern Tirol and Trentino parts of the Parco Nazionale Stelvio, which is Italy's biggest park. The park boasts the Ortles-Cevedale massif, along with numerous glaciers and valleys and abundant wildlife and alpine flora. The four-day tour has well-marked, well-maintained paths – and nearly 4,000 m (13,000 ft) of height gain. Several variants are available to shorten the hike or make it easier.

MONT VISO
Walking in the Alps, 2004, Lonely Planet
This circuit hike is in both Italy and France, but the massif itself is in Italy. Access is easier from the French side. It is a challenging three or four-day 62-km (39-mile) walk that climbs four high passes. It is an extremely scenic walk, passing glaciers, mountain tarns, and the headwaters of the Po river. It is located next to the Queyras natural park (see p.244).

DOLOMITES

VIA DELLE BOCCHETTE
Via Ferratas of the Italian Dolomites: Volume 2, by Graham Fletcher and John Smith, 2003, Cicerone

Some call the Dolomites the most beautiful mountains in the Alps. Accessible from June to September, the Via delle Bocchette leads across the Brenta massif at elevations of 2–3,000 m (6,500–9,800 ft). The trail takes from two to three days to complete; accommodation can be found in four trail-side refuges. The trail includes sections of via ferrata iron paths, and while you do not have to be an experienced climber, you may appreciate having a harness, especially if you are afraid of heights. The route starts at the cableway from Madonna di Campiglio to the Groste Pass.

SCILIAR CIRCUIT
www.parks.it/parco.sciliar
A network of trails in and around the Parco Natural dello Sciliar lends itself to a variety of itineraries from day-walks to multi-day excursions. Jagged peaks provide a dramatic backdrop, mountain huts provide lodging, and the trails range from gentle walks to via ferrata and technical climbing.

NORTHERN DOLOMITES TRAVERSE
Via Ferratas of the Italian Dolomites: Volume 1, by Graham Fletcher and John Smith, 2004, Cicerone
This seven-day 70-km (43-mile) traverse begins in Ortisei and ends in Sesto. It passes through spectacular scenery including the Tre Cime di Lavaredo, a mountain that some have called the most beautiful in the Dolomites. Although long, the trail is not difficult, and the route is well-marked.

ALTA VIA NUMBER 1
www.dolomiti-altevie.it/inglese/
altaVia/Home.asp
This 120-km (75-mile) week-long traverse is a classic walk through the Venetian Dolomites, starting in the Lago di Braies in Val Pusteria and travelling south along a superb trail. Refugios offer lodging along the length of the route. Views include the Fanes and Civetta mountains and the

spectacular peak of Tofana di Rozes.

ALTA VIA NUMBER 2
www.dolomiti.it/eng/itinerari/
altevie/altavia2.htm
185 km (115 miles) long and taking 15 days to complete, this route is not recommended for those who suffer from vertigo! It is a spectacular alpine route along ridges between the Isarco and Piave rivers. It connects the northern tip of the Dolomites to the Pre-Alps, which overlook the Venetian plain. The route links two lovely alpine towns (Bressanone and Feltre) and passes through three provinces. Recommended for advanced hikers.

MEDITERRANEAN COAST

THE CINQUE TERRE
www.cinqueterre.it/en/cta1.html
Once known as the via dell'amore (love path), this trail connects the five villages of Riomaggiore, Manarola, Corniglia, Vernazza, and Monterosso on Italy's northwest coast. It was once the area's only route on land. The villages are still connected by ferry, and each are four to five hours' walk apart. You can walk from one to the next as a day excursion, or walk the entire route in about four days.

ALTA VIA DEI MONTI LIGURI
www.altaviadeimontiliguri.it/
eng/home.html
This month-long route follows the ridges of the Appennines, which run parallel to the sea for 300 km (186 miles) from Ventimiglia on the French border, to Spezia. Because the trail's elevation ranges from 500 to 2000 m (1,600 to 6,500 ft), the environment varies dramatically, from lush deciduous and fir forests to barren rocks. Views range from the snow-capped Alps to the Mediterranean Sea, sometimes even to Corsica, and there are frequent opportunities to leave the trail and head for villages and towns along the coast. The route is accessible all year round.

AUSTRIA

It may be a small country, but Austria has more than 1,000 mountain huts and an equal number of hikes. Each of the routes described is included in **Walking in the Alps**, 2004, Lonely Planet. The Austrian National Tourist Office (**www.austria-tourism.at**) has a helpful site with lots of walk links and contact information.

RATIKON HOHENWEG NORD

This 24-km (15-mile) hike near the Austria/Switzerland/Lichtenstein border takes three days. It is a well-known route that crosses three high passes, but offers a surprising variety of terrain. In good weather, the ascent via a sidetrail to the 2,800-m (9,200 ft) Sulzfluh is a treat.

LECHTAL HOHENWEG

The Lechtal Hoehenweg wanders through 1,200 km (745 miles) of the Austrian Tirol, and the entire hike takes about 15 days. Shorter sections can also be hiked; a popular section is the first few stages starting from the Fufbahn cable car. Some sections are quite precipitous, but may have easier alternative routes.

OTZAL ALPS TRAVERSE

This challenging 32-km (20-mile) walk takes three days and climbs over two 3,000-m (9,800-ft) passes. This region of Austria has more snowfields than any other, as well as Austria's second-highest peak, and the hiking is demanding, requiring long ascents and descents. Snow lingers quite late in the summer, and if it has been a particularly snowy year, you may need a pair of instep crampons.

STUBAI HOHENWEG

www.stubaier-hohenweg.at
This nine-day circuit route is one of Austria's classic walks. It is approximately 80 km (50 miles) long, broken up by stops at alpine refuges. The terrain includes glaciers, lakes, tarns, valleys, and rocky peaks.

However, some sections of this hike are rather treacherous due to loose rock and require a strong stomach for exposure at heights.

SUDENDEUTCHER HOHENWEG

This highly scenic route offers hikers a chance to see some fine Alpine scenery and climb to a 3,200-m (10,500-ft) side summit, all in a two-day 20-km (12-mile) hike. The top of Kleiner Muntanitz provides one of the best views to be found in the country.

VERWALL CIRCUIT

This four-day loop hike in the Tirol is challenging and includes the ascent of a 3,000-m (9,800-ft) peak. It is accessed from St. Anton, which can be conveniently reached from Innsbruck.

GERMANY

Hiking opportunities in Germany range from the Alps to the green forests and fields of Thuringia, in the centre of the country. Single-day walks are especially popular, and information about them can be found in local outdoor gear shops.

BERCHTESGADEN NATIONAL PARK

www.nationalpark-berchtesgaden.de
There are dozens of hiking trails in the Bertchesgaden National Park. The landscape includes dramatic mountains and lakes, and some of the trails are best reached by ferry. The park is very popular, so book accommodation in huts in advance. It is possible to combine shorter trails to make routes of four to five days or more. The limestone landscape is porous, so surface water is scarce – carry enough for each day's walk.

RENNSTEIG

www.natureparktravel.com/hiking/hiking.htm#steig
The popular 167-km (104-mile) Rennsteig ridgeway crosses the Thuringian Forest and the Schiefer Mountains in central Germany. The route passes the Vessertal Biosphere Reserve, the watersheds of the Elbe and Rhine rivers, and the old border between East and West Germany. This is an ancient route, following the footsteps of Celtic and Germanic tribes, Roman legionaries, missionaries, as well as Martin Luther, Goethe, and Napoleon. The complete hike takes six to ten days. Accommodation should be booked in advance.

RHOEN HOEHENWEG

www.natureparktravel.com/hiking/hiking.htm#rhoen
The 137-km (85-mile) ridgeway crosses the Rhoen Biosphere Reserve and Nature Park. Starting at Bad Salzungen, the path passes through the mountains and moors, from Franconia to Thuringia, across the former East and West German border.

Index

Author's acknowledgments

The author would like to thank everyone from The Bridgewater Book Company and Dorling Kindersley who contributed to this book.

Publisher's acknowledgments

The Bridgewater Book Company would like to thank Ellis Brigham Ltd, Lowe Alpine, Peglers Expedition Advisors and Suppliers (www.peglers.co.uk), The North Face, and Yaktrax UK for the provision of outdoor clothing and equipment; the Alfriston Tennis Club & Camp Ground; and the following people for their contributions:

Editors: Alison Bolus, Sarah Doughty, Nicky Gyopari, Philippa Smith, Howard Spencer
Designers: Kevin Knight, Ginny Zeal, Barbara Zuniga **Picture Researcher**: Maria Gibbs
Indexer: Ann Barrett **Photoshoot Art Director**: Jo Grey **Prop Hunter**: Amy Jeavons
Models: Natalie George, Andy Hillion, Miranda Hunt, Nicholas King, David McCormick, Hayley Miles, Paul Zimmerman

Dorling Kindersley would like to thank Dr Viv Armstrong of the Red Cross, Jemima Dunne, and Jill Hamilton for their advice and help on the first aid section; Lettie Luff for assistance with the resources section; and Eadaoin Hutchinson and the staff at The North Face store Covent Garden.

Picture Credits

The publisher would like to thank the following for their kind permission to reproduce their photographs:

Picture Key: a = above; b = below; c = centre; l = left; r = right; rh = running head; t = top; f = far

Picture source code:
Co = Corbis
GB = Gerard Brown
GI = Getty Images
KB = Karen Berger
NG = Neill Gilhooley
NGI = National Geographic Image Collection
PM = Paul Milligan

1 Co/Jonathan Andrew; **2–3** Co/Charles Mauzy; **4–5** Co/Mark E. Gibson; **6–7** Co/Tom Bean; **9t** Co/Bob Krist; **9c** GI/Joe Cornish; **10–27, 238–256**rh GB; **10c** Co/David Stoecklein; **11** Co/Lee Cohen; **12–13** GI/Richard Price; **14** GI/David Madison; **15** GI/ Cheyenne Rouse; **16–17** Co/Stephanie Maze; **18**cfl Co/David Muench; **19b** NGI/Warren Marr/Panoramic Images; **19**crb GI/Thomas Del Brase; **20b** Co/Galen Rowell; **21**ca Co/Charles O'Rear; **21**br Co/Francesc Muntada; **22**bl GI/Cyril Isy-Schwart; **22–23** GI/James Balog; **23**br GI; **23**cbl GI/Jeremy Walker; **24**cr NGI/Bobby Model; **24**bl Co/Reuters; **25**clb GI/Robert Stahl; **26**bcl GI/China Tourism Press; **26**cfl GI/Keren Su; **27**cfr NGI/Todd Gipstein; **27b** GI/John Lamb; **28–29b** Co/Layne Kennedy; **28**bl Royalty Free; **28–45**rh PM; **30** Co/S.P.Gillette; **31** PM; **32** GI/Jenny Pate; **33** Co/ML Sinibaldi; **34t** Co/Gunter Marx Photography; **34b** Co/Macduff Everton; **35t** Co/ Anthony Bannister; Gallo Images; **35b** GI/Michael Melford; **38**c KB; **38–39** Co/Tom Bean; **39**tl, tr KB; **39**tc GI/Andrea Booher; **40** Co/David Samuel Robbins; **41b** Co/Galen Rowell; **41t** Co/Howard Davies; **42**cr KB; **42**bl Co/Ken Redding; **43** Co/Galen Rowell; **44** GI/Frank Herholdt; **45**t Co/Caroline Penn top; **45b** Co/Jeff Vanuga; **46–47** Co/Duomo; **48** Co/Michael DeYoung; **48–105**rh GI/Monica Dalmasso; **49b** Co/Layne Kennedy; **49**t GI/Karl Weatherly; **54**c Snow & Rock; **56**r Snow & Rock; **58**r Snow & Rock; **71**t Canadian Recreation Products; **86** Co/Paul A.

Souders; **99**bl Co/Galen Rowell; **106–107** Co/Carl Schneider; **109**t Co/Scott T.Smith; **110** GI/John Kelly; **119**b Co/Tom Stewart; **120–121b** PM; **121**t PM; **123b** Co/Picimpact; **125**t Co/Paul A. Souders; **125b** Co/Richard T.Nowitz; **126** KB; **127**b,t KB; **128** Co/David Samuel Robbins; **129t** Co/Dave Bartruff; **129b** Co/Scott T.Smith; **137** Co/Tim McGuire **140–141** Co/Layne Kennedy; **142–179**rh Co/David Arky; **142b** GI/David Madison; **143b** Co/Phil Schermeister; **149t** GI/Ken Chernus; **149c** GI/Stuart Hughs; **151**br Co/Michael DeYoung; **156c** Co/Darrell Gulin; **156t** Royalty Free; **157l** GI/Michael Melford; **158**br,c,cl,cr KB; **158**bl Co/ Paul A.Souders; **162**tr KB; **164** GI/Jerry Kobalenko; **165b** Co/David Samuel Robbins; **166b** Co/Carl & Ann Purcell; **166c** Co/Kevin Fletcher; **167b** Co/ Galen Rowell; **167**tr PM; **168c** Co/Chris Rainier; **168t** GI/Tom Stock; **168b** Co/Michael DeYoung; **169t** GI/Grant Dixon; **169b** NG; **170** Co/Craig Tuttle; **171**tl KB; **171**tc Co/Lester Lefkowitz; **171b** Co/Royalty Free; **171**tr Co/Scott T.Smith; **172**bl Co/Royalty Free; **173t** KB; **173b** Co/Craig Tuttle; **174b** Co/Dennis di Cicco; **174**cb Co/Jeff Curtes; **174**ca Co/Richard Berenholtz; **174t** Co/Richard Bickel; **175**ca,cb Co/ Craig Aurness; **175t** Co/W.Perry Conway; **176–177b** Co/PicImpact; **177**tr KB; **177l** GI/Bobby Model; **179** GI/Philippe Poulet/Mission; **180–181** Co/Randy M. Ury; **182–183b** Co/Robert Y. Ono; **183**cr Co/Layne Kennedy; **183**br Co/Phil Schermeister; **186b, t** KB; **188** PM; **189t** Co/O.Alamany & E.Vicens; **198** KB; **199** PM; **200–201** Co/Galen Rowell; **202–219**rh Co/Royalty Free; **204** Co/David Meunch; **206–207** Co/A&J Verkaik; **206l** Co/Raymond Gehman; **207**tr Co/Layne Kennedy; **208–209b** Co/Raymond Gehman; **210–211** Co/Bill Stormont; **211**t Co/Paul A. Souders; **212** PM; **214** Co/Lee Cohen; **215**t KB; **216** Co/Ron Sanford; **217** Co/Paul A. Souders; **218** GI/Brian Stablyk; **220–221** GI/Mike Timo; **222–237**rh Co/Layne Kennedy; **223** Co/Royalty Free

All other images © Dorling Kindersley.
For further information see **www.dkimages.com**